Ro n.e . 7.11

Feminism, the State
and Social Policy

rp

D1321790

Also by Nickie Charles:

Gender Divisions and Social Change
Women, Food and Families (with M. Kerr)
Practising Feminism (co-edited with F. Hughes-Freeland)
Gender, Ethnicity and Political Ideologies (co-edited
  with H. Hintjens)

Feminism, the State and Social Policy

Nickie Charles

Consultant Editor: Jo Campling

First published in Great Britain 2000 by
MACMILLAN PRESS LTD
Houndmills, Basingstoke, Hampshire RG21 6XS and London
Companies and representatives throughout the world

A catalogue record for this book is available from the British Library.

ISBN 0–333–65555–9 hardcover
ISBN 0–333–65556–7 paperback

 First published in the United States of America 2000 by
ST. MARTIN'S PRESS, INC.,
Scholarly and Reference Division,
175 Fifth Avenue, New York, N.Y. 10010

ISBN 0–312–22675–6

Library of Congress Cataloging-in-Publication Data
Charles, Nickie.
Feminism, the state and social policy / Nickie Charles ;
consultant editor, Jo Campling.
p.   cm.
Includes bibliographical references and index.
ISBN 0–312–22675–6 (cloth)
1. Feminism.   2. Women's rights.   3. Women—Government policy.
I. Campling, Jo.   II. Title.
HQ1154.C458   1999
305.42—dc21   99–29988
                                                                              CIP

© Nickie Charles 2000

All rights reserved. No reproduction, copy or transmission of this publication may be made
without written permission.

No paragraph of this publication may be reproduced, copied or transmitted save with
written permission or in accordance with the provisions of the Copyright, Designs and
Patents Act 1988, or under the terms of any licence permitting limited copying issued by
the Copyright Licensing Agency, 90 Tottenham Court Road, London W1P 0LP.

Any person who does any unauthorised act in relation to this publication may be liable to
criminal prosecution and civil claims for damages.

The author has asserted her right to be identified as the author of this work in accordance
with the Copyright, Designs and Patents Act 1988.

This book is printed on paper suitable for recycling and made from fully managed and
sustained forest sources.

10   9   8   7   6   5   4   3   2   1
09   08   07   06   05   04   03   02   01   00

Printed in Hong Kong

 The Sheffield College
Peaks - Learning Resource Centre
(0114) 260 2462

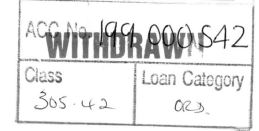
ACC No. 199 000 542
WITHDRAWN

Class	Loan Category
305.42	ORD.

Contents

Preface and Acknowledgments

Writing about social and political processes means that the certainties you are penning one day may be totally out of date the next. This has now happened to me twice. When I was writing about gender divisions in socialist societies for my last book, *Gender Divisions and Social Change*, the Berlin Wall fell, transforming what I was writing about. And when I was finishing Chapter 4 of this book bewailing the low representation of women in parliament, we had a general election which resulted in the proportion of women MPs doubling from 9.2 per cent to 18.4 per cent. This increase can be seen as a direct result of second wave feminism and, specifically, as an outcome of the move into the Labour party of many feminist activists in response to the election of the first Thatcher administration in 1979. It also demonstrates that it is hazardous to commit yourself to paper because you never know exactly what is round the corner. However, I have chosen to take the risk.

I have been helped in this endeavour by various friends and colleagues. Charlotte Davies and Margaret Kenna have provided much needed support and encouragement in the face of the ever-increasing workloads associated with modularisation, 'efficiency gains' and growing numbers of students; Paul Ransome has provided critical comment on several of the chapters and Lis Parcell has been the most wonderful subject librarian and friend, ferreting out all sorts of books and articles for me when time was running short and appearing with food at my door when I hadn't managed to get to the shops. I must also thank Stephanie Jones, who has read the manuscript from cover to cover to see if it makes sense, and Chris Harris, who has suggested many judicious cuts and rephrasings and has helped me clarify my ideas on states and social movements; their critical readings and support have been much appreciated. I am also grateful for the study leave I had when I began work on this project and the willingness of my colleagues (in what was then the Department of Sociology and Anthropology in Swansea) to facilitate my temporary absence from teaching and administration. Finally, I must thank Jo Campling who was enthusi-astic about this project from the beginning and who has smoothed the passage from book proposal to book, Val Bryson whose comments I have found extremely helpful, and Catherine Gray from the publisher who has provided excellent editorial support.

Life, of course, continues even when you are trying to write a book and can often make writing very difficult. Solva did her best to stop me starting this book and Inka almost stopped me finishing it. But my two best friends continue to enrich my life.

NICKIE CHARLES
Swansea

Introduction

This book explores the impact of feminist social movements on social policy. In order to do this it is important to understand the relationship between feminist social movements and the state. This is because, at the level of practical politics, feminist social movements have engaged with the state and expected a response from it in terms of changing policies. And, at a theoretical level, feminists have identified the state as upholding oppressive gender relations which are in need of change. Feminist social movements are said to occur in waves. In Britain the first wave is dated to the period 1870–1930 and was concerned chiefly with women's political and property rights. Here I focus on western women's liberation movements which constitute the second wave. These began to emerge in Western Europe and North America at the end of the 1960s and are associated with profound changes to the lives of women and men in the past 40 years. During the 1970s, the movement formulated seven demands. These were for equal pay; equal education and job opportunities; free contraception and abortion on demand; free, 24-hour nurseries; financial and legal independence; an end to all discrimination against lesbians and a woman's right to define her own sexuality; freedom from intimidation by threat or use of violence or sexual coercion, regardless of marital status, and an end to all laws, assumptions and institutions which perpetuate male dominance and men's aggression towards women. These demands focused on the state, attacking its control of women's fertility, its construction of women as dependants of men and its control of female sexuality and implicit support for male violence against women.

In these early years the movement was concerned with public policy as well as emphasising the politics of the personal. Indeed, the slogan that the personal is political linked the so-called private domain of the home to the public domain of politics and the state. Feminists argued that domestic tasks are constructed as women's work through social and economic policies and that it is not simply a matter of personal choice that means women rather than men give up their jobs to look after children. Indeed, the state itself constructs the private sphere to which women are ideally confined. The idea that the personal is political also implied that women active in the women's movement tried to live out their political beliefs in their personal lives and, through talking to other women in conscious-ness-raising groups, came to realise that what they had defined as something unique to them was in fact something that was shared by other women in similar social circumstances. In other words those of us involved in the movement began to develop a sociological and political understanding of the ways in which our personal lives were profoundly shaped by the politics and policies pursued by the state; we began to develop a sociological imagination.

This understanding involved our trying to change state policies: by setting up alternative forms of provision and organising campaigns in support of our demands. We demanded rights that were hitherto denied and we exposed the way that the state supported male power over women in the most intimate areas of our lives. Alongside this political activity there developed an analysis of the state and the way it supported gender relations that women expe-rienced as oppressive. Thus the state was seen by the women's movement as capable of responding to pressure by granting rights but also as pursuing policies which restricted women's rights and gave men power over women. It was also seen as having the power to give women greater access to resources by legislating for equal pay and through removing the assumption, written into much social security legislation, that married women were financially dependent on their husbands. Policy changes affecting women both preceded and succeeded the women's movements of the 1970s and there has also been profound cultural change. Such changes may not have been the revolutionary transformation of a capitalist and patriarchal society that some of us wanted, but they are nonetheless significant and the way they were brought about is worthy of study.

Towards the end of the 1970s the movement fragmented and it became obvious that its apparent inclusivity actually excluded women who were not white, relatively young, heterosexual and middle class. Feminist organisations, however, continued to exist and new ones came into being, spreading the influence of feminism throughout society. Feminisms such as black feminism produced critiques of liberal, socialist and radical feminism and, through their political practice, broadened out feminist understandings of society and the state. Thus although the feminist social movements of the 1970s with their transformative goals have ceased to exist, feminist politics and ideology have had and continue to have a profound effect on society. It is my intention, in the pages that follow, to explore this effect in terms of policy change and to develop a theoretical understanding of the ways in which social movements and the state relate to each other and to changing social policies.

The book is divided into two parts. The first brings together theorisations of the state and social movements in order to develop a conceptual framework within which to analyse specific policy developments. In the first chapter, I explore the way the state has been theorised and the difference feminist social movements and feminist analysis have made to state theory. In particular I show that conventional state theory conceptualises states in terms of class or in terms of power and bureaucracy, ignoring the salience of gender as a category that helps explain the nature of states and their development. In the second chapter I focus on the way social movements have been theorised. I show that most analyses are unable to explain feminist social movements because they either attempt to understand the development of social movements in terms of class or in terms of organisations and resources. In other words they suffer from the same epistemological and theoretical shortcomings as does state theory. Chapter 3 explores the detailed ways in which social movements affect social policies and, conversely, how states affect the form taken by social movements. Thus states and social movements influence each other through their forms of organisation and representation and the policies they pursue. In these three theoretical chapters I show how feminist theory and practice have changed sociological understanding of the state and society.

The second part of the book explores how feminist theory and practice have changed the practical politics of social policy formation. In Chapter 4 I discuss the conditions of emergence of women's liberation movements in Western Europe and North America, showing that they are both cause and consequence of profound socio-economic and cultural change. Thus, as with the state and social policy, there is a dialectical relationship between structural and cultural change and social movements. The next five chapters explore the impact of feminist social movements on the specific areas of policy which were identified by the seven demands of the women's movement. In Chapter 5, I look at the so-called equality legislation and the implementation of equal opportunities policies within organisations. This shows that the state, in passing legislation, can contribute to the mobilisation of social movements. It also explores the way in which policies are implemented within bureaucratic, capitalist organisations and shows how working within such organisations can transform feminist demands. In Chapter 6 I focus on poverty and explore the way in which feminist research and participation in policy-making networks affects the policy agenda. This discussion relates to the demand of the women's movement for an end to the assumption by the state, particularly in social security policy, of women's financial dependence on their male partners. In the next chapter I discuss the response of feminist social movements to male violence against women. As well as exploring the rights granted to women by the state in response to feminist pressure, such as the right to be rehoused away from the threat of violence, I explore the alternative feminist forms of organisation that were set up and their effect on women's access to resources. This chapter provides a counterbalance to Chapters 5 and 6 because it explores feminist organisations and their impact on policy and the state rather than the ways feminist-inspired policies are implemented within male-dominated organisations.

In Chapter 8 I discuss the issue of abortion, highlighting struggles over definitions and meaning and the limitations imposed on the movement by a largely defensive struggle waged on hostile territory. Finally, I turn to family policy and pro-family counter-movements, focusing particularly on child care and reproduction. Here feminist social movements have met with considerable resistance which, I argue, relates to the threat that changes to the control of sexuality and the organisation of child care pose to the gender order and the power and legitimacy of the state. I discuss the resistance to feminist social movements posed by counter-movements and the way their interactions affect the policy agenda. These chapters provide an exploration of the way feminist social movements actually engage with the state and the results of this engagement in terms of policy. In the final chapter I return to a discussion of processes of policy change, the nature of social movements and theories of the state, drawing together the argument of the book and revisiting the issues with which I began.

Chapter 1

Theorising the State

During the 1970s, feminist social movements identified the state as having the power to change policies which affect women and to give women certain rights. Demands for equal pay and equal opportunities, for child care provision, for reproductive rights and for sexual self-determination and an end to male violence were directed at the state in the belief that it could implement the desired changes. At the same time, the state was identified as supporting social relations which are oppressive to women. Thus women demonstrating in defence of abortion rights chanted, 'Not the church and not the state, women will decide their fate'. This suggests that the state is central to feminist politics. But it also reveals an ambivalence towards the state which is seen, at one and the same time, as enabling and constraining, as a potential ally and as an oppressive force. This ambivalence towards the state has been characteristic of second wave feminism and, as we shall see, has shaped the tactics adopted by feminist social movements in their engagement with the state.

A similar ambivalence can be found in state theory which is the focus of this chapter. I shall argue that this reflects a real problem with the state in both political and theoretical terms, a problem which has been illuminated by feminist political practice. The problem is that the state is defined and experienced both as a set of institutions standing over and above us *and* as something which permeates our everyday lives and in which we all, wittingly or unwittingly, participate. This has led some to question both the existence of the state and its utility for feminist political practice (Abrams, 1988; Allen, 1990).

Because the state has the power to implement policy change and to grant rights, and because this power was recognized by second wave feminism, it is important to understand what the state is and how it relates to social movements. Indeed, the state provides the political framework within which social movements develop and is itself shaped by social movements. Theorisations of the state are also influenced by social movements and, because of the continuing importance of class-based analyses, I begin by discussing class-based state theory. I explore two particularly influential variants of this – Marxist and social democratic. Both conceptualise class-based social movements as affecting the form taken by the state and explore the relation between the state, the economy and class politics. Both are representational theories of the state. This means that they see the state as representing interests that are constituted elsewhere, usually at the economic level. Thus political power is a representation of economic power and is derived from it. Representational theories tend to be society centred. That is, they explain the structure of the state as arising from the nature of the society within which it exists. Thus class, gender and racial inequalities both structure and are shaped by the state through the policies it pursues. Society-centred approaches are associated with Marxist and Marxist-derived analyses.

I also explore non-representational theories which see the state as constituting political interests. Such theories focus on political power and forms of organisation and are often referred to as state-centred approaches. State-centred approaches analyse the way states are organised, seeing them as a specific form of political association in their own right. They focus on the means used by states to achieve their ends (Pierson, 1996: 7) and conceptualise them as bureaucratic organisations exercising domination over society and having a monopoly of legitimate violence. State-centred approaches tend to employ Weberian analyses of the state.

Having explored these different understandings of the state, I focus on the way feminist theory has developed them in order to understand the nature of the state with which contemporary feminist movements engage. I explore the key concepts of conventional state theory which have been put to use and argue that the most fruitful analyses transcend the dichotomy between representational and non-representational theories, developing a gendered understanding of state organisation, forms of representation and policies and recognizing the dialectical relation between states and social movements. Such an approach enables us to see what difference feminist practice has made to our understanding of the state through engaging with it and attempting to bring about change.

Representational theories – class

Marxism and the state

Within classical Marxism the state is seen as contradictory. On the one hand it is conceptualised as part of the political superstructure arising from the economic class structure of society and as representing the interests of the economically dominant class; it is based on the domination of one class over another, a domination which derives from its economic position and which is supported by the state's monopoly of violence. On the other hand, within Marx's writings, some actions of the state are conceptualised as a response to working-class pressure and as being in the interests of the working class. Marx shows this in his analysis of the struggle over the length of the working day in 19th-century Britain. The working class organised to press for a reduction in the length of the working day. At the same time landed and urban capital, represented by the two main political parties, were divided over the issue of free trade. Both attempted to gain working-class support by promising concessions on the length of the working day. Working-class pressure for a shorter working day, in the context of contradictions within the bourgeoisie, eventually resulted in state regulation of hours of work (Therborn, 1977: 26). Thus, according to Marx, pressure from the organised working class led to state intervention in the economy on behalf of the working class, despite the fact that he conceptualises the state as representing the interests of the capitalist class.

There are two issues which arise from this: first, if the state is indeed a class state representing the interests of the dominant minority within society, how does it manage to engender both the consent of the population to its rule and their belief that it represents them and rules in all their interests? In other words, how is class rule legitimated? Second, how can the intervention of a capitalist state in the interests of the working class be explained? Marx and Engels argued that consent to class rule is achieved through ideology, specifically legal ideology. This is because in law individuals are defined as equal no matter how unequal they are in class terms (Marx and Engels did not take into account other bases of inequality such as gender). This legal equality is taken as the reality rather than the economic inequalities which structure society and make a state necessary in the first place; it therefore legitimates state power. Antonio Gramsci developed this argument further, suggesting that the ruling class not only requires a monopoly of force in society in order to maintain power but also needs to hold ideological sway; it needs to exercise hegemony over subordinate classes thereby ensuring their consent to class rule.

Contemporary Marxists argue that state provision of welfare also legitimates state power. Provisions that are universal and available to all give the impression that the state 'cares' about its citizens and give them a reason to support the existing system. Citizens derive certain benefits from the existing political order; this makes them reluctant to upset it. Consent to class rule, that is, hegemony, is thereby ensured. The state is thus an important factor of cohesion in class-divided societies. Its juridical and welfare practices and ideologies defuse potential conflict by masking the class nature of the state and giving citizens real rights and a stake in the existing system.

The concept of reproduction has been developed in order to explain the intervention of a capitalist state in the interests of the working class (Althusser, 1971). In order for capitalism to survive, the working class needs to continue to exist and reproduce itself. The state is conceptualised as functioning in order to ensure that this reproduction takes place and, in the case of state welfare provision, takes on many aspects of social reproduction. This idea of reproduction helps to explain the state's intervention in the economy to limit the length of the working day. In the long run, this intervention ensured the reproduction of the working class, even though in the short run it was seen as being against the interests of particular capitalists. The concept of reproduction is central to many contemporary Marxist analyses of the state which emphasise both its class structure and its ability to be changed by human action in the form of class struggle (Ginsberg, 1979; Gough, 1979; Doyal, 1981).

Within this sort of analysis the state is conceptualised at two levels: an abstract level where the structural relation between it and the capitalist economy is specified, that is, it reproduces labour power, maintains the non-working population and legitimates state power, and at a concrete historical level where class struggle assumes importance in determining the nature of state intervention in welfare provision. The state is conceptualised as functioning so as to reproduce the conditions necessary for capitalist production and accumulation and, in order for these to continue, class inequalities must be maintained. Within these constraints class struggle has some effectivity. In this type of analysis, however, the centrality of political power to the state almost vanishes. It is the economy and the way the state functions for the economy that are seen as important.

Social democracy

The social democratic approach to the state, in contrast, stresses the role of political parties in the process of representation of classes within the state and in determining state policies. This type of analysis is based on the assumption that industrial capitalism requires state intervention in order to be able to function (Therborn, 1989; Pierson, 1991). However, there is a variation in state forms which can be explained by the classes and class alliances which exercise political power (Moore, 1967; Mishra, 1981) and this, in turn, relates to different phases of industrial development (Flora and Heidenheimer, 1987; Therborn, 1989). These two elements are combined by Goran Therborn who relates changes in the nature of the state to changes in its main function. Over the last 800 years the main functions of states have changed from establishing boundaries in relation to other states by means of war and military exploits, through the development of their own territories and the infrastructure necessary for industrial production, to ensuring the reproduction of their populations. The first stage is associated with the absolutist state and the transition from feudalism to capitalism; the second with early industrialisation, the emergence of liberal democracies, restricted suffrage and limited citizenship rights; and the third, which is associated with mass democracy, a widening of citizenship rights and the development of welfare states, emerges once industrial production is fully established (Marshall, 1950; Therborn, 1977; Flora and Heidenheimer, 1987). It is in this third phase that feminist social movements came into existence.

These changes are related to class and class alliances. During the 19th century the bourgeoisie was in the ascendant and state intervention was directed towards the provision of a stable infrastructure for industrial production; in the 20th century, however, welfare state expansion is due to the decline of 'bourgeois and traditional power and an increase of working class and other popular power, but a power always delimited by capitalist relations of production' (Therborn, 1989: 77). Thus the development of states and the different forms they take are linked to class-based movements and alliances which are themselves derived from the economic structure of industrial capitalism (Esping-Anderson, 1990); a position not dissimilar to that of some contemporary Marxists.

Another and highly influential version of this type of theory is that of Gøsta Esping-Anderson who argues that different forms of the welfare state embody different structural relationships between the state, the economy and the family. In common with much mainstream analysis, however, he focuses most analytic attention on the relation between the state and the economy. Following T.H. Marshall, he argues that state provision of welfare, particularly the provision of welfare as of right, represents a process of de-commodification and a reduction of people's dependency on the market for their subsistence needs (Esping-Anderson, 1990: 23). He distinguishes between different welfare state regimes by the extent to which they facilitate de-commodification and how they distribute welfare provision between the state, the market and the family (which are of course not unrelated). These regimes relate to class in two ways: first, their emergence is dependent upon the economic class structure and the class interests and class alliances to which it gives rise and, second, they reproduce particular forms of stratification.

He distinguishes three different welfare state regimes: social democratic, conservative-corporate and liberal. In *social democratic* welfare state regimes the basis of entitlement to state welfare is citizenship (Daly, 1994: 106); these regimes are based on principles of universalism and de-commodification and they reduce class differentiation in access to welfare provision. They also socialise the 'costs of familyhood' by taking over responsibility of caring for children and other dependants. In other words, they take over the tasks of social reproduction, enabling women to choose paid employment rather than unpaid domestic labour should they so wish.

In *conservative-corporate* welfare state regimes the basis of entitlement is performance based and state provision of welfare maintains class and status differentials. In addition they are committed to preserving the 'traditional' family and expect women, once married, to be dependent on their partners and to raise children with no state provision of day care or other family services.

In *liberal* welfare state regimes the basis of entitlement is need; they are dominated by the logic of the market, benefits are very limited and are generally means tested. This results in divisions between recipients of state welfare (who are all equally poor) and the rest of society, whose access to welfare is dependent on the market and therefore differentiated according to market position. This creates a society polarised between classes and characterised by inequality.

For Esping-Anderson these three welfare state regimes are the outcome of a class-based political process. Classes and class alliances, which are structured by economic processes, form the basis for political alliances which, in the context of specific institutional arrangements, affect the type of welfare state regime which develops and the policies it pursues. In his argument it is the relation between the economy and the state which has explanatory power. Thus in both his characterisation of regime types and in his discussion of their formation and their effects in terms of stratification, class and class alliances are central. It is only in his discussion of the conservative/corporatist welfare state regime that the state-family relation assumes importance. His analytical focus is on the effect of different packages of citizenship entitlements for class stratification and the impact of different class alliances on the development of regime types (Sainsbury, 1994). It is however clear that the three welfare state regimes have different effects in terms of gender relations, with social democratic regimes taking on responsibility for the tasks of social reproduction (including child care) while the other types assume that women within the family will retain this responsibility (see also Chapter 9). Thus class structures and the class alliances to which they give rise can have a significant impact on the distribution of the tasks of reproduction between the state, the family and the market and hence on gender relations. Despite this, or perhaps because of it, his argument has provoked considerable debate among feminists who have been particularly critical of his concept of de-commodification (see O'Connell, 1993; Sainsbury, 1994; Lister, 1997) and his typology; I discuss this further later.

Both Marxist and social democratic representational theories focus on the relation between classes and the state. Classes and class interests are constituted within the economy and structure the state and state policies, either directly, as in many versions of Marxism, or indirectly, through the representation of their interests by political parties. States are conceptualised as agents of stratification, and it is through their welfare policies that class inequalities are reproduced and/or modified. For both these types of analysis (even for writers such as Esping-Anderson) class is the significant social division determining the form taken by the state and it is the state-market relation which is of fundamental theoretical importance. Gender, ethnicity and 'race' are virtually unmentioned except by recent writers who have begun to take feminist and anti-racist critiques of this sort of analysis into account (see for example Ginsburg, 1992; Williams, 1994).

Non-representational theories – states and power

Weber, unlike Marx, does not conceptualise the state as an embodiment of class power. The state is centrally about power but Weber argues that it is only possible to *define* the state sociologically in terms of the means it uses, that is its monopoly of physical force. A state is 'a human community that (successfully) claims the *monopoly of the legitimate use of physical force* within a given territory' (Weber, 1970: 78). Thus, for Weber, central to the definition of the state are notions of violence, territory and legitimacy. He also says that the 'right to use physical force' is bestowed by the state and that 'the state is a relation of men dominating men, a relation supported by means of legitimate (that is, considered to be legitimate) violence' (Weber, 1970: 78). The state is about power and domination which have to be seen to be legitimate and require that subjects are obedient to the authority of the state. Such obedience is secured through emotions, such as 'fear and hope', and by means of interests. Furthermore, in order to organise domination, administration is necessary which needs to be resourced; the state therefore requires a revenue base in the form of taxation (Weber, 1970: 80; Pierson, 1996: 8). Discussing the emergence of the modern state Weber writes:

> The modern state is a compulsory association which organises domination. It has been successful in seeking to monopolise the legitimate use of physical force as a means of domination within a territory. To this end the state has combined the material means of organisation in the hands of its leaders, and it has expropriated all autonomous functionaries of estates who formerly controlled these means in their own right. The state has taken their positions and now stands in the top place. (Weber, 1970: 82–3)

This process of the monopolisation and expropriation of 'the means of administration, warfare and financial organisation' is '*a complete parallel to the development of the capitalist enterprise through gradual expropriation of the independent producers*' (Weber 1970: 82). Thus it is not dependent upon class power at the economic level but is an autonomous process involving political power *per se*.

The modern state takes a bureaucratic form. Indeed, for Weber, bureaucracy is fully developed 'only in the modern state' and 'in the most advanced institutions of capitalism' (Weber, 1970: 196). These parallel processes of bureaucratisation arise from the rational basis of capitalist society; bureaucracy being the most efficient way of organising and administering on a large scale. Whether it be the organisation of power or the organisation of economic production is irrelevant, they are both manifestations of the same drive towards the rational mode of organisation, a drive which Weber argued was a defining characteristic of modern societies.

It is important to note that Weber defines the state as a form of concentrated power which is not derived from elsewhere. This means that he does not conceptualise state power as deriving from economic class power; there may be a relation between the two empirically but conceptually they are totally distinct. This has led to his being criticised for failing to theorise the link between capitalism and forms of the state (Held, 1983: 38). However, this is tantamount to criticising him because he fails to adopt a Marxist analytical framework. He conceptualises struggles for political power as occupying the political realm which is distinct from the realm of economic power. Thus lifestyle-based status groups and parties as well as classes are important actors in struggles for power. This differentiates his analysis from Marxist and social democratic approaches which prioritise class-based social movements. As long as action is political, even if non-class based, it can be effective at the level of the state. Weber's focus is on the way the power and authority of the state are organised and legitimated and the extent of the state's jurisdiction. Thus states are territorially bounded, exist in relation with other nation states, enjoy a monopoly of the legitimate use of physical force within their boundaries, and are administered by officials organised in bureaucracies.

Weber's ideas on the modern state have influenced contemporary analyses by fostering a renewed interest in the internal organisation of the state and the possibilities of working for change within state bureaucracies (London Edinburgh Weekend Return Group, 1980; Franzway *et al.*, 1989; Cooper, 1995). This development shifts the focus from the relation between the state and the social order to the social order as it is manifest within the institutions of the state. One of the consequences of focusing on the internal organisation of the state is that its contradictions become apparent, and instead of appearing as a monolithic entity its unity is seen as something which is continually having to be achieved (Franzway *et al.*, 1989; Cooper, 1995). Thus, viewed externally the state can be seen as a set of institutions which together constitute the state apparatus which has power over civil society. Viewed internally the state appears as a set of social relations which are in continual flux, it is seen as a process rather than a thing (London Edinburgh Weekend Return Group, 1980: 59; Burton, 1985: 104–5; Franzway *et al.*, 1989: 45; Cooper, 1995: 59–60).

This conceptualisation of the state and political power is made explicit in the work of Foucault who has been widely cited as supporting the argument that a concept of the state is not useful and that power in modern societies is ubiquitous and, tentacle-like, reaches into every area of our lives (Allen, 1990; Pringle and Watson, 1992). Power is apparent in its effects, the ability to act denotes power (Cooper, 1995: 20). It is not clear, however, that Foucault's arguments support the abandonment of the concept of the state.

> I don't want to say that the state isn't important: what I want to say is that relations of power, and hence the analysis that must be made of them, necessarily extend beyond the limits of the state. In two senses: first of all because the state, for all the omnipotence of its apparatuses, is far from being able to occupy the whole field of actual power relations, and further because the state can only operate on the basis of other, already existing power relations. The state is superstructural in relation to a whole series of power networks... I would say that the state consists in the codification of a whole number of power relations which render its functioning possible. (Gordon, 1980 cited Held *et al.*, 1983: 312)

This view ties in with the slogan of the women's movement that the personal is political which, in common with Foucault, alerts us to the power relations which structure (or invest) our daily and most intimate interactions. What has emerged from Foucault's analysis of sexuality, for instance, is the concept of the state as a regulatory agency and this, together with a Weberian emphasis on bureaucracy, informs some recent explorations of the state.

Civil society and the state

Some contemporary theorists attempt to move beyond the dichotomy of representational and non-representational approaches to the state, arguing that political interests have a basis in society but are constituted by the state. Bob Jessop, for instance, tries to incorporate non-class-based interests in his theorisation of the capitalist state by arguing that it relates both to the structure of the economy and civil society. In this he follows Gramsci, arguing that one of Gramsci's most important contributions to understanding the state and the interests that it represents is his 'emphasis on the social bases of state power in civil society as well as in political society' and his 'anti-reductionist' incorporation of social forces other than those based on class into a hegemonic bloc or 'popular-democratic struggle' which can, under the leadership of the working class, undermine and challenge state power (Jessop, 1982: 209). It is probably worth noting here that there is disagreement about what exactly the term civil society denotes, whether it can be differentiated from the economy and how it relates to the 'private' realm of the family (Pateman, 1989: 183; Ransome, 1992: 139); I return to this in Chapter 3.

Jessop argues that it is the social categories of civil society as well as the classes constituting the mode of production which provide the basis for the state's constitution and shaping of political interests. He thus distinguishes between political interests and social and economic categories, arguing that class relations are determined by the relations of production while political class interests are constituted within the state and associated forms of representation. Similarly, forms of domination in civil society (some of which may be patriarchal) provide a basis for the constitution of political interests. Political interests therefore have their social basis in forms of class exploitation at the economic level *and* in forms of domination in civil society. Thus economic and social categories can be represented within the state, the state provides a terrain for struggle, but political interests are in a fundamental sense constituted by processes within the state, understood as a set of institutions involving specific forms of representation, organisation and intervention (Jessop, 1982: 228).

Jessop also makes the point, following Foucault, that power is apparent in its effects; however he points out that because the effects of power are 'overdetermined' it follows that it is extremely difficult to attribute political outcomes to particular agents. This points to the difficulty of coming to definite conclusions concerning the impacts of feminist social movements on state policies. His analysis, however, permits a theorisation of the relation between social movements and the state by stressing their base in civil society and the constitution of political interests in relation to the state (see also Keane, 1993). Thus he avoids prioritising the links between the economic class structure, the 'needs' of capital and the state and neglecting the relationship between the state and civil society.

Feminism and the state

Feminists are critical of the focus on class and the gender blindness of most conventional state theory (see for example Pateman, 1988). They argue that gender, sexuality and 'race'/ethnicity are important dimensions of states and state activity and have been neglected hitherto. These different types of analysis can be linked to social movements and the new knowledges and meanings that they produce (Eyerman and Jamison, 1991). Thus class-based theorisations are a product of the labour movement while analyses of the state in terms of gender, sexuality and 'race'/ethnicity have emerged from the 'new' social movements of the 1970s and 80s and the epistemological shifts associated with them. Such analyses explore not only the relation of states to class and the economy, but also their relation to the family and to ideas of nationality and ethnicity.

The epistemological challenge mounted by contemporary social movements has also transformed state-centred approaches, revealing the gendered nature of bureaucratic hierarchies and political power. Although early feminist attempts to theorise the state were heavily influenced by Marxism and took a representational form, more recent analyses combine representational and non-representational approaches. Insights from both Marxist and Weberian analyses have also been brought together in contemporary understandings of the state that see it as both a set of institutions and as being made up of social relations which are themselves contested, that is, that the state is itself a terrain of struggle as well as being the object of struggle (Jessop, 1982). This theoretical development derives from political practice. Whereas for Lenin the state was viewed externally as an oppressive and coercive set of institutions, for contemporary socialists and feminists who are employed by the state and work within state bureaucracies it has become apparent that the state is contradictory and that working within the state can present opportunities to influence the direction of state policy and the form of organisation assumed by state institutions (London Weekend Edinburgh Return Group, 1980; Franzway *et al.*, 1989; Connell, 1990; Yeatman, 1990; Eisenstein, 1991; Cooper, 1995). These experiences are reflected in feminist understandings of the state. I argue that this better reflects the ambiguities of the state which are confronted by social movements seeking to enlist its support in bringing about social change.

Feminist analysis of the state has focused on its forms of intervention rather more than its internal organisation or forms of representation, leaving it open to the charge that it has no theory of the state (Franzway *et al.*, 1989). Thus feminists have tended to concentrate on social policies and their effects on gender relations rather than the way in which gender interests are constituted and represented at the political level.

Representational theories – gender

Capitalism and gender

Feminists defining the state as capitalist have developed and expanded Marxist and social democratic theories, focusing particularly on the concepts of social reproduction and citizenship. Marxist-feminists have argued that the male breadwinner family and women's dependence within it are supported by capitalist states because they have to ensure the reproduction of labour power and that women's unpaid domestic labour is the cheapest way of doing this. This arrangement also means that women are available as a source of cheap and flexible labour for capital if and when they are needed (Wilson, 1977). It is therefore because of the state's relation to capitalist production that it supports gender relations which are oppressive to women (McIntosh, 1978). This structural analysis is, as we have already seen, combined with an analysis of the way in which human action in the form of class struggle affects the state and the policies it pursues. Thus Marxist-feminists argue that the historical process of class struggle in Britain during the 19th century institutionalised a specific form of gender divisions and led to the development of social policies which support the dependent-breadwinner family (Wilson, 1977; Barrett, 1980). These struggles were informed by gender ideologies which assumed women's economic dependence upon men within family-households and resulted in the very structures which are defined as oppressive by contemporary feminists (Barrett, 1980; Banks, 1986; Dale and Foster, 1986; Koven and Michel, 1990; Brenner and Laslett, 1991).

Feminists also argue that class struggles (in which women as well as men are involved) have resulted in the state taking over some of the tasks of social reproduction from the family, specifically from women within the family, and that the distribution of these tasks between the state, the market and the family provides a material basis for the construction of gender interests. In the words of Brenner and Laslett:

The distribution of the work of social reproduction between families, markets, communities, and states – and between women and men – has varied historically. (Brenner and Laslett, 1991: 315)

The distribution of this work affects women's access to resources. Thus the allocation of responsibility for the work of social reproduction to women within the family-household reduces their independent access to resources within the labour market, the family and the welfare state and provides a basis for men's power over women (Millar and Glendinning, 1987). Conversely, the greater the involvement of the state in tasks such as child care the less likely it is that women will be dependent on individual men and the more likely it is that they will be in paid employment (Borchorst and Siim, 1987; Dahlerup, 1987; Hernes, 1987; Meyer, 1994). Increased state involvement in social reproduction has not altered the fact that the bulk of care work is undertaken by women; it merely moves from the private into the public domain. This has been seen by some as representing a shift from private to public patriarchy (Borchorst and Siim, 1987; Siim, 1987, 1988; Allen, 1996).

This recognition that state activity can have positive outcomes for women, in so far as it introduces measures which increase their independent access to resources, has modified Marxist-feminist analyses of the state. The initial claim that the dependent-breadwinner family form was functional for capital and therefore supported by capitalist states has also been shown to be empirically and theoretically unsound. Instead states vary in their relation to families and gender relations, some of them supporting a breadwinner form of family while others facilitate women's independence and increase their access to resources. Indeed, even within the same state, policies differentiate between women on the basis of class, ethnicity and sexuality. Black feminists, for instance, have argued that the state constructs families differently on the basis of 'race' and that women of different ethnicities have differential access to power and resources. Thus, while women from the majority ethnic group in Britain have a right to state support if they leave their partner because of actual or threatened violence, ethnic minority women may be denied these rights and their dependence on their abusive husbands reinforced (Patel, 1997: 261–2) or they may experience abuse from the state if they involve the police in a violent domestic situation (Mama, 1989). Moreover immigration laws operate to divide black families rather than keeping them together. Similarly, it is only heterosexual families that are supported by the welfare state, same-sex partnerships are not sanctioned. State policies therefore reflect institutionalised racism and heterosexism and deny some women rights on the basis of ethnicity and sexuality (Bryan *et al.*, 1985; Mama, 1989).

What emerges from feminist elaborations of Marxist analyses is that welfare state intervention in social reproduction has important effects on gender relations and that welfare states differentiate between women on the basis of class, 'race' and sexuality (and, one might add, age and disability). Central to this approach is the conceptual distinction between social production and reproduction and the idea that power is based on access to and control over resources. Thus it is argued that the form of the state is created and changed by the collective action of women and men, but that this action is conditioned and constrained by the social relations and ideologies within which these collective actors are located. In addition, many measures which are of benefit to women, such as the provision of child care facilities and minimum wage legislation, are outcomes of labour movement involvement in the formulation of social policies (Ruggie, 1984; Allen, 1996). Thus class as well as gender is seen as important to an analysis of the relation of the state to gender divisions, and the extent to which states facilitate women's independent access to resources is conceptualised as an outcome of struggle over the distribution of reproductive tasks between the state, the market and the family. The strength of this sort of analysis is that it shows how *class-based social movements are gendered*, that is, they represent not only class interests but also gender interests, and that these class and gender interests arise from the relations of production and reproduction. The representation of these interests within the labour movement results in the institutionalisation of specific gender divisions of labour and their incorporation into social policies. Its weakness is that other bases of division, such as ethnicity and sexuality, have not been fully incorporated into their analyses (see, for example, Barrett and McIntosh, 1985).

In light of variations in the distribution of the work of social reproduction between state, market and family (although not between women and men), feminists have developed a critique of class-based typologies – particularly Esping-Anderson's – and attempted to generate typologies which are based on gender as well as class (see for example Leira, 1993; Sainsbury, 1994). If welfare states are distinguished according to the extent to which they take on responsibility for social reproduction and *reduce* gender inequalities, typologies can be produced which take into account both gender and class. Such typologies distinguish between welfare states based on a breadwinner model of social policy and those based on an individual model (Sainsbury, 1994: 153) or between egalitarian, ecclesiastical and liberal regimes of gender relations (Mosesdottir, 1995). What is important in developing these typologies is that consideration needs to be given to the extent to which motherhood or participation in care work is recognized as a basis of entitlement or, to put it another way, whether child care is seen as an individual and private matter or as something for which society has a collective responsibility (Sainsbury, 1994). It is important, however, not to lose sight of class in developing such typologies as the effect of welfare states on gender relations varies depending on the class alliances that have shaped the welfare state (Esping-Anderson, 1990). And it is those welfare state regimes that bear the stamp of the working class that are more likely to be associated with policies which do not treat women as dependants of men (Norris, 1987).

These socialist-feminist analyses relate the different ways in which states organise social reproduction to class and gender interests which are constituted within the relations of production and reproduction and which give rise to social movements. They thereby retain the insights of class-based analyses that class struggles and alliances have affected the form taken by welfare states, but show that such struggles embody particular gender relations and associated ideologies and incorporate dominant definitions of sexuality and ethnicity.

Patriarchy

An alternative approach is provided by those who conceptualise the state as patriarchal and who relate changes in its forms of representation to feminist movements. In contradistinction to a capitalist mode of production and its associated classes of producers and non-producers, it is argued that a patriarchal or domestic mode of production exists which is structured in terms of male dominance and female subordination (Walby, 1986). This patriarchal structuring is represented at the political level and leads to a characterisation of the state as patriarchal as well as capitalist, that is it 'represents patriarchal as well as capitalist interests and furthers them in its actions' (Walby, 1986: 57). More recently Sylvia Walby has moved away from such an obviously representational account by suggesting that the state has a 'systematic bias towards patriarchal interests' (Walby, 1990: 21) and that political struggles have a 'degree of autonomy' from the 'material basis of patriarchy and of capitalism' (Walby, 1990: 159). She therefore retains the notion of patriarchal interests but it is not altogether clear where or how they are constituted.

Feminists have also argued that the basis of patriarchal power lies in male violence. This approach has been particularly associated with radical feminism and brings together the structuralism of Marxist approaches with a focus on the relation between the state and violence. The state is conceptualised as representing 'the interests of the dominant group, that is, men' rather than as representing class interests (Hanmer, 1977, 1978). Male control of women (and hence male dominance) is dependent on force – the state therefore supports male violence against women (Hanmer, 1978: 227, 231). This analysis, however, has been shown to be partial by black feminists who argue that it is the dominant group of men whose interests are represented by the state and that its response to male violence against women is shaped by 'race' and class. Thus although violence towards women on the part of white men may be tolerated, when it comes to black and/or working-class men's violence towards white, middle-class women the situation is very different; in these circumstances the violence is taken as an affront to the ethnically dominant group (Davis, 1982; Collins, 1990). This points to the importance of recognizing that 'race' and ethnicity, as well as class and gender, shape state policies. It has also been argued that the state's monopoly over legitimate violence involves the acceptance of certain levels of male violence towards women; in other words the state gives to men the right to be violent towards women (Franzway *et al.*, 1989: 16; Walby, 1990) and, indeed, makes citizenship rights dependent on (some) men's ability to exercise violence in defence of the nation.

Despite Walby's recent disclaimers (Walby, 1996) these analyses remain representational.[1] That is, they argue that gender interests are constituted outside and represented within the state in a way analogous to class interests. MacKinnon's celebrated analysis of the structure of reproduction and heterosexuality as providing the material basis for law provides an example of this type of approach as does Walby's earlier analysis of the patriarchal mode of production (MacKinnon, 1989; Walby, 1986).

Citizenship

Feminists have also developed an analysis of citizenship, arguing
that it is structured by gender and ethnicity, and provides the basis
for certain forms of political representation (Jessop, 1982). The
gendering of citizenship rights was recognized by T.H. Marshall,
who argued that limitations on the hours of work of women and
children during the 19th century in Britain were not extended to
men because of men's status as citizens and their freedom,
enshrined in law, to 'conclude a free contract of employment'
(Marshall, 1950: 24). Women and children were not full citizens and
did not enjoy the same civil rights therefore it was entirely appropriate and not regarded as an infringement of their liberty to curb a
right which they did not have. Indeed, the state owed women protection precisely because of their lack of citizenship rights which,
according to Pateman, are constructed on the basis of ownership of
property in the person, something enjoyed by men but not women
(Pateman, 1988: 139). The exclusion of women from full citizenship rights, such as the right to own property and the right to vote,
was challenged by first wave feminism and resulted in such rights
being extended to women. This enabled their direct representation
as individual citizens within parliamentary democracies and,
according to Walby, ended state support for men's exclusionary
strategies (Walby, 1990: 191).

Feminists have developed a cogent critique of citizenship,
arguing that the remaining obstacles in the way of women exercising full citizenship rights are their responsibility for care work
within the family-household and their gendered integration into
paid employment. They point out that many social rights of citizenship are dependent on participation in paid employment, hence
gendered patterns of employment ensure that women's social rights
differ from those of men (Pateman, 1992: 23–4; Bryson and Lister,
1994). Indeed, Pateman has argued that citizenship is structured on
the gendered distinction between public and private and that citizenship rights are associated with the former (Pateman, 1988). This
means that, with a few notable exceptions, women's care work
within family-households does not carry with it citizenship entitlements in the way that paid employment in the public domain does.
Feminists, therefore, argue that women's care work within the
family-household should be a basis of entitlement to rather than
exclusion from various social rights and for measures to facilitate
their full inclusion in paid employment and the entitlements that go

with it (Lister, 1990, 1997; Walby, 1994). In addition, black feminists point out that citizenship rights are based on nationality and that this has implications for black women's (and men's) citizenship status. Thus, even though black women are more likely than their white counterparts to be in full-time employment, this does not guarantee their access to citizenship rights which are limited by racialised definitions of national identity (Williams, 1990; Allen, 1997). Such critiques have led to a characterisation of the state as capitalist, patriarchal and racist within the economy, the family and imperialism respectively (Williams, 1990).

Thus feminists have argued that forms of representation based on the exercise of individual rights of citizenship, such as a parliamentary democracy, are based on a series of exclusions, and that challenging these exclusions can result in changes in the form of patriarchy. Walby argues that women's access to political rights enabled them to fight for an extension of their civil and social rights, thereby challenging private patriarchy and transforming it into public patriarchy (Walby, 1990, 1994: 384–5). It is feminist social movements that have undermined state support for private patriarchy and forced the adoption of a new patriarchal strategy of inclusion and control. However, even in Walby's analysis, irrespective of whether the state is supporting private or public patriarchy, it is structured by the same patriarchal interests; indeed it is defined as one of the structures of patriarchy (Walby, 1990). In this sort of analysis, therefore, feminist social movements are seen as having an impact on forms of representation and through this on state activity. And the political activity of women within the labour movement and in feminist organisations is seen as being 'critical in the development of the welfare state' (Walby, 1990: 187–8; Lister, 1997: 169).

Beyond dichotomies

Thus far we have concentrated on feminist theorisations of the state that conceptualise it as representing interests that are constituted elsewhere. Little attention is given in these analyses to the forms of organisation of the state; their primary focus is on forms of state intervention and, to a lesser extent, forms of representation.

Latterly, attention has turned to the state itself, seeing it as in process rather than as a 'thing'. The focus has shifted from external determinants of state action to the organisation of the state and the way in which state employees are themselves active in shaping state policies. This shift can be seen as reflecting the resurgence of Weberian sociology in the wake of the declining influence of Marxism but it has also to do with the shift from structural analyses to those which emphasise social action and individual agency.

An important analysis of the state which uses concepts derived from Weber and Foucault, combining them with insights from representational approaches, is provided by Franzway *et al.* (1989; Connell, 1990). They conceptualise the state as the 'central institutionalisation of social power' and as 'involved with the overall patterning of gender relations, the "gender order" of the society as a whole'. It is a 'regulatory, managing agency... [and] takes a prominent role in *constituting* gender categories... and regulating the relationships among them by policy and policing' (Franzway *et al.*, 1989: 52). The relationship between the state and society is conceptualised as being two way with the state both constructed by and constructing gender relations (Connell, 1990). Thus the form of the state and the policies it pursues are affected by gender politics; the state institutionalises and regulates power relations elsewhere in society, often through its ability to legitimate the use of violence by certain social groups (for example husbands, soldiers); and it is marked by a politics of masculinity.

Here the internal organisation of the state is seen in terms of institutionalised masculinity. Connell argues that different forms of state are associated with different hegemonic masculinities. Absolutist states are associated with a masculinity that values honour and the ability to defend honour through fighting duels while, in the 19th century, with industrialisation, personal violence (at least between men) was eschewed and masculinity became associated with rationality, calculation and orderliness. These changes in hegemonic masculinity were associated with the ascendancy of the bourgeoisie and their notions of respectable manliness (Mosse, 1985) as well as with the increasing bureaucratisation of society and the state (Connell, 1990). Gender and sexuality, as well as class, are central to understanding and theorising the state. Indeed, as well as being marked by class hierarchies, European states have been marked by the equation of authority with a dominating masculinity; they have been effectively controlled by men and they are biased towards the interests of heterosexual men. Thus Connell links changes in the form taken by states to changes in hegemonic masculinity, the gender order and sexual politics, while, as we have seen, mainstream theorists of the state link the same changes to class-based politics and the extension of citizenship rights. It is of course the case that certain forms of masculinity and gender ideologies are associated with certain classes; which aspect is prioritised in explaining variations in state form depends on the conceptual framework being adopted.

Although different types of state are dominated by particular forms of masculinity, different branches of the same state are more or less masculinised. Thus the state directorate is overwhelmingly male in all liberal democracies and the coercive sectors of the state are male dominated in comparison with those concerned with human service work such as health and education. Moreover state hierarchies are structured along lines of gender with men predominating at the higher levels. Franzway *et al.* argue that there is an overall gender structuring of the state such that the more peripheral state institutions and activities are less masculinised than the central ones of coercion, political leadership and decision making (Franzway *et al.*, 1989: 42–3; Connell, 1990). This masculinisation is apparent in both the personnel and culture of the state apparatus (Franzway *et al.*, 1989: 42).

In addition, state organisations are bureaucracies which embody patriarchal or masculinist assumptions, practices and values (Franzway *et al.*, 1989; Connell, 1990; Halford, 1992). Connell observes that the ostensibly gender-free concept of rationality on which bureaucratic organisations are structured opens the possibility for women within bureaucracies to argue, on the basis of equal opportunities, that they are capable of doing the same jobs as men, thus making inroads into previously masculinised areas of the state. However, those who have power within state bureaucracies are overwhelmingly men and male networks remain significant in recruitment and promotion. Men also resist women's advancement, ensuring that should they attain positions of power and authority, the power and authority shift elsewhere (Cockburn, 1991; see also Chapter 5). Within organisations there is also a gender patterning of emotional attachments, what Connell refers to as 'the structure of cathexis'. This echoes Weber's discussion of the way in which obedience is secured and is a reference to the personal and emotional investments that are made in gendered jobs and identities and hence in the gender order within the state.

The issue of legitimacy is also relevant in discussing the impact of feminist social movements on state policy. Connell argues that gender struggles, within and outside the state, can have an effect on the gender order within the state and on the way in which the state regulates gender relations in society. Because of this the state is constantly changing. Thus although the state may be patriarchal and represent male power at a certain historical conjuncture, it is not essentially patriarchal and can therefore be changed. As we have already seen, the possibility of change is demonstrated by the successful struggles of women using the liberal-democratic concept of citizenship rights to claim a whole range of rights previously denied them (see also Walby, 1990). Connell links these successes to the need of the state to maintain its legitimacy and to the way in which demands for change are framed. The liberal-democratic state, which is ostensibly gender neutral, is obliged to respond to demands which are phrased in the discourse of liberalism (Franzway *et al.*, 1989; Connell, 1990). If it does not, such demands have the potential to call into question its legitimacy. However, in responding to feminist demands there is the danger of a backlash and a destabilisation of the gender order which can also jeopardise its legitimacy (Franzway *et al.*, 1989: 53). An illustration of this is the debate over abortion which has mobilised social movements on both sides of the debate (Franzway *et al.*, 1989; Staggenborg, 1991; see also Chapters 8 and 9). Although there are dangers to legitimacy involved in granting feminist demands, making concessions can serve to mute the feminist challenge. By playing according to the rules of the game (and perhaps changing them a little in the process), feminists contribute to the legitimation of the liberal-democratic state and the rule of law and may even strengthen it (Smart, 1989). As Hester Eisenstein puts it in her discussion of femocrats, a term coined in Australia to describe feminists working within state bureaucracies:

> Whatever its virtues, the femocratic experiment has proceeded via an acceptance of the bureaucratic form of politics, and therefore at some level has served in turn to legitimize, rather than to contest, state power. (Eisenstein, 1995: 43)

As well as institutionalising a certain gender order within its own organisations, the state constitutes the political categories which support and contest that gender order. Franzway *et al.* argue that the state regulates gender relations and sexuality thereby constituting the social categories of gender. Underpinning this analysis is a Foucaultian conception of the state as a concentration and institutionalisation of power which is continually contested both internally and externally. The state regulates power relations through the constitution of subjects within its discursive practices. Part of the way this is achieved is through social policies which define people in certain ways, for example as dependants, claimants, workers, mothers, wives, and it disciplines the population so that they behave appropriately, for example prefer to work in paid employment rather than claiming Job Seekers Allowance. Ideology and discipline are also dimensions of power (Cooper, 1995: 21). Dominant ideologies naturalise social relations which might otherwise be perceived in terms of unequal power relations, thus relations of class exploitation or gender oppression are masked by ideologies of equality and citizenship, while disciplinary power is associated with processes of surveillance, management and control (Cooper, 1995: 22). Subjects are vested with power within their relationships in order to carry out the work of the state, for example mothers socialise their children which involves power backed up by the surveillance of health visitors, midwives and social workers (Donzelot, 1979). Similarly it could be argued that the state vests power in men in order to keep women in their place and to maintain the gender order. What is interesting about this way of theorising the state is that it is understood as constituting social groups and collective actors; a view which is important when considering the relation between social movements and the state. As Franzway *et al.* put it:

> A social category may exist in a dispersed form, with the political mobilisation being part of what *constitutes* the category as a social group with a shared identity and a capacity for collective action. In this sense the state, as the focus and antagonist of mobilisation for the suffrage, is involved in the constitution of the sociopolitical group 'women' as protagonist... The role of the state in the constitution of the collective actors in sexual politics has been overlooked in almost all theoretical work in the area. (Franzway *et al.*, 1989: 39)

Much recent work on the state, whether feminist or not, has attempted to transcend the dichotomy with which I began this chapter. Thus the state is conceptualised as representing interests constituted elsewhere and as reproducing the social divisions and inequalities which structure it. However, it is also argued that the state plays a part in constituting these social divisions and political categories through its forms of representation and intervention and the operation of its social and legal policies (Jessop, 1982; Esping-Anderson, 1990; Cooper, 1995). Thus, in the words of Esping-Anderson:

> The welfare state is not just a mechanism that intervenes in, and possibly
> corrects, the structure of inequality; it is, in its own right, a system of strat-
> ification. It is an active force in the ordering of social relations. (Esping-
> Anderson, 1990: 23)

This dialectical process between state and society is one that is
mediated by social movements and its recognition and incorporation into analyses of the state enable the dichotomy between representational and non-representational theories to be overcome. The
state constitutes political interests, but this constitution takes place
on the basis of the material social relations which structure the
unequal access to resources characteristic of capitalist societies.

Thus contemporary feminist understandings of the state, along
with those of Jessop and Esping-Anderson, attempt to transcend the
representational/non-representational dichotomy, seeing the state as
constituted by and constituting the political interests of gender and
class. This theoretical recognition of the chameleon-like nature of
the state has been facilitated by the political practice of feminist
social movements. Thus feminist social movements engage with the
state by confronting it *and* by working within it; it is experienced as
both enabling and constraining, as oppressive and responsive to
pressure for change. Engaging with the state courts the danger that
feminist interests will be lost sight of and issues redefined in non-
feminist terms, but it also holds out the promise that feminist
demands will be met and feminist interests represented within and
by the state. This means that the state has to be engaged with both
internally and externally in order to change its policies and to challenge the gender order. The ambivalence of second wave feminism
towards the state, and the competing theorisations of the state that I
have outlined here, could therefore be seen as arising from the
contradictory nature of the state itself rather than constituting mutually exclusive ways of theorising it.

As well as moving beyond these dichotomous understandings of
the state, 'conventional' state theory has been influenced by the
critiques of the class paradigm emanating from contemporary social
movements. Thus Esping-Anderson recognizes the importance of
the family as well as the economy, although he is less successful in
integrating this into his theorisation of welfare states, and Jessop
attributes importance to civil society as the basis for relations of
domination represented at the level of the state. However, they both
retain the split between economy and family or civil society, linking
class interests to the former and gender interests to the latter. In

order to overcome this public–private division between class and gender, it is important to recognize that social movements, such as the labour movement, which are generally seen as representing class interests, also represent gender interests; a feminist insight that has not been absorbed into mainstream state theory. As we shall see, these criticisms can also be levelled at social movement theory. This is explored in the next chapter in order to develop a fuller under-standing of the relationship between social movements, the state and social policies.

Chapter 2

Theorising Social Movements

Having explored different ways of analysing the state, I now focus on social movement theory in order to assess its usefulness for understanding feminist social movements and their impact on social policies. There are two main variants of social movement theory, new social movement theory (NSMT) which is European in origin and resource mobilisation theory (RMT) which emanates from the US. I look first at NSMT with its emphasis on the cultural dimensions of contemporary social movements and the structural conditions which explain their emergence. I then discuss RMT with its focus on organisations and the notion of rational action. Finally I explore the limitations of these theories focusing specifically on the difficulties they encounter when dealing with feminist social movements.

New social movement theory

NSMT defines contemporary social movements as new, but there is considerable debate about whether and in what ways they are significantly different from other social movements (for example Melucci, 1980, 1985, 1988, 1989; Olofsson, 1988; Rucht, 1988; Tilly, 1988; Plotke, 1990; Bagguley, 1992; Eder, 1993; Tarrow, 1994; Buechler, 1995). Many books and articles contain the question, 'What is new about new social movements?' and most of the answers relate to the difference between new social movements and the allegedly central social movement of capitalist industrial societies, the labour movement. Thus new social movements are not based on 'traditional forms of class conflict' (Melucci, 1985: 335), their values are distinct from those of the labour movement and they embody a fundamental critique of modernity and rationality. However, the most important dimension of new social movements is that they belong to a 'different systemic location' from previous social movements (Melucci, 1989: 42). Thus new social movements are associated with systemic change, whether this be conceptualised as a transition to a post-industrial or programmed society (Touraine, 1981), a transition to disorganised capitalism (Lash and Urry, 1987) or the emergence of post-modernity (Melucci, 1989; Eyerman and Jamison, 1991). Their structural location means that they are primarily cultural rather than political, bringing about social change through the transformation of cultural codes and collective identities. They are concerned with 'cultural reproduction, social integration, and socialisation' and seek to defend the life world from encroachment by the system (Habermas, 1981: 33). The 'new politics' is about 'quality of life, equality, individual self-realisation, participation, and human rights' whereas the 'old politics' is based on 'economic, social, domestic and military security' (Habermas, 1981: 33). New social movements arise not from relations of production and distribution but within the sphere of reproduction or the life world, hence issues of resource distribution are said to be irrelevant to them (Kriesi *et al.*, 1995: xix). Their action is allegedly directed not towards the state but primarily concerns civil society which needs protection from an ever expanding, interventionist state.

Similarly, Alain Touraine argues that in post-industrial societies 'social movements form around what is called consumption in the name of personal or collective identity... not in relation to the system of ownership' (Touraine, 1977: 323) and that the struggle between 'capital and labour in the factory' which characterised industrial society has been superseded by the struggle between 'social forces for the control of historicity[1] and of the action of society upon itself' (Touraine, 1981: 9). These social forces are social movements and their struggles are about culture and meaning. Some NSM theorists distinguish social movements from political movements; the latter being concerned with the state and state power, the former with cultural codes, specifically 'the production of symbolic goods... of information and images, of culture itself' (Touraine, 1985: 774). Thus, '*social movements*, in a strict sense, represent conflicting efforts to control cultural patterns... in a given societal type' (Touraine, 1985: 776). New social movements are therefore located in civil society and are involved in bringing about cultural change (Scott, 1990: 19).

The structural location of new social movements is also reflected in their social base which is no longer the working class but the 'new class' (Kriesi, 1989; Eder, 1993) or the new middle class in association with the old rural classes and those who are peripheral to or outside the labour market (Melucci, 1988). The new middle class is drawn from the human service professions and/or the public sector and their activism is explained by their relatively high levels of education and their access to information (Offe, 1985). This may lead them to question the way society is run and the decisions that are taken thus motivating them to participate in collective action. Those who are marginal in terms of the labour market – students, housewives, unemployed people – have the resource of time at their disposal, are often on the receiving end of bureaucratic control and manipulation and are unable to participate fully in a society based on employment and consumption. For instance women, as mothers, sisters and partners, far outnumber men as clients of social services. Their experience thus predisposes them towards action. It is precisely the main protagonists in old social movements and conflict that are absent from new social movements, the industrial working class and those who wield economic power. Thus new social movements are class based, as are old social movements, but their base is middle class rather than working class. This has led some to argue that new social movements represent a 'new politics of class' rather than a new form of politics which has no relation to class (Eder, 1993; Kriesi, 1989). Their politics is the politics *of* a class but not *on behalf of* a class (Offe, 1985: 833). The demands of the new movements are not class specific but universalistic or particularistic and cannot be understood as representing class interests. Interestingly, however, the issues which are taken up by the new social movements featured on the agenda of working-class movements in the past, issues such as cooperative organisation of production, pacifism and so on, but were abandoned in the interests of material security and institutional participation.

The social base of new social movements, their structural location and their orientation towards cultural change are also reflected in the values that they embody which are allegedly post-material. Thus Melucci characterises contemporary complex societies as post-material, information societies. They are post-material in so far as they 'develop a cultural production not directly connected to the needs for survival or for reproduction' (1985: 804) and 'material production is increasingly replaced by the production of signs and social relations' (1989: 45). This latter formulation is problematic; in the words of Mooers and Sears: 'One wonders what people might eat in such societies... Of course, they eat signs'! (Mooers and Sears

1992: 64). The lack of concern with material values which is said to be a characteristic of new social movements may not be unrelated to their social base which is largely middle class and youthful (Offe, 1985; Johnston *et al.*, 1994). To be fair, Melucci is *inter alia* directing attention to the importance of symbolic and cultural practices for contemporary social movements and linking this to the spread of what Inglehart has termed post-material values, especially among younger generations in western societies (Inglehart, 1990). This refers to the questioning of modern notions of growth and progress and the adoption of 'alternative' values which characterise the new social movements. In this sense post-material values may better be understood as a rejection of the materialistic orientation of consumer capitalism rather than indicating the development of a society where material production is replaced by the production of signs.

The transition with which new social movements are associated is manifest in the changing technological basis of advanced capitalist society, the spread of information technology and the increasing significance of knowledge as a resource; all of which affect the form taken by social movements (Touraine, 1981; Melucci, 1989; Eder, 1993). Thus, new social movements operate primarily on the symbolic level. The movement is the message, the form taken by the movement is itself a challenge to dominant cultural codes and embodies different ways of understanding and relating to the social world. Social movements 'perceive' and 'name' the world in new ways, ways which make visible previously invisible power relations (Melucci, 1989: 75). Although these movements do not directly address the state or demand political power, one of their effects is to 'render visible the power that lies behind the rationality of administrative or organisational procedures' (Melucci, 1989: 76–7). Following Foucault, Melucci argues that power is dispersed in complex societies and is invisible, 'playing a crucial role in shaping all social relationships' (1989: 76–7). Once this power becomes visible it becomes negotiable.

This raises the issue of the relation of social movements to ways of seeing and the production of knowledge; a question which is addressed by Eyerman and Jamison (1991). They argue that social movements are 'producers of knowledge' and translate 'scientific ideas into social and political beliefs' (Eyerman and Jamison, 1991: 43, 92). They focus their attention on environmental and peace movements and the workers' movements of the 19th century; however the claim that social movements create new knowledge finds resonance within feminism. Thus as we have already seen, new ways of understanding power and the state have emerged from the feminist movement.

Eyerman and Jamison also argue that new social movements present a fundamental challenge to the:

> Established routines of 'doing politics'... Redefining situations, opening up new conceptual spaces, and framing new issues in political terms – this is politics in its primary form and is the core around which the cognitive praxis of social movements revolves... all social movements originate as attempts to redefine the accepted boundaries of the political. (Eyerman and Jamison, 1991: 149–50)

This position is also adopted by Claus Offe who argues that new social movements represent a new paradigm of politics which has the potential of transforming the political order (Offe, 1990). 'Old' social movements were also involved in social transformations. Thus they were carriers of the project of modernity and helped mediate the transition from traditional to modern society by creating new individual and collective identities and new forms of politics. Now, however, they have become institutionalised and new social movements have taken their place. These new social movements:

> Occur at a distinct stage in societal development, involve new actors equipped with different orientations and identities, and aim at achieving quite different ends than the old movements. In addition, they take these older movements as part of the Other, a responsible party in the formation of the values and the institutions they react against. (Eyerman and Jamison, 1991: 153–4)

Thus the commitment to economic growth, increasing productivity and rising living standards which characterise industrial capitalist societies and their working-class movements is rejected. This may help to explain the antagonism that has been noted between the labour movement and new social movements, the new movements question the very foundations on which the labour movement has been based (Offe, 1985; Eder, 1993; Buechler, 1995: 455). New social movements therefore challenge accepted definitions and political practice and embody a critique of the ideas of growth and progress constituting the project of modernity of which old social movements were part.

Thus far I have discussed the way new social movements are theorised as arising from and contributing towards major social transformations at the macro-level. New social movement theory is also concerned to link these changes to social processes occurring at the micro-level of society. This is attempted by using a concept of collective identity in order to explain the way structural change is translated into collective action. Melucci, who has developed this concept within NSMT, conceptualises social movements as action systems which are constrained by the system in which they exist. The system creates possibilities for action and sets limits on it, it is thus enabling and constraining, but it is the negotiation and renegotiation of collective identities by social actors which provides the link between individuals and social structures or systems. He defines collective identity as 'a shared definition of the field of opportunities and constraints offered to collective action' (Melucci, 1985: 793). It is not, however, fixed but is subject to a continual process of construction and reconstruction. Collective identity involves the development of shared cognitive frameworks, the activation of social relationships and emotional commitment. Cognitive frameworks define the 'goals, means and environment of action', social relationships mean that actors can 'communicate, negotiate, and make decisions' and 'emotional investments enable individuals to recognize themselves in each other' (Melucci, 1989: 35). The negotiation and interaction necessary to construct a collective identity take place in recruitment networks which are found in 'that part of the population which, because of its situation, has attitudes favourable to a movement or a certain issue' (Melucci, 1988: 339).[2]

The construction of collective identities involves change on an individual and personal level which is seen by social movement participants as an intrinsic part of wider social change. In addition the forms of organisation adopted within new social movements prefigure a different way of organising society and embody a different set of values. Melucci stresses that contemporary social movements:

> Do not fight merely [sic] for material goals, or to increase their participation in the system. They fight for symbolic and cultural stakes, for a different meaning and orientation of social action. They try to change people's lives, they believe that you can change your life today while fighting for more general changes in society. (Melucci, 1985: 797)

Although new social movements are primarily cultural in orientation, they may also bring about policy and institutional change through the formation of new elites and cultural innovation (Melucci, 1985: 75; 1989: 79). Melucci thus acknowledges that contemporary social movements can have political effects although these come about primarily through their challenging of cultural codes.

Restructuring the political order

The authors considered so far understand new social movements as arising from and contributing to a major structural change in capitalist industrial societies, a change which involves the lessening importance of class conflict rooted in the sphere of economic production, and an increasing importance of other forms of conflict based in civil society or the 'life world'. Thus struggles for political integration and over the distribution of resources are being replaced by struggles over values and meaning and in defending civil society from encroachment by the state. Indeed, Melucci argues that new social movements are functional for contemporary societies in so far as they draw attention to fundamental problems, such as pollution or the danger of nuclear catastrophe, problems which are products of the system and remain invisible until social movements ask hitherto impermissible questions. In this way movements function to facilitate 'the adaptation of complex systems to the transformation of the environment and to the accelerated pace of internal change they are exposed to' (Melucci, 1985: 810) thus assisting systems to adapt and change. Other writers, however, do not conceptualise new social movements in quite the same way, retaining an emphasis on politics, class and the state as well as recognizing the importance of the cultural dimensions of new social movements. Thus Claus Offe (1985) argues that new social movements should be conceptualised as part of the project of modernity rather than facilitating any transition to a post-modern society and situates their emergence in the context of increasing levels of state intervention in civil society. Following Habermas, he argues that as the state seeks to control more and more aspects of daily life, citizens resist this control and seek to defend civil society and the spaces of everyday existence from the encroachments of the state. This resistance has given rise not only to new social movements but also to the new right, both of which are involved in restoring/reconstituting civil society albeit in different ways.

    Although new social movements question the ideas of progress and economic growth on which old movements were based, Offe argues that there is nothing post-modern in these values, on the contrary they have been evident in social movements of both the bourgeoisie and the working class throughout the modern period (see also Eder (1993) who points to the romantics as embodying similar values to new social movements). He prefers to call the critique mounted by new social movements a modern critique of modernity:

> Rather than an 'antimodernising' or 'postmaterialist' one, since both the foundations of the critique as well as its object are to be found in the modern traditions of humanism, historical materialism, and the emancipatory ideas of the Enlightenment. (Offe, 1985: 850)

The values of new social movements are a selective radicalisation of 'modern' values rather than a wholesale rejection of them. They thus provide:

> A non-reactionary, universalist critique of modernity and modernization by challenging institutionalised patterns of technical, economic, political and cultural rationality without falling back upon idealised traditional institutions and arrangements such as the family, religious values, property, state authority, or the nation. (Offe, 1990: 233)

This latter is, of course, precisely what is done by right-wing movements, an issue that I explore in Chapter 9. Here Offe points to the centrality not only of a critique of modernity but also of rationality to new social movements; I discuss this later.

Offe argues that new social movements have the potential to transform the political order, but such a transformation is not inevitable and depends on the development of political programmes in alliance with other (class-based) sectors of the population (Offe, 1990). For Offe, therefore, a political transformation is possible but only if new social movements form an alliance with 'old' social movements representing class interests. This position shares many similarities with that adopted by neo-Gramscians who argue that new social movements are involved in counter-hegemonic struggles which challenge the relations of domination by creating alternative cultural practices and forms of organisation. Their analysis is derived from Gramsci who argued that the working class would play a central role in the overthrow of capitalism but only if it succeeded in building alliances with other popular forces to wage the necessary cultural as well as economic struggle. Instead of confronting the state and seizing state power, as was advocated and achieved by Lenin in Russia, Gramsci argued for a war of position in which the working class and its popular-democratic allies would undermine the hegemony of the ruling class within the institutions of civil society (Ransome, 1992: 146). Carroll observes that neo-Gramscian analyses of social movements 'retain this view of counter-hegemony as a unification of class and popular-democratic struggles that prefigures a new order' (Carroll, 1992: 12). However, cultural resistance in itself is not enough to constitute a counter-hegemonic struggle, what is needed is a strategy that takes account of the nature of power in advanced, capitalist societies (Boggs, 1986). As Boggs puts it:

> If social movements carry forward a revolt of civil society against the state – and thus remain largely outside the bourgeois public sphere – they typically have failed to engage the state system as a part of a larger democratising project. In the absence of a coherent approach to the state, political strategy is rendered abstract and impotent. (Boggs, 1986: 56–7)

For Boggs, as for Offe, new social movements on their own are not capable of transforming capitalism precisely because of their location in civil society. However they have what he calls a counter-hegemonic potential because they challenge 'ideologies that legitimate the power structure' (Boggs, 1986: 243). In his view a Leninist strategy of seizing state power is no longer viable, but a combination of social-democratic strategies of democratising and expanding the liberal-democratic state and the anarchist tradition with its emphasis on 'prefigurative activity within local autonomous forms, directed against the multiple forms of domination' (Boggs, 1986: 238) would transform the state by, at one and the same time, creating alternative loci of power and working within the state to democratise it: as we shall see, this strategy was adopted by feminist social movements. Thus social movements are counter-hegemonic in so far as they challenge relations of domination and 'subvert the dominant patterns of thought and action' (Boggs, 1986: 5).

Although recognizing the different structural location of new social movements and their important cultural dimensions, these authors conceptualise them as having to engage with the state and other class-based movements in order to bring about the social transformation for which they are aiming. In their view cultural struggle which does not take account of the state is unlikely to achieve its aims of undermining dominant structures of power.

NSMT, in both its cultural and political forms, attempts to develop macro-explanations of why social movements emerge in particular historical conjunctures but does not generally concern itself with how these structural factors are translated into social activity through the action of groups and individuals. An exception to this is provided by Melucci who recognizes the importance of the micro-level of analysis in his development of the concept of collective identity. Even he, however, discusses collective identity in highly abstract terms with little reference to empirical research. NSMT therefore operates on the macro- and micro-level, albeit at a rather high level of abstraction. In contrast, RMT's focus is on the meso-level and it is primarily concerned with processes of mobilisation of social actors into social movements. As Melucci has put it, its focus is on the 'how' of social movements while NSMT's is on the 'why'.

Resource mobilisation theory

There are two variants of resource mobilisation theory, the 'organisational-entrepreneurial' model and the 'political-interactive' model (Canel, 1992: 39). Organisations and resources are central to both approaches but the latter develops RMT to take account of the interaction of social movements with the political process (Tarrow, 1983 and 1994). This is particularly important when considering the effect of social movements in terms of policy development. I briefly outline the 'organisational-entrepreneurial' model before exploring the 'political-interactive' model.

Organisations and rational actors

RMT was initially developed by McCarthy and Zald (1987). They write from the perspective of movement activists who face problems of strategy and tactics, agitation and mobilisation, and identifying those sectors of the population which will be most easily mobilised. Their emphasis is on the social environment of social movements and the way in which it supports and constrains them and their central question is the tactical one of how people are mobilised (McCarthy and Zald, 1987: 16).

Social movements are defined as 'a set of opinions and beliefs in a population representing preferences for changing some elements

of the social structure or reward distribution, or both, of a society'
(McCarthy and Zald, 1987: 20). In order to translate these preferences into collective action this population, or sectors of it, have to
be mobilised into social movement organisations. A social movement organisation 'identifies its goals with the preferences of a
social movement... and attempts to implement those goals'
(McCarthy and Zald, 1987: 20). This mobilisation is facilitated by
the fact that the population is already organised into institutions
such as churches, communities, and social groups and networks of
many different kinds. However, RMT assumes that social actors act
on the basis of instrumental rationality, weighing up the costs and
benefits of any particular course of action before deciding to pursue
it. This means that there have to be incentives in order to persuade
them to participate in social movement organisations because they
will benefit from the outcome of a movement whether or not they
actually participate themselves.

McCarthy and Zald distinguish two types of social movement
organisation, professional and classical, both of which need
resources in order to attain their goals. Resources take the form of
labour, money, premises, transport and legitimacy. Professional
social movement organisations appeal for resources mainly from
supporters who may not themselves benefit directly from the
success of the movement and who are unlikely to contribute their
labour to the organisation; such supporters are termed conscience
adherents. Classical social movement organisations rely for
resources, including labour, on those who support the movement's
goals and are likely to benefit from its success; they are termed
beneficiary adherents. McCarthy and Zald suggest that the
resources available to social movement organisations will increase
with increasing disposable income in society and that this will
encourage a larger number of social movement organisations and
social movement industries to develop. Thus the growing affluence
of US society can account for the upsurge in social movement activity during the 1960s. They further argue that conscience
constituents are becoming increasingly important to social movement organisations in the US, to the extent that social groups 'with
serious objective deprivations... have been underrepresented by
social movement organisations' (McCarthy and Zald, 1987: 28).
Thus they point to the predominance of professional social movement organisations in the US.

They also discuss the relation between organisational structure,
resource mobilisation and incentives. Social movement organisa-

tions function like any other organisation, their primary goal being to ensure their own survival. Individual involvement is based on an assessment of costs and benefits, hence the availability of selective incentives can increase the likelihood of involvement. The incentives available depend on the structure of the social movement organisation. Thus some social movement organisations set up local groups while others do not, these are termed federated and isolated organisations respectively. The existence of local groups provides members with 'solidary incentives' thereby increasing their commitment to the group and, hence, to the social movement organisation. In contrast, social movement organisations with an isolated structure communicate with their supporters directly but there is no contact between supporters therefore no 'solidary incentive' to maintain their commitment.

The more successful a social movement organisation is in mobilising resources the more likely it is to become professionalised and develop specialised skills. They suggest that this process of bureaucratisation is essential in order to be able to lobby, to raise funds and to keep the accounts of a large organisation. Thus professional, bureaucratic social movement organisations are likely to be the most successful in terms of achieving their goals.

Unlike the new social movement theorists who stress the non-institutional nature of social movements, McCarthy and Zald assume that 'collective action is supported by and occurs in institutional settings' (1987: 12). They thus assume the normality of collective action and that rational action describes fully individual participation in social movements and organisations (Buechler, 1993: 218). Their approach is instrumental in that it adopts the point of view of organisations and movement entrepreneurs 'looking outward for resources and reflexively looking at constituents and the authorities for tactics and opportunities' (Zald, 1992: 333). It is about how to mobilise people in order to attain movement goals.

Finally social movement organisations not only represent the preferences of a social movement, they can also shape them; this is relevant to the question of the constitution and representation of interests discussed in Chapter 1. This process has been investigated by Snow and Benford (1992) who use the concept of framing (derived from Goffman, 1974) to describe the way in which situations previously accepted as natural, such as women's pay being lower than men's, can be redefined as unjust and therefore in need of correction through action (Snow and Benford, 1992).[3] This constitutes frame transformation and is analogous to various concepts developed within NSMT which point to the ways in which social movements create new ways of understanding the world and, like them, it draws attention to the importance of culture and meaning in effecting mobilisation. This is something which is very underdeveloped in McCarthy and Zald's version of RMT, relying as it does on rational actors, costs and benefits and selective incentives to explain mobilisation and discounting the effects of grievances on the grounds that they are a permanent feature of society.

Cycles of protest and political opportunity structure

The second variant of RMT concerns itself much more with political processes and with the way social movements relate to the state and it incorporates many of the insights of NSMT into its understanding of social movements (Tilly, 1984, 1988; Tarrow, 1983, 1994). Tarrow defines social movements in a very different way from McCarthy and Zald. According to him movements are 'collective challenges by people with common purposes and solidarity in sustained interaction with elites, opponents and authorities' (Tarrow, 1994: 3–4). He argues that what triggers collective action is not an increase in the availability of resources but changes in the political opportunity structure. By this he means:

> Consistent – but not necessarily formal, permanent or national – dimensions of the political environment which either encourage or discourage people from using collective action. (Tarrow, 1994: 18)

People are encouraged to use collective action when their prospects of success increase. Thus electoral instability, divisions among elites, policy changes, the successful challenges of previous social movements and state form and activity may all 'create incentives for collective actions' (Tarrow, 1994: 6). Indeed, as we saw in Chapter 1, Marx's analysis of the struggle for the shortening of the working day in 19th-century Britain demonstrates that divisions over the issue of free trade between the landed and manufacturing classes created a situation which enabled the working class to achieve its goal of a reduction in working hours.

In this version of RMT, social structure is seen as important in creating the mobilisation potential of a movement (mobilisation potential is analogous to McCarthy and Zald's definition of a social movement). Thus in Marx's terms the class structure of capitalist society creates the potential for the mobilisation of the working class. Echoing McCarthy and Zald, Tarrow argues that mobilisation potential needs to be activated through organisation but, going beyond them, collective action also requires the mobilisation of consensus (Klandermans, 1988) and a favourable political opportunity structure. Gramsci's discussion of the cultural dimension of collective action and the need for a broad alliance relates to the need to mobilise consensus (Tarrow, 1994: 13). Indeed, 'consensus mobilisation comes up against the cultural power of capitalist society – especially of the kind that requires no conscious manipulation but results from the ordinary business of the media and the state' (Tarrow, 1994: 23). Consensus mobilisation, therefore, could also be conceptualised as the construction of a counter-hegemonic movement, particularly if frame transformation is accomplished (Snow *et al.*, 1986: 474).

Tarrow thus locates himself within the European structuralist tradition of analysis as well as the American RMT framework. And he is primarily concerned with the political aspects of collective action, both in its effects and in its causes. He suggests that the emergence of collective action is a response to changes in the political opportunity structure and that these changes, in addition to macro-structural changes, explain when and why social movements emerge (Tarrow, 1994: 17). Like McCarthy and Zald he argues that it is the social organisation of actors into networks, groups and institutions which provides the basis for 'activating' and 'sustaining' collective action. But mobilisation also requires trust, cooperation and shared understandings between movement participants and the negotiation of a collective identity (Tarrow, 1994: 22).

Tarrow also discusses the fact that social movements occur in waves, hence first and second wave feminism (Brand, 1990). For instance, the wave of social movements which began in the 1960s includes the civil rights movement, the student movement, the peace movement, the green movement, the women's movement and the counter-movements spawned by them. These waves constitute cycles of protest which are:

> A phase of heightened conflict and contention across the social system that includes: a rapid diffusion of collective action from more mobilised to less mobilised sectors; a quickened pace of innovation in the forms of contention; new or transformed collective action frames; a combination of organised and unorganised participation; and sequences of intensified interaction between challengers and authorities which can end in reform, repression and sometimes revolution. (Tarrow, 1994: 153)

If collective action is seen to be successful this creates opportunities for other opposition groups to mobilise. This has an effect on oppositional elites, who may demand changes, and on the state, which may respond with repression, reform or a combination of both. Thus, for Tarrow, social movements occur in cycles and have effects in the political sphere. However, these effects may be out of the control of the movements which precipitate them because it is 'policy-making elites' who actually implement policy change. He comments:

> From the point of view of the outcomes of social movements, the important point is that, although movements almost always conceive of themselves as outside of and opposed to institutions, collective action inserts them into complex policy networks, and, thus, within reach of the state. (Tarrow, 1994: 25)

It is important to note that Tarrow attaches great importance to the political dimensions of a social movement's environment, something to which McCarthy and Zald refer but do not analyse. He also places emphasis on forms of organisation based on 'autonomous and interdependent social networks linked by loosely coordinated mobilising structures' rather than the rational-bureaucratic model of organisation which is seen by McCarthy and Zald as necessary for achieving the goals of a movement. In addition he argues that the effects of social movements in terms of policy change are mediated by the state and by 'policy-making elites' and are therefore indirect and possibly unintended.

Further modifications of RMT have been attempted in order to understand more fully the way in which structural factors are translated into collective action. The concept of mobilisation, denoting the process which transforms structure into action, is seen as key to understanding this problem and, as we have seen, Tarrow argues that the formation of collective identity is part of the mobilisation process (Klandermans, 1986; Klandermans and Tarrow, 1988; Johnston and Klandermans, 1995). Others have also attempted to incorporate conceptions of collective identity into the RMT framework (for example Hunt *et al.*, 1994; Morris and Mueller, 1992) and to take account of the cultural practices of social movements (Johnston and Klandermans, 1995). Thus within RMT there is a recognition that issues of meaning, culture and identity are crucial to understanding processes of mobilisation and the link between social structure and social action.

The women's movement

Having explored the two main variants of social movement theory it is now appropriate to assess their relevance to feminist social movements. As we have seen the main argument of NSMT is that new social movements are symptomatic of major social transitions occurring in contemporary societies and that their social base and values reflect this transition. However the evidence on which these arguments are based has been heavily criticised and when attempts are made to analyse feminist social movements within this framework its limitations become apparent.

New social movement theories have been criticised on several counts. First, many critics have argued that new social movements are not new at all. This is argued on both empirical and theoretical grounds. Empirically, new social movements differ considerably from each other and display far more continuity than discontinuity with movements of the past (Tilly, 1988; Scott, 1990; Tucker, 1991; Bagguley, 1992; Eder, 1993; Tarrow, 1994). The theoretical claim for the newness of new social movements rests on the conceptualisation of contemporary societies as undergoing profound structural transformations. As we have seen, there is no agreement among new social movement theorists about the nature of these changes but it is a strength of the theories that they attempt to link the emergence of contemporary social movements to structural change. As Sasha Roseneil (1995) has pointed out, however, the changes that are invoked are changes in capitalism, industrialism or modernity, there is no mention by any of the new social movement theorists of changes in gender relations and thus no means of explaining the emergence of feminist social movements.

New social movement theories have also been criticised for being ethnocentric. This relates particularly to the claims that new social movements are based on post-material values and the almost exclusive focus (with the exception of Castells) on social movements in the advanced industrial world (Gamson, 1992: 58; Mooers and Sears, 1992). Moreover, the claim that material production is being replaced by the production of signs can be seen as resulting from a process of theoretical abstraction which is gendered and which bears little relation to the material reality experienced by most women and many men. Dorothy Smith, for instance, argues that whereas men of the non-labouring classes can abstract themselves from the material production of daily life this is not so easy for women and the labouring classes, even in societies characterised as affluent (Smith, 1988). Women in particular are involved in the material production and reproduction of bodies and things. In order for material needs to be met, the labour of women and the working class is necessary. These needs cannot be wished, or socially constructed, out of existence. This is even more pertinent when applied to third world societies where significant proportions of the population live in conditions of material scarcity. Thus issues of distribution, which NSMT claims are of no concern to new social movements, are crucial to many contemporary social movements including the women's movement. In the words of Tilly and Gurin, these movements are concerned with politics defined as 'efforts to affect the distribution of power and resources in a state community' (Tilly and Gurin, 1990: 6).

One of the main reasons cited for the newness of new social movements is the critique of modernity that they embody. As we have seen, this does not mark new movements off from older movements, indeed a critique of modernity is an intrinsic part of modernity itself (Giddens, 1990; Eder, 1993). The stress on the anti-modern or post-modern nature of new social movements also renders invisible the contradictory nature of contemporary social movements, the fact that they can embody values associated with modernity at the same time as representing a critique of some aspects of its development (Rucht, 1988). This is particularly pertinent to feminist social movements and is something which NSMT finds difficult to accommodate.

Habermas, for instance, defines the youth movement, the peace movement, the ecology movement, ethnic movements and movements based on the preservation of community unequivocally as 'new'. They represent 'resistance to tendencies to colonise the life world' and are about creating social spaces and searching for 'personal and collective identity' (Habermas, 1981: 35–6). The women's movement, however, presents him with a problem. It has the character of 'bourgeois-socialist liberation movements' but is new in so far as it is concerned with lifestyles as well as with rights. Touraine's comments on the women's movement share the ambiguity expressed by Habermas. On the one hand, women's liberation movements are modernising movements because they aim to extend the social and political participation of women but, on the other hand, they include:

A more radical tendency which rejects an equality which appears to be imitative of the dominant male model and asserts the specificity of women's culture, experience and action. (Touraine, 1985: 777)

In his view 'leftist-inspired... feminist movements... are not clearly social movements' (1992: 144). This ambiguity results, presumably, from his distinction between social and political movements. The fact that women's movements are concerned with political as well as social and cultural change makes it difficult to define them strictly as social movements. As my central concern is the development of a framework of analysis through which to understand feminist movements it is significant that, for Touraine and Habermas, contemporary feminist movements are not considered to be (new) social movements.

Melucci also has problems with the women's movement which he resolves by separating it into two distinct parts. He argues that what he calls the women's movement has gone beyond demands for equality and inclusion in the masculine world to stress difference and people's right to be different:

[It] has raised a fundamental question concerning everyone in complex systems: how communication is possible, how to communicate with 'another' without denying the difference by power relations. (Melucci, 1985: 311)

He argues that changes in social policy brought women into the public sphere by providing resources for their mobilisation. Second wave feminism resulted from this and, in turn, affected social policy such that many of its demands were met; sections of the movement became institutionalised, new elites were created and institutions incorporated feminist practices. Rather than diffusing the movement, however, this led to the spread of a grassroots movement concerned with cultural production and issues of difference. He makes an interesting and somewhat idiosyncratic distinction between feminism and the women's movement arguing that feminism concerns those women who were active in the early years of second wave feminism and have subsequently created feminist institutions and contributed to the transformation of institutional life generally: an equal rights feminism. While the women's movement:

Comprises a much more articulated variety of submerged phenomena, in which the cultural dimension predominates over direct confrontations with political institutions... It is within these submerged networks that the female difference becomes the basis for the elaboration of alternative symbolic codes at odds with the dominant cultural and political codes. (Melucci, 1989: 95)

Thus he is arguing that visible public mobilisations of women no longer exist, but women's collective action persists in daily life, occasionally surfacing in single issue campaigns. The women's movement has become mainly symbolic and exists in submerged networks, supporting an alternative 'women's culture' (Melucci, 1988: 95). By separating these two dimensions of the women's movement and naming them differently, he manages to fit the 1980s' women's movement to his theoretical construction of new social movements as cultural and symbolic rather than political. This avoids his having to modify his theory, but it constructs the women's movement in a way which is not recognizable to feminists of either the 1970s or the 80s (see, for example Roseneil, 1995).

One of the central critiques of new social movement theorists relates to their focus on culture at the expense of politics. As we have seen, most of the theorists discussed here do discuss politics and some, such as Offe and Boggs, regard the focus of new social movements on culture as an intrinsic weakness. However, new social movement theorists largely agree that social movements represent cultural rather than political challenges to society and function in the realm of civil society rather than directing their activity towards the state. This conceptualisation of social movements seems inappropriate for the women's movement, either of the 1970s or the 80s, where politics and the state, as well as cultural innovation, have always assumed a central importance (Charles, 1993; Lovenduski and Randall, 1993). It is also not entirely clear that 'the' old social movement was political rather than cultural, particularly as detailed historical analysis of older movements provides ample evidence of their cultural as well as political dimensions (Tucker, 1991).

Despite the claim that new social movements are distinct from old social movements in so far as they are not class based in the sense of representing class interests, the class basis of new social movements is explored extensively. Thus the predominance of the middle classes in new social movements is analysed while the predominance of women is not. Women's high levels of participation in new social movements is linked to their marginal position in relation to the labour market. This, however, is insufficient to explain the participation of young women, students, relatively highly educated and professional women in contemporary movements and their preponderance in some of them. Explanations which do not take into account gender relations remain partial. Similarly there is no exploration of the relation between collective identity formation and structural inequalities, even those of class. A remedy to this lacuna has had to await attempts to integrate new social movement theory with resource mobilisation theory.

Resource mobilisation theory, however, is also problematic, particularly for an analysis of feminist social movements. This is most evident in the concepts of organisation and rational action which are central to it (Ferree, 1992; Buechler, 1993). Ferree argues that the centrality of rational choice theory to RMT betrays a fundamental gender bias (Ferree, 1992). Thus RMT sees potential participants in social movements as devoid of social characteristics such as gender, ethnicity, class or age. In effect this means that the rational actor, unencumbered by ties of any sort and free of emotions, demonstrates 'universal attributes of human nature' (Ferree, 1992: 41). Countless feminist theorists have pointed out that these supposedly universal attributes are actually those associated with white, middle-class males in western societies (Smith, 1988; Hekman, 1990). Rational choice theory assumes that self-interest, with its attendant problems of costs and benefits and selective incentives, is the only motivation for action. Ferree argues that people are motivated by all sorts of things apart from self-interest and that a recognition of this is essential for a theory of social movements. She comments on the irony of a situation where many of the movements studied, including the women's movement, have developed a critique of instrumental rationality, and yet a large body of theorists have failed to incorporate this into their theorising. This leads them to assert a particular point of view as universal and objective. Human action is based on other types of rationality such as value rationality and the motivation for action is broader and more diverse than self-interest. Neglecting this impoverishes RMT and means that it cannot explain satisfactorily people's commitment to social movements.

Problems have also been identified with the concept of organisation used within resource mobilisation theory. It is argued, for instance, that the emphasis on the organisational nature of social movements leads to a neglect of poor people's movements which, in practice, often lack the resources to form organisations and therefore fall outside the scope of analysis. Because of this the theory is said to be class biased (Piven and Cloward, 1992: 318). Similarly, the women's movement demonstrates that formal, bureaucratic organisation is not necessary for a movement to operate effectively. In contrast, it is informal networks, communities and organisations which are crucial (Buechler, 1993: 223). Unlike bureaucratic organisations, these are not necessarily based on formal or instrumental rationality.

Feminists have developed this idea, arguing that cooperatives, women's refuges and so on are often organised as collectives. Such organisations are non-hierarchical, reach decisions through a process of consensus building and practice direct democracy. There are thus no leaders and followers and no specialisation of tasks. Skills are shared and everyone knows how to do all the tasks associated with the organisation. Unlike bureaucratic organisations the incentives to participate are not only material but consist more importantly of value fulfilment and 'solidary incentive such as friendship' (Rothschild-Whitt, 1979: 515). These collectivist organisations are common within contemporary social movements and it is argued that they are based on substantive or value rationality rather than on the instrumental or formal rationality associated with bureaucratic organisation (Rothschild Whitt, 1979; see also Ramsay and Parker, 1992 for a very similar argument). Within RMT most discussions of organisation focus on the latter and this renders it difficult to analyse the forms of organisation and action that characterise the women's movement (Cohen, 1985: 675; see also Buechler, 1993).

A third and related criticism of RMT concerns the focus on strategic action and the assumption that all social movements develop strategies. Resource mobilisation theory is based on an elitist model of politics and society as pluralistic, social movements are explained solely in terms of the availability of resources and favourable political opportunities, and their success is measured in terms of their strategic effectiveness (Meyer, 1995: 177). Strategy is, however, associated with 'instrumental rationality, cost-benefit analysis and military-like planning' and is particularly inappropriate in analysing movements such as the women's peace camp at Greenham where there was no discernible strategy (although there were goals) and action was often based on 'affective and emotional impulses' (Roseneil, 1995: 98; c.f. Cooper, 1995). The idea that the success or failure of social movements can be measured is also problematic, particularly when the cultural effects of movements are considered. Indeed some authors argue that the disappearance of a movement, often taken to mean failure, may indicate the normal-isation of movement issues and their incorporation into the polity (Scott, 1990).

One of the most frequent criticisms of RMT is its lack of attention to meaning, identity, solidarity, culture and the emotional basis of action, those aspects which have been stressed by NSM theorists like Melucci. Indeed, McCarthy and Zald made a conscious decision to consider neither beliefs (ideology) nor grievances when they developed their focus on organisations and resources. Buechler, in his research on women's movements in the US, found that grievances were just as important as resources in mobilising women in both first and second wave feminism and that the development of feminist ideology enabled grievances to be politicised and women to develop a feminist collective identity. He suggests that 'the social construction of grievances may be the critical step which allows members of socially dispersed groups to begin to mobilise for action' (Buechler, 1993: 222).

Despite these problems with RMT, several analyses of the women's movement have emerged from the US which mobilise many of the central categories of this approach (for example, Freeman, 1975; V. Taylor, 1989; Buechler, 1990; Meyer and Whittier, 1994). Having said this, though, Jo Freeman adapts RMT so that it incorporates issues of meaning, consciousness, ideology and spontaneity (Freeman, 1983). She also suggests that the movement entrepreneurs or leaders so beloved by RMT are only necessary to a movement if there is no crisis or situation of strain to galvanise the network into spontaneous action. This notion is missing from the original formulations of RMT although the spontaneity of movement activity has been discussed within this paradigm and is clearly an important aspect of social movements (Klandermans, 1988; Rosenthal and Schwarz, 1989). In contrast little empirical research on the women's movement or, indeed, other contemporary social movements, has emerged from NSMT (Epstein, 1990: 39; Canel, 1992). As Tarrow points out, general theories linking system or state development to the emergence of social movements need to be supported by comparative research on social movements in different societies with different political formations (Tarrow, 1983).

Neither NSMT nor RMT – nor the recent amalgamations of the two – have responded to the challenge of feminist social movements by producing a gendered theory of social movements. This is particularly ironic in the case of NSMT as one of its claims is that social movements create new knowledges and meanings which may have epistemological implications (Eyerman and Jamison, 1991; Snow and Benford, 1992). Clearly the new knowledges and meanings which have emerged from second wave feminism have not yet been incorporated into social movement theory and, as a result, it has difficulties in accommodating feminist social movements. This is true for both variants of social movement theory as feminist social movements can neither be defined unequivocally as new social movements nor do their forms of organisation and action correspond to those identified within RMT as characterising social movement organisations.

Despite these shortcomings, there are several insights arising from social movement theory which are important when considering feminist social movements and their relation to the state and social policy change. First, within NSMT, new social movements are conceptualised as being located in civil society or the life world rather than in the economy. They are comprised of social actors who are not directly involved in the capitalist production process. They are young people (students, unemployed), 'housewives' and employees of the welfare state rather than the industrial working class; those who are involved in processes of social reproduction rather than production. Second, the emergence of new social movements is seen as a response to state activity, specifically the expansion of state control of the institutions of civil society and, at a different level, as a response to changes in state policies. Third, they are defined as primarily cultural in orientation, thus their challenge to the increasing and inappropriate use of state power takes the form of a challenge to the cultural hegemony of the ruling class. They expose hidden power relations by naming them, thereby questioning dominant definitions of social reality and creating new ways of knowing the world. New ways of being in the world arise from the formation of collective identities whose very existence poses a challenge to the values on which capitalist society is based and often involves the transgression of hitherto unquestioned boundaries. Within RMT the construction of collective identities is seen as part of social movement formation and mobilisation and has been linked to structural inequalities. This provides a means of theorising the connection between social structure and processes of mobilisation (Gamson, 1992; Taylor and Whittier, 1992). RMT focuses attention on the social environment of social movements; specifically the organisations which facilitate collective action and the political opportunity structure which affects both the emergence of and the form taken by social movements. Both theories, however, are marred by their reliance on gender-blind concepts.

Feminist social movements defy categorisation either as new social movements or as displaying the forms of action and organisation identified within RMT.

There are, therefore, aspects of both variants of social movement theory which can contribute to an understanding of feminist social movements but they need to be developed in a way which takes account of the gendered nature of social movements and social relations. I return to this issue in Chapter 10; meanwhile, in the next chapter, I develop a more detailed analysis of the relation between social movements and policy change.

Chapter 3

Social Movements and Policy Change

In this chapter I focus on the relation between social movements and developments in state policies. This involves analysis of a more detailed kind than has been undertaken hitherto and the need to unpack the complex relationship that exists between states and social movements. This relationship has two aspects: on the one hand, states have been theorised as structured by social divisions and the political conflicts arising from them – primarily those of class although gender, sexuality and ethnicity are now being given more attention – and, on the other, states are involved in constituting the social and political categories that form the basis for social movement formation and they provide the conditions necessary for the emergence of social movements. Thus the forms of organisation, representation and intervention of states relate dialectically to social movements as well as to the social and economic relations which structure society. Moreover, social movements take place in the context of nation states. They are influenced by their structure, the power relations characterising them and their modes of operation. In other words the existence of social movements is intimately bound up with the existence of nation states, nation states which are liberal democratic in character (Tilly, 1984; Kaplan, 1992). Here I discuss ways of understanding the relationship between states and social movements, bringing together the arguments of the previous two chapters and exploring the concept of political opportunity structure. In particular I look at comparative studies of the way states affect the emergence of social movements and the way social movements affect social policies. From this discussion I draw out elements that are important for a consideration of the relationship between social movements and policy change.

States and social movements

As we saw in Chapter 1, some theorists argue that states are histor-ically constituted by conflicts and alliances which arise from the main social divisions within society and that the state is an 'arena of routinized political competition in which class, status and political conflicts, representing both elite and popular interests, are played out' (Bright and Harding, 1984: 3–4). These divisions have been seen by mainstream theorists in terms of class, but there are other bases of social cleavage such as ethnicity, religion, urban-rural and centre-periphery which are also important (Esping-Anderson, 1990; Kriesi *et al.*, 1995: 10). Gender, however, is only recognized as a significant social division by feminist scholars, a recognition which is itself due to the emergence of a gender-based social movement. Indeed, feminists argue that the sexual division of labour is funda-mental to the structuring of liberal-democratic states and the public–private distinction on which they rest (Pateman, 1989: 184).

In the first chapter we saw that struggles for representation and over the distribution of resources – in the spheres of production and reproduction – have led historically to state intervention in the economy and the family. In the course of these struggles gender ideologies have been incorporated into policy. Thus in the 1942 Beveridge proposals for the British welfare state women's economic dependence on their husbands was assumed while in Sweden an individual model of social policy shaped state interven-tion (Ruggie, 1987; Kaplan, 1992; Sainsbury 1994). However, much mainstream theory conceptualises the impact of social move-ments on states in terms of class rather than gender or any other social cleavage. In order to incorporate other social divisions into theorisations of the relationship between state formation and social movements it is important to conceptualise the state as relating to the organisation of reproduction as well as production, something which is stressed within NSMT as well as by feminist and some Marxist theorisations of the state. This is facilitated by taking state–civil society relations into account as well as the relation between the state and the economy. However, as we have already noted, there is a problem in defining what it is that constitutes civil society. As Carol Pateman points out, contemporary political theo-rists define the state as the public domain and the economy is defined as private. Hegel, in contrast, categorises both the state and civil society as the public domain while the family is located in the private sphere. There are thus two separations for Hegel, that between civil society and the state, which is the contrast between private enterprise and the 'public power' economic 'man' and citizen, and is a class division, and what Pateman calls a 'patriarchal separation between the private family and the public world of civil society/state' (Pateman, 1989: 183). In much contemporary state and social movement theory, civil society is conceptualised as encompassing the family and is contrasted with the state and the economy (see for example Jessop, 1982). Thus struggles over reproduction derive from the structure of civil society while struggles over production derive from the structure of the economy. The social divisions characterising these spheres provide the basis for the formation of political interests, represented by social movements and/or political parties, which then affect the form of the state and the policies it pursues. The mechanisms linking policies to social movements remain unspecified at this general level of theory although an unproblematically direct relationship is often assumed (see Esping-Anderson, 1990: 108 for a useful critique).

States also react back on society, operating as agents of stratification/regulation. They influence inequalities through their impact on the distribution of resources, partly through specifying the bases of entitlement to the rights of citizenship and partly through their support for the unequal distribution and control of productive and reproductive resources. They are also involved in the constitution of 'social identities, status communities, and solidarities' (Esping-Anderson, 1990: 109) which together form the basis for grievances/mobilisation. But the basic lines of cleavage, arising from the socio-economic structure of society, are given by the unequal distribution of resources which gives rise to struggles over rights, resources and meanings.

Social movement theory has relatively little to say about the relation between social movements and the state at this abstract level of theorisation although, as we have seen, changes in the class structure of society and/or the all-encompassing nature of state intervention are important elements for NSMT in explaining the emergence of so-called new social movements. At a more concrete level, both NSMT and RMT argue that states can have an impact on social movement emergence. Thus Melucci suggests that feminist social movements emerged in the wake of policy changes which provided them with 'institutional resources and motivations' (Melucci, 1989: 93) and RMT argues that the state may provide resources to social movement organisations which facilitate their mobilisation (Canel, 1992: 39). However, the almost exclusive focus of NSMT on the cultural dimensions of social movements means that this school of thought has little to say about the effect of social movements on policy; by definition social movements are not political but cultural phenomena. In contrast RMT has assumed that the success of social movements can be measured in terms of policy change. However, even here there is relatively little that has been written about the way social movements influence policy and even less about their impact upon the state (Huberts, 1989; Jenkins, 1995). Indeed, it has been argued that it is not possible to state categorically that a specific policy change has been caused by a social movement (Kriesi *et al.*, 1995: 212). Further, the question as to whether policy change is caused by social movements or whether both it and social movements are a response to socio-economic and cultural change is far from resolved. For instance, the British feminist movement emerged after legislation legalising abortion and is said to have had little impact on the so-called equality legislation (Banks, 1986; Ruggie, 1987; Gelb, 1989; see also Chapter 5). Similarly, in the US, equal pay legislation and the outlawing of sex discrimination in employment in the Civil Rights Act took place in 1963 and 1964 respectively, predating the emergence of second wave feminism. In Sweden similar policy changes have taken place in the absence of a significant feminist movement (Kaplan, 1992). This is not only the case for gender issues. In Holland policy change reflecting a heightened consciousness of the environment occurred at the same time as the emergence of the environmental movement (Huberts, 1989). Existing research on the impact of social movements on social policy either conclude that it is almost impossible to determine the impact of social movements upon policy change or assume that the coexistence of movements and policy change mean that the former caused the latter (Gelb and Palley, 1982; Gelb, 1989; Huberts, 1989; Staggenborg, 1991; Kriesi *et al.*, 1995: 207–8). Indeed several authors seem to adopt both positions. Some attempts have, however, been made to theorise the relation between social movements, the state and policy change more closely by using the concept of political opportunity structure derived from RMT (Tilly, 1988; Tarrow, 1994; Jenkins, 1995; Kriesi *et al.*, 1995). Here I explore how this concept has been used to understand both the emergence of social movements and their effect on social policies.

Political opportunity structures

A considerable body of literature now exists which relates the emergence of social movements to political processes and to the nature of the state and shows how social movements vary depending on the political context in which they are operating (Birnbaum, 1988; Gelb, 1989; Jenkins and Klandermans, 1995; Kriesi *et al.*, 1995). Some authors concentrate entirely on political processes while others link them to the social structures which provide the basis for the formation of political interests. Here I briefly explore the arguments which relate the emergence of social movements to the nature of the state at a fairly abstract level before going on to look at more detailed analyses of the relationship between states, feminist social movements and policy change.

In a comparison of labour movements in Britain, France, Germany and the US, Birnbaum (1988) distinguishes between strong and weak states. He argues that strong states which are centralised and highly differentiated from society have a different effect on social movements, specifically the labour movement, from those which are weak. Strong states are those which approximate to an ideal type of state, one that is differentiated from:

> A set of social, religious, ethnic and other peripheries. This differentiation implies the institutionalisation of the state, the formation of a tightly-knit bureaucratic apparatus which is both meritocratic and closed-off to various external intrusions, an administrative law and a secular approach – all of which are barriers marking off the boundaries of the space of the state. (Birnbaum, 1988: 6)

States cannot be capitalist but social groups, such as the bourgeoisie (or men?), can 'attribute state power to themselves' hence wield it in their own interests (Birnbaum, 1988: 6). Birnbaum argues that different types of state generate different types of collective action. Thus strong, bureaucratic states fused with a capitalist ruling class facilitate either an anarchist or Marxist-inspired working-class movement while weak states, like Britain, produce reformist, labourist movements. Weak states encourage reformism because they facilitate representation of the peripheries at the centre thus avoiding any confrontation or challenges to state power; they are inclusive rather than exclusive (Kriesi *et al.*, 1995). Strong states adopt tactics which are repressive and this leads to social movements which are violent and which threaten the state. Furthermore, weak states are likely to provoke collective action based on individualistic calculations of interest while in strong states there is likely to be a sense of solidarity and collective identity based on social networks (Birnbaum, 1988).

In a comparative study of the peace movement, the solidarity movement, the squatters' movement and the gay movement in Western Europe, Kriesi *et al.* also distinguish between strong and weak states. Like Birnbaum their classification of states as strong or weak is based on whether they are autonomous from their external environment (their degree of differentiation from society) and whether they have the capacity to act. In addition they suggest that in order to understand the way political opportunity structures affect social movements, it is important to consider whether political systems are open or closed and the strategies they use to deal with the challenges mounted by social movements. Thus a political system that is open can incorporate new political actors, such as Green parties or women, more easily than one which is closed, and oppositional social movements are therefore less likely to develop. The strategies adopted by states are formal and informal and are either inclusionary or exclusionary. These strategies affect the mobilisation and strategies of social movements because they determine how social movements can be politically effective and whether they can hope to achieve reform by being included in political processes. Thus the form taken by social movements and whether they emerge at all are shaped both by their chances of success in influencing the system and by threats to existing rights. For instance, the threat of more restrictive abortion legislation in Britain and the US contributed to the continued mobilisation of the pro-choice movement and the different strategies it adopted at different times (Staggenborg, 1991) and, in Germany, provoked the mobilisation of the women's movement in the 1970s (Ferree, 1987). Conversely, if desired reforms are being introduced by established political actors then movement mobilisation may also be affected, either becoming less likely (which was arguably the case in Sweden (Ruggie, 1987; Gelb, 1989; Kaplan, 1992)) or being facilitated as Melucci has argued.

These insights are useful, particularly the differentiation between open and closed political systems. There is, however, a major problem with the typology of Kriesi *et al.* as their classification of the four states which form the object of their study is not consistent. Thus Germany is classified as both an intermediate state in terms of institutional strength (Kriesi *et al.*, 1995: 37) and as weak (215) while the Netherlands changes from being intermediate to strong. Unhappily they also arrive at a different classification of states from Birnbaum. He characterises Britain and the US as having weak states while France and Germany have strong states (Birnbaum, 1988) while Kriesi *et al.* classify Britain as having a strong state and Germany as intermediate (Kriesi *et al.*, 1995: 37). A similar problem arises in discussions of the relation between forms of representation and social movement emergence. Thus it has been suggested that the degree of corporatism exhibited by states affects social movement formation, with neo-corporatist states being less likely to experience social protest than those with pluralist forms of representation (Gelb, 1989; Nollert, 1995). In contrast, it is also suggested that while corporatism creates channels of access and representation for institutionalised social movements, the labour movement being the prime example, and institutionalises class conflicts, at the same time it excludes groups, such as women or those constituted outside the economic sphere, from the political process. This leads to their organising in unconventional ways to press for access and inclusion (Offe, 1985; Wilson, 1990). Indeed, as Wilson points out, due to the 'lack of reliable measures of either the extent of corporatism or the incidence of new social movements' any attempt to relate the one to the other at a general theoretical level is fraught with difficulty (Wilson, 1990: 72). Perhaps this underlines the difficulties of developing general theories of the links between states and social movements and the importance of analysing different political configurations and their impact on social movements at a less abstract level.

Another important dimension of the political opportunity structure is provided by what Kriesi *et al.* call social cleavages which are either traditional or new. They make this distinction because they are concerned to explain the emergence of 'new' social movements. For them it is the cleavages in society which provide the basis for social movement mobilisation. Traditional cleavages are those arising from class relations, from religion, from centre–periphery relations and from rural-urban divisions. In the past these have provided the basis for the political mobilisation of social movements such as the labour movement. The subsequent pacification (or institutionalisation) of these movements and conflicts provides the space in which new social movements can emerge. If traditional conflicts have not been pacified then new social movements are unlikely to surface because the traditional cleavages, 'still dominate the political agenda in movement politics, absorb public attention, and provide master frames for the interpretation of political mobilization in general' (Kriesi *et al.*, 1995: 25). For instance, in France politics is understood in terms of class struggle and those who are potential new social movement supporters are actively involved in class politics leaving no time for new social movement politics. Thus the dominance of the class struggle paradigm and the so-called old left can inhibit the independent organisation of new social movements such as the women's movement (J.A. Hellman, 1987: 129). Similarly, where nationalist movements are strong, new social movements are unlikely to emerge because they draw on the same pool of supporters. Thus an active political issue based on traditional social cleavages simply does not allow the space for new social movements to develop.

For social movements to emerge social actors need to be mobilised, and this mobilisation takes place on the basis of collective identity, solidarity and consciousness raising. One of the reasons that the continued vigour of traditional social cleavages inhibits the emergence of new social movements is that if the dominant social cleavage is based on class or national identity, then individuals will define themselves as working class or as Welsh or Scottish rather than as feminists or peace campaigners. This means that issues to do with women or nuclear disarmament are interpreted as class issues or as national issues because of the ways of seeing associated with traditional cleavages. In the analysis of Kriesi *et al.* therefore it is not only the structure of the state which shapes social movements but also major cleavages within society. Together they constitute important dimensions of the political opportunity structure.

There is, however, a problem with their classification of traditional and new, particularly when considering feminist social movements. Gender is arguably an example of a traditional social cleavage, albeit one which has been ignored by mainstream social movement theorists, and it has given rise to earlier social movements throughout the western world which declined with the advent of the First World War and the achievement of universal suffrage. It may be middle-class women who are mobilised into feminist movements, but it is their gender as well as their class which is significant; this suggests that gender should be considered as a significant social cleavage which is both new and traditional and questions the pertinence of this dichotomy to understanding the emergence of social movements.

It is also argued that the political opportunity structure faced by social movements is crucially shaped by parties of the left, either social democratic or communist parties. This is particularly the case in Western Europe where political parties are one of the main channels available for effecting policy change. It is not so relevant in the US where there has never been a strong labour movement, where interest group politics is far more important than in Europe and where political parties are of declining significance (Gelb, 1989: 21). Thus, analyses of the peace movements in Britain and Italy show how their fortunes have been affected by the fortunes of the Labour Party and the Italian communist party (PCI) respectively (Maguire, 1995). Similarly, strong socialist or social-democratic parties or trade unions 'provide potential organisational vehicles for implementing feminist policies' but can also be hostile to feminist demands (Klein, 1987: 41; Buechler, 1995: 455). Where access to policy making is mainly through political parties, feminist demands may be diluted and transformed by them at the same time as feminist involvement in parties may contribute to changes in both their organisation and policy agenda. Thus in Italy the PCI took on board feminist demands for the legalisation of abortion (S. Hellman, 1987) but, in the process, changed them so that the eventual legislation did not reflect the original demands (Beckwith, 1987; see Chapter 8). In effect this means that contemporary social movements face the political legacy of the labour movement, both in terms of potential allies as well as in terms of the welfare state and its social policies.

Social movements are also affected by parties of the right, particularly if they support repressive measures against them and, as in the case of Italy in the 1970s, neo-fascist counter-movements (Della Porta and Rucht, 1995). Indeed opposition to social movements often takes the form of counter-movements and can result in restrictions on rights that have previously been gained if they are not effectively resisted (see for example Staggenborg, 1991). Such counter-movements, as well as being allied with parties of the right, may have links with big business and religious organisations (Chafetz and Dworkin, 1987; Buechler, 1990; Staggenborg, 1991). They also form part of the political opportunity structure and may have a significant impact on the ability of social movements to influence social policies, not least because of their effect on public opinion and the fact that their existence demonstrates that an issue is controversial and therefore likely to be a vote loser.

It is also important to consider pre-existing organisations, some of which may emanate from other social movements. Thus Anne Costain argues that the support of voluntary women's groups was important in the transformation of some women's movement organisations in the US into interest groups (Costain, 1981), while Verta Taylor demonstrates the importance of support from organisations which were a legacy of first wave feminism to the emergence of second wave feminism (V. Taylor, 1989). Other social movement organisations and networks can provide support such as those associated with the labour movement (Lovenduski and Randall, 1993) or the population movement (Staggenborg, 1991). Indeed, the emergence of women's peace movements during the 1980s was profoundly influenced by the existence of both women's and peace organisations and networks associated with earlier movements (Meyer and Whittier, 1994).

From the discussion so far several dimensions of the political opportunity structure have been isolated as important in influencing the emergence of social movements. They are the nature of the state, whether it is strong or weak, open or closed, and the strategies it adopts towards challengers. Forms of representation, such as corporatism and pluralism, are also significant but there is considerable disagreement about how they operate. The social cleavages within society and political parties and other social movement organisations are important aspects of the political opportunity structure, as is the policy context which may inhibit or facilitate the emergence of a social movement. What is notable by its absence from this sort of analysis is any discussion of the role of structural and cultural change in the emergence of social movements. Kriesi *et al.* mention that the 'structural and cultural potentials for political mobilisation' are important but do not dwell on them in their analysis. This lacuna is a result of the development of the concept of political opportunity structure within RMT and its focus on the organisational environment of social movements rather than their structural and cultural roots.

Social movement outcomes

Measuring the success or assessing the outcomes of social movements is fraught with difficulty, especially when dealing with movements concerned with cultural as well as political change. However, there have been attempts to do precisely this by analysing their trajectories or mobilisation outcomes, their effect on political processes and policies, and their impact on cultural identities and consciousness (Katzenstein and Mueller, 1987; Gelb, 1989; Kriesi *et al.*, 1995; Roseneil, 1995; Staggenborg, 1995: 341). It is important to take into account all these dimensions when attempting to theorise the relation between social movements and policy change, as cultural change and the mobilisation of activists may contribute – albeit indirectly – to processes of policy change. Thus social movement organisations that ostensibly fail because they cease to exist, a fate of many women's liberation groups during the 1970s, can succeed in terms of mobilisation and cultural outcomes. The women who were involved in them may go on to become active as feminists in other organisations, and the ideas and ways of thinking that they developed within these groups may contribute to wider changes in consciousness thereby leading to cultural change. They also contribute to the creation of social movement communities and new forms of collective identity, all of which are relevant to policy change (Staggenborg, 1995). Similarly, the transformations of identity and consciousness noted by Roseneil among Greenham women can be seen as a movement outcome (Roseneil, 1995).

Changes in forms of organisation, identity and consciousness are defined by Kriesi *et al.* as internal outcomes. These need to be differentiated from external impacts which relate to the political system and to changes in public attitudes (Kriesi *et al.*, 1995: 212). They construct a typology which defines the different outcomes that may be expected and their relation to different types of state. They suggest that there are four sorts of impact social movements can have on the political system: viz., sensitising, procedural, substantive and structural. Their sensitising impact takes the form of getting new issues onto the political agenda and influencing public attitudes. Their procedural impact is to do with gaining access to the political system and being accepted as a legitimate political actor; such access can either be ad hoc or permanent. Substantive impacts refer to gains made by social movements or 'new advantages', such as the recognition of domestic violence as a legitimate cause of homelessness in the 1977 homelessness legislation in Britain. Structural impacts occur when social movements affect the political opportunity structure, either by producing institutional change or changes in the pattern of alliances (Kriesi, 1995: 210). This can also involve changes in the forms of organisation of states and in forms of representation and is something that needs to be taken into consideration when discussing the effect of social movements on policy change. Others have suggested a different typology which includes agenda setting, policy formation and policy implementation (Norris, 1987; Gelb, 1989: 90). Agenda setting is equivalent to

sensitising impact and policy formation involves both a consideration of procedural and substantive impacts; policy implementation
is not included in the typology developed by Kriesi *et al.*

What is missing from both these typologies is any notion that
social movements might result in a transformation of the social
structure, something which is an important consideration when
exploring feminist or revolutionary social movements which have
as their ultimate aim the transformation of gender relations and/or
capitalism and which is an intrinsic part of NSMT. As we have seen,
Walby suggests that an important outcome of first wave feminism
was just such a transformation (Walby, 1990). Whether or not her
analysis is accepted, it suggests that any discussion of feminist
social movements which attempts to assess their outcomes has to
take into account their relation to the structuring and restructuring
of gender relations.

The effectiveness of movements in bringing about policy change
also depends on the issues which they address; it is much easier to
influence some policies than others (Boneparth, 1982; Gelb and
Palley, 1982; Kriesi *et al.*, 1995). Thus Kriesi *et al.* distinguish
policy domains on the basis of whether they are high profile or low
profile and whether they involve a redistribution of resources, a
challenge to the power of established political actors, their electoral
relevance and their relation to the national interest. If the issues
addressed by social movements are high profile it is likely that the
system will be relatively closed and the state response will be more
repressive; if they are low profile then the state will be more open
to movement influence, there will be less repression and more facil-
itation. Policies have also been distinguished according to whether
they are distributive, regulatory or redistributive; changes to distributive policies being less threatening than changes to redistributive
ones (Boneparth, 1982: 11). However, it seems most useful for an
analysis of policy change and feminist social movements to utilise
the distinction between role equity and role change issues. Gelb and
Palley argue that role equity issues, such as equal pay and equal
opportunities, appear to operate within the dominant framework of
liberalism and do not challenge basic societal values or threaten to
redistribute power and resources. However role change issues have
the potential to redistribute power and resources and challenge the
values underpinning 'traditional' gender divisions of labour. Thus
the issues of abortion and women's control over their own fertility,
central concerns of second wave feminism, challenge basic societal
assumptions about women's role and, indeed, the legitimacy of the

public–private divide. They also raise the spectre of women's taking control over fertility into their own hands, thus denying men or the state control over the resources necessary for reproduction. This could significantly alter the balance of power between women and men and, because of this, policy change is much more difficult to sustain and much more controversial than in the area of equal rights (Staggenborg, 1991). However, even here a clear cut line cannot be drawn between issues of role equity and those of role change, what begins as the former may eventually have serious implications for the latter as seems to have happened with the Equal Rights Amendment in the US (Gelb and Palley, 1982). Thus demands for equal treatment advanced by liberal feminism, at least initially, fit within a liberal framework and maintain the distinction between public and private on which the liberal democratic state is based. Gender equality in the public domain can be granted. However the granting of equal rights reveals that gender inequality in the public domain is structured by the sexual division of labour in the private domain and thus threatens to turn into a role change issue. Citizenship is a case in point. Equal citizenship rights exist within the public-political domain, but it is the inequalities of gender, class and 'race' within the economy and civil society that prevent women, the working class and minority groups from exercising those rights. Policy changes which affect these inequalities raise issues of redistribution and threaten the maintenance of class and gender power. They are therefore more likely to meet with resistance.

Feminist social movements and policy change

Most studies of second wave feminism and its impact on social policies have used the framework provided by RMT and/or concepts of the political opportunity structure and political process (see for example, Gelb and Palley, 1982; Katzenstein and Mueller, 1987; Gelb, 1989; Staggenborg, 1991; Costain, 1992). In addition they tend to focus on US feminism (for example Freeman, 1975; Klein, 1984; Buechler, 1990). Little empirical analysis of feminist social movements has emerged from within the new social movement paradigm. Indeed, analysis of feminist social movements emanating from Britain and Europe is scarce and tends either to engage only tangentially with the social movement problematic (for example Bouchier, 1983; Banks, 1986; Bassnett, 1986; Lovenduski, 1986a; Kaplan, 1992; Lovenduski and Randall, 1993) or to draw on elements of both traditions. Such studies attempt to combine an understanding of the political opportunity structure with an analysis of the impact of feminist social movements on individual and collective identities and consciousness (Roseneil, 1995). They are, however, few and far between and the majority utilise the RMT approach. A full consideration of their analyses of feminist social movements and the impact of different political opportunity structures on them is provided in Chapter 4. Here I wish to explore the factors involved in an assessment of feminist social movements' effects on social policy, focusing initially on the political level.

Agenda setting and policy formation

It is unquestionable that social movements have raised the public profile of many issues and established them as legitimate political concerns; that is they have influenced the policy agenda. It is much more difficult to ascertain the effect they have had on policy formation and implementation. Policy formation differs in different countries and is dependent on the policy-making process. Thus, in the US interest groups are influential while in Britain the closed and centralised political system relies on political parties in Parliament to initiate policy reform and the professional civil service to implement and monitor it. Indeed, this has led some commentators to argue that policy change and implementation in Britain have come about without any direct input from the feminist movement (Gelb, 1989: 120, 135). This conclusion is premature and ignores the indirect, but nonetheless significant, influence of feminist social movements on policy change. It is also a product of a reliance on RMT and its insistence that the only effective form of organisation, in terms of having an input into the political process, is a professionalised, hierarchical and bureaucratic one, an assumption which has been seriously questioned by studies of the women's movement (Buechler, 1990). Thus the impact on social policy formation needs to be analysed in different social contexts without making prior assumptions about the superiority of one form of organising over another.

The openness of a political system is clearly important in affecting the way feminist social movements organise and their effectivity at the level of policy change. Thus in systems which are open, where states and political parties are weak, and where interest groups have a major impact on policy formation, social movement organisations are likely to develop in the direction of lobbying and creating policy networks (Costain, 1981; Gelb and Palley, 1982; Costain and Costain, 1987: 210; Staggenborg, 1991). The absence of a state-employed body of expertise and the resultant need for political representatives to rely on experts external to the organisations of the state also creates favourable opportunities for social policy networks to have an impact (Finegold and Skocpol, 1984: 168). The creation of a policy network involves social movement organisations working with sympathetic members of the political elite (Costain, 1981; Gelb and Palley, 1982; Costain and Costain, 1987; Ferree, 1987: 174). Successful lobbying, on the American model, involves the bureaucratisation and professionalisation of social movement organisations (Freeman, 1975; Gelb, 1989). This partly explains the almost exclusive focus of RMT, at least initially, on this form of organisation and its assumption that all social movements are instrumental. However it also leads those working within this framework to underestimate the impact of social movements organised on a different basis, and sometimes to dismiss them as ineffectual in bringing about desired change, an observation that is particularly relevant to second wave feminism (Gelb, 1987, 1989; Buechler, 1990; Roseneil, 1995).

Gelb has argued that the creation of alternative services and, one might add, alternative forms of organisation and loci of power, is one of the ways in which feminist social movements have influenced the policy agenda. Thus the setting up of women's refuges and rape crisis lines in the 1970s put the issue of sexual violence towards women on the political agenda. And the provision of alternative feminist services, with minimal financial support from the state, demonstrated that organisations based on value rationality and direct democracy rather than instrumental rationality and hierarchies can be effective (Charles, 1995). Such organisations also serve to legitimise feminist social movements as political actors and demonstrate that the problems they identify, such as male violence towards women, exist and create needs which require policy and legislative change. Such effects correspond to sensitising impacts as defined by Kriesi *et al.*

Social movements have an ambivalent position in relation to the political system and effecting policy change. It is often argued that social movements are outsiders or challengers to the political system, however Staggenborg argues that this is inaccurate; they are neither insiders nor outsiders, they are both. In her words, 'both spontaneous mass mobilisation and institutionalised groups are important to social movements' (Staggenborg, 1991: 153). Thus the success of social movement organisations in gaining backing for their policies in the policy-making domain often depends on the amount of support they can point to in the form of membership and public events such as mass demonstrations. Specialised 'lobbying, research, and litigation groups' need to be backed up by membership organisations in order to be seen as legitimate political actors (Gelb and Palley, 1982: 52). In addition, the social networks of movement 'leaders' are important in enabling social movements to have access to political elites and, in the case of women's movements, women's presence in positions of power affects the likelihood of their being given a sympathetic hearing. Evidence suggests that the presence of women within political institutions is significant as they are more likely than men to support feminist issues (Gelb and Palley, 1982: 180; Mueller, 1987; Staggenborg, 1991). It is therefore important for the achievement of policy change that women are involved both within the system, as officials or representatives, and outside it bringing pressure to bear (Flammang, 1987: 290).

Thus far we have identified several important variables affecting the impact of feminist social movements on social policy. These are the presence of broad-based support, the formation of policy networks, a caucus of women officials or representatives within the political system, the development of different types of feminist organisation and the perception of such organisations as legitimate political actors (Gelb and Palley, 1982). In addition it is important to recognize that policies do not only have to be changed, they also have to be implemented, and in order for policies to be effective they need to be backed up by resources. A good example of this is provided by the difference between granting women legal rights and providing them with the resources to make those rights effective. Thus, granting women the legal right to be rehoused if they become homeless as a result of domestic violence, or the right to exclude violent men from their home, has to be backed up by resources; and this is often achieved through feminist organising within and outside the state (Barron, 1990; Charles, 1995). Similarly, there is a difference between granting women the legal right to terminate an unwanted pregnancy and providing the material resources that will enable them to put this right into practice. Thus, although Italy has one of the most liberal abortion laws in Western Europe, its implementation involves confrontation with social actors who are opposed to the provision of abortion and who may control the resources necessary to translate paper rights into rights which are realisable (Norris, 1987: 107). I have argued elsewhere that feminist politics can influence the distribution of resources through the inter-action of feminist organisations with the state (Charles, 1995). Thus an assessment of the impact of feminist social movements on social policy has to take into account not only policy formation but also the way it is implemented. The role of feminist organisations in policy implementation and increasing women's access to resources is explored in Chapter 7.

Cultural values and structural change

Social movements have a complicated relationship to policy change, not least because it is often policy change, either positive or negative, that prompts their mobilisation. Thus, as we have already seen, in Germany the threat of restrictive abortion legislation served to mobilise women while in the US and Britain progressive equal-ity and abortion legislation served the same purpose (Gelb and Palley, 1982; Gelb, 1989; Melucci, 1989; Buechler, 1990). Simi-larly changes in identity and consciousness, as well as being outcomes of social movements are also their precursors (Klein, 1987; Buechler, 1990). These issues are explored more fully in Chapter 4. Here it is important to note that cultural change may also be significant in affecting the ways in which social movements can bring about policy changes. Thus feminist movements have stressed the importance of consciousness raising as a means of creating collective identity within the movement, while propaganda and education are aimed at raising the awareness of non-activists about feminist issues. Together these contribute to changes in cultural meanings, life-styles and ways of seeing the world, that is, cognitive frameworks or master frames, which can in turn have an effect on actors within the policy domain. This also involves the formation of social movement communities which 'provide a basis for ongoing mobilization and progressive reform of dominant institutions' (Buechler, 1990: 76). Thus, in Britain in the 1970s, local women's groups used cultural forms as a means of transforming conscious-ness. They wrote plays and staged street theatre as part of the campaign against attempts to reduce the upper time limit on abor-tion and in an effort to raise women's awareness of the issues involved. These cultural interventions were often combined with more conventional forms of political organising such as public meetings addressed by sympathetic women MPs. British refuge groups continue to be involved in educational work with state organisations such as local authorities, social services and police forces in an attempt to change their responses to women who are threatened with domestic violence. Indeed, it has been argued that refuge groups and their networks of supporters constitute a social movement community and, as such, are involved in contributing to policy change (Charles and Davies, 1997). Gelb suggests that the importance of educational campaigns is recognized in the US but not in Britain but this is not an accurate assessment of the state of feminist politics in the UK (Gelb, 1989: 122; Charles, 1995). Thus cultural change needs to be taken into consideration in assessing the impact of social movements on social policies.

In addition value change and identity transformation affect both the likelihood of women running for political office and the number of women within organisations. There are increasing numbers of women in political parties and elected to local and central government. There is also evidence of a change in consciousness and identity in a feminist direction among women in public office in the US (Mueller, 1987). These developments are likely to have an impact on policy because an increase in the number of women above a certain 'critical mass' within organisations affects the likelihood of their raising and pursuing feminist issues (Flammang, 1987: 304; Lovenduski and Norris, 1993; Lister, 1997: 158). Individuals who identify with the values of social movements are also found within the organisations of state and are often state employees. This is particularly the case with the expansion of welfare state employment since the Second World War and the associated changes in the gender composition of the workforce. State employees constitute the new middle classes, the constituency of the new social movements. Thus, as well as influencing the policy agendas of political parties and, through them, government, social movements also contribute to cultural change within organisations of the state. This is evident in developments such as the introduction of equal opportunities policies and outlawing sexual harassment within organisations, together with women's increasing participation in heavily masculinised state organisations such as the police and the military. These issues are the focus of Chapter 5.

Feminist social movements have also affected forms of representation which are changing throughout Western Europe and North America with increasing numbers of women participating in the political process at formal as well as informal levels (Kaplan, 1992;

Lovenduski and Norris, 1993). Thus political parties are increasingly recognizing gender as a basis for representation and are taking seriously the need to address issues of importance to women. This, together with women working within parties for organisational and policy change, may lead to a change in the bases of representation such as the weakening of links between the British Labour Party and the trade union movement. However, systems of political representation, such as parliamentary democracy and proportional representation, together with the incorporation of interest groups into decision-making processes, remain unchanged. It is the input into these processes which has changed, particularly in the US with the formation of feminist policy networks and in Britain and Europe with the increasing participation of women in political parties. Resulting from this, and from socio-economic and demographic changes, policies have developed in the direction of increasing gender equality in the sphere of production and increasing women's control over their sexuality in the sphere of reproduction. And even in Britain, feminist policy networks have been influential in shaping the political agenda and, on certain issues such as domestic violence and abortion legislation, lobbying effectively (Gelb, 1989). The role of feminist policy networks is explored further in Chapter 6 with a discussion of policy debate relating to poverty.

Limitations of the concept of political opportunity structure

There is evidence, however, that both social movements and related policy change may be precipitated by broader socio-economic and cultural developments. Thus the increasing participation of women in the workforce, the impact of two world wars on women's perceptions of their own capabilities, the advent of the contraceptive pill and decreasing fertility levels (not necessarily linked in that order), may be sufficient in themselves to produce policy change and/or social movements; and policy change may itself precipitate social movements. It may also be the case that social movements have the effect of bringing social policies into line with the needs of the economy (Mitchell, 1986) and that changes in gender identity and consciousness, as well as being outcomes of feminist social movements, are also the necessary precursors of their emergence (cf. Buechler, 1990; Kaplan, 1992). There is, therefore, considerable debate about the extent to which policy change results from events in the political domain or whether it is caused by socio-economic developments. Analyses which focus on the political opportunity structure tend to neglect the effect of changes at the socio-economic level while the reverse is also true. This reflects the difference between state- and society-centred approaches and returns us to the different understandings of the state discussed in Chapter 1. Thus some theorists suggest that given certain economic developments, states are likely to pursue similar policies independent of political differences (Norris, 1987: 6). Equal pay policies are therefore a result of economic developments, such as the expansion of the service sectors of advanced industrial economies post-Second World War and associated labour shortages, rather than arising from the impact of the labour movement and social democracy or women's movements (Norris, 1987: 8). However, evidence shows that political parties do have an impact on policy formation and implementation, with social democratic parties being more likely than others to introduce policies which reduce social, including gender, inequalities and which support feminist demands (Norris, 1987: 11). This suggests that it is important to take both socio-economic and political developments into account when attempting to explain changing social policies. Thus in all advanced industrial societies divorce and abortion laws have been liberalised, women's access to fertility control and maternity and child welfare services have been improved, and women's ability and right to control their own sexuality have been recognized (Norris, 1987: 105; Walby, 1990). However, the form taken by this process of liberalisation has been affected by feminist social movements and the political complexion of the reforming government.

In order to assess the impact of feminist social movements on social policies it is therefore important to take into account the socio-economic, cultural and political changes which precede the emergence of particular movements as well as those which can be attributed to their existence. It may be that social movements are part of a process of social change which is in train before their emer-gence. The contribution of feminist social movements to this process is assessed in the following chapters which focus on the conditions which gave rise to second wave feminism (Chapter 4) and the policy changes with which it is associated.

Chapter 4

The Emergence of Second Wave Feminism

In this chapter I focus on the socio-economic and demographic changes which gave rise to second wave feminism as a social movement in Western Europe and North America and the political opportunity structures which affected the form of the movements. The chapter is divided into two parts, focusing first on the societal changes which preceded the emergence of women's liberation movements and, second, on the effect of different states and political systems on the form they took. I shall be concerned to bring together analysis of structural change with changes at the meso- and micro-levels of society which, together, created the conditions for the emergence of second wave feminism.[1]

Social movement theorists have identified various factors as conducive to the emergence of social movements. At the structural level these factors tend to be categorised as either political or cultural (depending on the theoretical orientation of the author) and to relate to changes in capitalism, industrialism or modernity; there is no attempt to theorise them in terms of gender. This is a particularly disabling omission when it is the women's movement which is being studied. Thus, on the political side, attention is focused on social cleavages, their political representation in the form of parties and/or interest groups and the strength or weakness and openness/closedness of the state, while the cultural factors identified as important are cultural codes, changing values, collective identities and consciousness. At the meso-level and for those using a resource mobilisation theory (RMT) problematic, the emergence of second wave feminism is often linked to the civil rights movement in the US and the New Left and the students' movement in Britain and Europe. It is conceptualised as being facilitated by previous social movements in a cycle of protest which began in the late 1950s and early 1960s. But what was happening to women which led them to take to the streets? What changes were occurring in their lives and what was causing these changes? In order to answer these questions I look at structural change, changing patterns of employment and family formation and changes in identity, consciousness and values.

Structural change

Whereas the emergence of the first wave of feminism has to be understood (at least partly) as the result of the completion of the transition from an agrarian to an industrial economy, the second wave was associated with a change occurring within established industrial-capitalist economies. After the Second World War the expansion of advanced capitalist economies was increasingly based on mass production of consumer goods which required mass employment, both for purposes of production and in order to ensure that people had enough wages in order to be able to consume the goods that were being produced. Alongside this was the expansion of the service sector and the welfare state, both of which recruited large numbers of women. In the late 1960s and early 1970s, however, capitalism entered a period of crisis. The consequent restructuring involved a move to more capital intensive forms of production and a shift from mass, whole-product production generating a stable demand for labour to globalised and fragmented forms of production undertaken by 'flexible' firms. This, together with the growing importance of information technology, has produced changes in the occupational structure such that 'traditional' working-class jobs have declined dramatically while white-collar and service sector jobs have increased. What is significant about this for class theorists is the emergence of a 'new' middle class which provides the basis for 'new' social movements. However, from a feminist perspective what is significant are its gender and ethnic dimensions. 'Traditional' working-class jobs had been usually monopolised by white men (Beynon, 1975; Cockburn, 1983) whereas white-collar and service sector jobs rely largely on female and so-called 'immigrant' labour (Doyal, 1981). Thus the NHS, for example, is the largest employer of women in Britain and a significant proportion of its employees are from ethnic minorities (Doyal, 1981: 201–2; Pierson, 1991: 135). Indeed, the expansion of health, education and social services largely accounts for the increases in women's labour force participation since the Second

World War (Pierson, 1991: 73) and 'for between 47 per cent (US) and 89 per cent (Sweden) of the growth in female non-agricultural labour force participation in the period 1960–1980' (Pierson, 1991: 79). How can this shift in the gender and ethnic composition of the workforce be explained?

There are two types of explanation. One explains it by recourse to changes in the nature of capitalism while the other argues that it is due to changes in patriarchy or a combination of the two. Walby, for instance, suggests that the degree and form of patriarchy have changed in response to changes in capitalism and the requirements of economic production *together with* women's political mobilisation in the 19th and early 20th centuries. This mobilisation resulted in the legitimation of their participation in the public sphere and an associated shift from private to public patriarchy (Walby, 1990). Specifically Walby argues that the achievement of civil rights and access to higher education by women early in the 20th century facilitated and legitimated women's participation in the workforce which has, as a result, increased throughout the 20th century, particularly since the Second World War. Associated with the legitimation of women's entry to the public sphere is a change in state policy such that legislation to exclude women from certain forms of paid employment has been replaced by endorsement and even encouragement of women's paid employment. Walby's argument is weak, however, in so far as it fails to specify the material basis of this shift in the relations of patriarchy. She argues that it is a result of political struggles by women, struggles for the vote, for access to higher education, for the right to own property, that is, for civil and political rights, but she does not specify fully the changes in material circumstances which led to these struggles.

In contrast Steven Buechler argues that the material changes which led to the emergence of first wave feminism in the US were the decline in women's productive role together with decreasing fertility levels associated with industrialisation (Buechler, 1990: 13). He therefore links the emergence of first wave feminism to changes in the material organisation of production and reproduction. Declining fertility levels were also a feature of the last decades of the 19th century in Britain, and throughout north-west Europe; this was associated with the later period of industrialisation and the need for a skilled and literate rather than simply numerous labour force (Seccombe, 1993: 157, 182). At the same time protective legislation and restrictive practices excluded women from certain occupations and motherhood and domesticity were elaborated as full-time roles for women (Wilson, 1977). Thus declining levels of fertility and the exclusion particularly of middle-class women from productive activity outside the home are the material changes which underpinned first wave feminism (Buechler, 1990). During the 20th century fertility levels decreased even further (with the exception of the post-Second World War 'baby boom'). This means that fewer women are involved in child bearing and rearing and those who are have fewer children with the result that they are not fully occupied in domestic work throughout their adult lives. This has enabled women to move into those sectors of the economy which have expanded during the 20th century and where restrictive trade union practices did not result in their exclusion. These are precisely the service sector and the welfare state. Women's winning of the vote, the culmination of first wave feminism, legitimated women's participation in the public sphere. Decreasing fertility levels facilitated women's *actual* participation which has increased throughout the 20th century. This, however, says nothing about the terms of the participation and it is this, rather than the right to participate which was established by the first wave, which has been a central concern of second wave feminism.

While class relations and the organisation of capitalist production are theorised as being derived from the exploitation of labour by capital, it has been argued that oppressive gender relations arise from the dominance and control of men over women's labour, whether paid or unpaid, public or private, and their resulting control over women's sexuality and reproductive potential (cf. Coontz and Henderson, 1986; Hartmann, 1986). The reduction in fertility levels coupled with an increase in the availability of jobs (due to consumer capitalism, mass production, the expansion of the welfare state and labour shortages post-Second World War) provided the material basis for women to challenge this control in both the public and private spheres or, to put it another way, in the spheres of production and reproduction.

So how are these structural changes translated into the lives of women in such a way as to lead to their participation in feminist social movements? What changes occurred in women's lives in Western Europe and North America prior to the 1960s?

Employment, education and fertility

In his analysis of first and second wave feminism in the US, Buechler argues that the emergence of social movements has to be explained with reference to background factors and proximate causes (Buechler, 1990: 12). The background factors for feminist social movements are changing patterns of employment for women, declining levels of fertility and increasing levels of educational attainment, all of which can be related to economic change. The proximate causes are a heightened sense of collective identity, the emergence of a group consciousness and the pre-existence of other social movements. In addition attention has to be paid to the political opportunities, resources and forms of organisation which facilitate the emergence of a social movement. In what follows I look first at patterns of employment, participation in education, fertility levels and changing attitudes before exploring the ways in which the political context influenced the development (or not) of second wave feminism.

In Britain, Europe and the US after the war there was an expanding economy, based on consumer capitalism and an expansion of the welfare state. This resulted in acute labour shortages which could only be met by tapping the labour reserve constituted by married women and, in the case of Britain, calling on workers from commonwealth countries to immigrate (Freeman, 1975; Charles, 1979). In the Scandinavian countries this situation had arisen in the inter-war years and policies had already been developed to facilitate women's employment (Kaplan, 1992). Women's participation in the workforce of advanced capitalist societies had been increasing since the early years of the 20th century. This increase was largely due to the increasing numbers of married women involved in paid employment.

It is argued that married women's participation in paid employment led to frustration, conflict and strain (Freeman, 1975; Buechler, 1990). This was because they experienced limited opportunities at work, particularly in comparison to men, and conflicting demands at home. On the one hand they were expected to be perfect wives and mothers, happily consuming on behalf of their families and attending to their children 24 hours a day to prevent them from experiencing maternal deprivation. But, on the other hand, they were being exhorted to participate in paid employment by government and by an increasingly aggressive consumer capitalism. This schizophrenia is apparent at the level of policy. Thus in Britain, social policy assumed that men had a duty to support their wives and children and that women had a duty, once married, to stay at home fully engaged in domestic work and child rearing. These assumptions were enshrined in the Beveridge Report of 1942 and subsequent social security legislation. There was also concern about the family and the danger of population decline which reinforced the need to encourage married women to stay at home and have children (Lewis, 1992: 17–18). At the same time the government was encouraging married women to enter the workforce because of acute labour shortages. It was, however, very careful to ensure that the employment of married women did not interfere with their ability to carry out their primary role as domestic workers. Thus, married women were drawn into the workforce, but they were constructed, by government policy and by themselves, as temporary workers whose prime responsibilities were to their homes and families (Charles, 1979: 168). This position was supported by many women in the post-war labour movement and is associated with welfare feminism (Banks, 1986). In addition women were constructed as the prime targets of the burgeoning consumerism, women as housewives were assumed to make all the purchasing decisions on behalf of their families (Wilson, 1980). However, in order to be able to consume as much as possible, women had to earn a wage, and if they did this they were failing in their duties as mothers. Thus married women were subject to contradictory pressures.

Once in paid employment women experienced discrimination and a widespread disapproval of mothers working. Thus a survey in Britain in 1965 found that 89 per cent of women 'approved of a married woman working if she had no children, 39 per cent approved if her children were all at school, but only 20 per cent approved if she had children who were not yet at school' (Dex, 1988: 28). In addition, although women's rates of participation in the workforce had increased since the beginning of the century they had not experienced any lessening of gender segregation. And while women's share of clerical work increased between 1911 and 1966 their share of managerial and administrative jobs decreased. Similarly, the percentage of skilled female manual workers declined while the proportion of women working as unskilled manual workers rose substantially.

Pay for women was lower than for men, in Britain in 1965 for instance, women's average weekly earnings (full-time manual) were 49 per cent of men's. In the US full-time women workers earned

58.2 per cent of 'the median income of men. This varied from 40 per cent for sales workers to 66 per cent for professionals' (Freeman, 1975: 30). Indeed, women who had degrees were earning less than men who had dropped out of high school. Thus although women were increasingly to be found in paid employment, their status and pay were considerably lower than men's. In Gisela Kaplan's words:

> The gradual broadening of women's occupational and educational choices in the 1950s and 1960s amidst a host of discriminatory practices may well have contributed to women's growing awareness of and impatience with social injustices, and it may therefore have been instrumental in bringing about the second-wave mass movements. (Kaplan, 1992: 12)

Educational attainment was also changing for women and the proportion of women in higher education had increased over the century. Thus, in 1920s Britain women were less than a fifth of all university students but by 1965 this had risen to a quarter (Bouchier, 1983: 32–3). Despite this there was still resistance to women's entering some professions and in the late 1960s many medical and veterinary schools used quotas to restrict the number of women entrants. This bred feelings of injustice in young women inclined to pursue these careers. And the elitism of the British system of higher education meant that by the 1960s there were still only 5 per cent of British women at institutions of higher education compared with 30 per cent of women in the US (Bouchier, 1983: 33). Jo Freeman, in discussing the situation in the US, argues that feelings of relative deprivation were particularly acute for these highly educated women and that they were likely to experience the greatest strain. This is because they compared themselves to others with similar educational qualifications and those others were likely to be their husbands or other male relatives and friends. These women saw the occupational achievements of their male peers as something to which they themselves should be entitled but were hampered from achieving because of domestic commitments and barriers to their advancement within the occupational structure (Freeman, 1975: 31–2).

Similar discontent was voiced by middle-class women in Britain (Bott, [1957] 1971: 83–4). But across Europe there was another dimension to the problems faced by middle-class women. Due to the increase in the availability of jobs for working-class women, a trend that had started before the war, middle-class women could no longer rely on 'servants' to carry out their domestic work. Thus technological innovations, such as the washing machine, while lightening the burden of washday for those who had always done their own washing, actually increased the burden for those who had not because now they had to operate the machine, hang out the washing and so on rather than relying on domestic help to do it for them (Kaplan, 1992: 38). Thus, for many middle-class women, the burden of domestic work increased in the post-war years. This made it very difficult for them to continue with paid employment once they had children and a study published in 1957 showed that there was widespread dissatisfaction with domesticity (Hubback, 1957, cited in Wilson, 1980: 56–7). This was to be identified as the problem that has no name by Betty Friedan in 1965 in the US (Friedan, 1965).

The third trend that is important in considering the material basis for the emergence of second wave feminism is the decline in fertility rates which reduced the time women spent in child bearing and rearing, even if they had to look after their children themselves. There was a baby boom in the years immediately following the end of the Second World War, but this was over by the late fifties and the decline in fertility levels continued. This decline predates the introduction of the contraceptive pill which was not available until 1960 in the US and shortly after in Britain (Vaughan, 1970; Freeman, 1975: 28). In the US during the 1960s patterns of family formation were changing with young women being increasingly likely to live alone or with friends rather than getting married (Freeman, 1975: 29). In Britain and Europe similar trends were observable with divorce rates increasing and more women choosing to live alone or to have children outside wedlock (Kaplan, 1992; Lewis, 1992). Falling levels of fertility meant that women were likely to have completed their families by the time they were 30 and to have a considerable length of time free of the demands of small children when they would be able to take up paid employment (Kaplan, 1992: 14). Thus although domesticity and childrearing were supposedly full-time occupations for married women and the ideology of motherhood was trumpeted from the rooftops, the reality was that women were having fewer children and were increasingly participating in the workforce alongside men. They were therefore exposed to the unpalatable reality of their status as second-class citizens in the sphere of paid employment and could compare the way they were treated as a group with the way men were treated (Klein, 1984: 3). Women's increasing participation in the workforce also gave them access to an income of their own, even though their wages were so much lower than men's, and this, if women retain control over it, has been shown to be important in shifting relations of power within households in women's favour (Blumberg, 1991; Safa, 1996). Thus by the end of the 1960s in Britain women were able to control their own fertility and support themselves, either by access to a wage or through welfare benefits, far more effectively than ever before.

Consciousness and cultural change

For much social movement literature, particularly that which operates within an RMT paradigm, emphasis is placed on women's feelings of relative deprivation, the structural strains they experienced and their increasing access to resources. Together these led to the emergence of second wave feminism. What is missing from this sort of approach, however, is a consideration of the important part played by consciousness in the generation of discontent and in the subsequent mobilisation of women into a feminist movement. Subjective feelings of discontent need to be translated into a consciousness of the social and political structures that create this discontent before a social movement can emerge (Klein, 1984). This, as RMT points out, relates not so much to whether an objective situation of grievance exists (although it may well do) but to the way a situation is perceived and the means available (in the form of resources) to do something about it. Thus the changes outlined earlier resulted in the possibility of women's constructing a collective identity based on their shared experience of increased aspirations and the reality of gender segregated employment and restricted career opportunities. What Buechler refers to as proximate causes of second wave feminism, a heightened sense of collective identity and group consciousness, emerged as a result of the socio-economic and demographic changes that took place in Western Europe and North America in the post-war years (Klein, 1984; Buechler, 1990). Women also had access to greater resources, in the form of educational qualifications or cultural capital, wages and time because of the reduction in time spent bearing and rearing children. Thus values, consciousness and meaning – as well as access to resources – are vital in understanding the emergence of social movements (Mueller, 1987: 92).

There is evidence that advanced industrial societies are undergoing a significant cultural shift which first became apparent in the

1960s (Inglehart, 1990: 67). This shift is apparent in the emergence of post-materialist values on which 'new' social movements are based and it is taking place throughout the advanced industrial world (Inglehart, 1990: 373). It involves a move away from 'traditional religious social and sexual norms' and therefore has implications for gender relations (Inglehart, 1990: 177). Post-materialist values are associated with societies where material insecurity is a thing of the past and where welfare states and relatively high levels of prosperity mean that, for the bulk of the population, physical survival is taken for granted. They include a high level of concern with 'spiritual' values and a high regard for self-realisation and personal fulfilment (Inglehart, 1990). The reduction in importance of traditional religion is, in Inglehart's view, linked to a decline in the religious norms which have guided much social and sexual behaviour. Thus the decline of religious values is associated with an increasing tolerance of homosexuality, 'abortion, divorce, extramarital affairs, prostitution, and euthanasia' (Inglehart, 1990: 195). Additionally:

> Postmaterialists place more emphasis on self-fulfilment through careers, rather than through ensuring the survival of the species; but they are also more permissive towards single parenthood, perhaps because they are likelier to take the economic viability of the single mother for granted. (Inglehart, 1990: 199)

Inglehart points out that divorce rates, rates of illegitimacy and rates of abortion have been increasing since 1960 while fertility levels have now reached a level where they are not sufficient for population replacement in many advanced industrial societies (Inglehart, 1990: 201). Thus behaviour and values are changing and together constitute significant cultural change which predates and underpins the emergence of 'new' social movements (Inglehart, 1990).

Evidence of attitude change relating specifically to gender relations is also available. Thus a comparison of wartime surveys of British women's attitude to paid employment with evidence from the early 1960s shows that attitudes had become less 'traditional', that is, there was more of an acceptance of paid employment for married women (Dex, 1988). Similarly a higher proportion of husbands of women in paid employment were said to disapprove of their wives working in the 1940s than in the 1960s (Dex, 1988: 32). Significantly the survey carried out in the 1960s found that there was a generational difference between younger and older women with more younger women 'favourably disposed to the idea of going out to work' (Dex, 1988: 27). This ties in with Inglehart's evidence which shows that younger people are more likely than older people to espouse post-materialist values, part of which emphasises the need for women to find individual fulfilment through paid employment rather than through child rearing. These findings are replicated in the US where 'approval for the employment of married women increased dramatically, from 25 per cent in 1945 to 44 per cent in 1967' (Klein, 1987: 24).

This evidence suggests that cultural change was a precursor of second wave feminism and contributed to the changing identities and consciousness of women which are crucial aspects of social movements. Cultural change and changing consciousness and identities, however, can also be seen as an outcome of feminist social movements and are important when considering their impact on social policies and the state (Mueller, 1987). The cultural changes associated with the emergence of social movements are also associated with liberalising legislation and a period of social reform; these can, in turn, be conceptualised as constituting part of the political opportunity structure which affected the form taken by women's movements and whether or not they emerged.

Changing political opportunity structures

There are three aspects of the political opportunity structure which are important when considering the emergence of social movements. They are the policy context, the existence of other social movements and political parties, and the forms of representation characterising the state. Here I discuss each of these in turn.

The 1960s was a time of reform and liberalisation. Thus, in Britain, a reforming Labour government was elected in 1964 committed to implementing equal pay (Banks, 1986: 218; Carter, 1988: 113). The first British Race Relations Act was passed in 1965, in 1967 abortion was legalised and homosexuality between consenting adults was decriminalised and, in 1969, divorce reform was introduced. These reforms were preceded by government commissions and reports undertaken by the Church; they were thus subject to a long period of public debate and consultation (Wilson, 1980; Lewis, 1993) which 'served to raise consciousness and expectations' (Bouchier, 1983: 37). Many of these reforms can be seen as the outcomes of previously existing social movements. Thus the birth control movement had been advocating a reform of the abortion laws and wider availability of contraception since the beginning of the century and women within the trade union movement and the professions had been campaigning for equal pay throughout the post-war years.

The implementation of equal pay legislation was eventually brought about by the combined efforts of a woman Minister of Employment and a strike by women in the motor industry and coincided with the emergence of the women's movement in Britain. The strike was by 183 women machinists at Ford's Dagenham plant for an extra 5d an hour in June 1968:

> It is significant that the strike occurred in the motor industry because even though fewer than 200 women were involved it threatened to halt production. The women went on strike on the 6th of June and by June 13th articles were appearing in the press saying: 'Five thousand production workers at the Ford factory at Dagenham, Essex, may be sent home next week' (Times 13/6/68) and the next day: 'Over 40,000 car workers are likely to be laid off "imminently" at Ford factories throughout the country...' (Times 14/6/68). By June 15th the government was involved in the dispute, not because the demands of the women were of vital importance but because the lost production 'could lose export orders worth millions of pounds' (Times 15/6/68) and was also 'threatening to lead to thousands of *male* workers at the factory being laid off' (my emphasis) (Times 15/6/68). (Charles, 1979: 272)

This took place in the context of Britain's impending membership of the EC which required legislation on equal pay. Thus the Treaty of Rome (1957) stated that: 'Each member State shall... ensure and subsequently maintain the application of the principle that men and women shall receive equal pay for equal work' (Kaplan, 1992: 26). This had been introduced to ensure fair competition throughout the European Economic Community rather than for reasons of social justice (Kaplan, 1992: 26) and took place long before the emergence of second wave feminism. Thus countries such as Italy and Germany had constitutional commitments to equality for women in 1946 and 1953 respectively (Lovenduski, 1986a: 265, 272). The effectiveness of such commitments to gender equality is, however, another matter. This example illustrates the importance of the supranational as well as the national context in shaping the political opportunity structure faced by emergent social movements and the role that policy change can play in their emergence.

A different situation existed in Sweden, where the social democratic party had been in power continuously from 1932 to 1976. This meant that the issue of gender equality had a high political profile and, although there was no legislation until the late 1970s (Gelb, 1989: 164–5), the policy of wage solidarity eliminated:

> The (irrational) bases for unequal wages for women and other low-paid workers... as a result... the wages of all low-paid workers began to rise in relation to higher-paid workers, and women were the major beneficiaries. By 1970, women's pay as a proportion of men's in the industrial sector was 80 per cent, and by 1980 it was 90 per cent. (Ruggie, 1987: 261)

This policy was initiated in the 1950s and can be seen as a response to acute labour shortages and a desire to facilitate women workers' ability to combine paid employment with having children as well as to circumvent the need to rely on immigrant labour (Gelb, 1989: 157). In 1969 the Swedish social democrats committed themselves to the 'eradication of sex discrimination in recruitment, promotion, and wages' (Gelb, 1989: 12). Sweden had liberalised its abortion laws in the inter-war period, divorce by mutual consent became legal in 1915 and homosexuality was decriminalised in 1944 (Kaplan, 1992). Changes to family law were introduced during the 1960s which were based on the principles:

> That every adult ought to be responsible for his/her own support independent of marital status; ...that marriage is a voluntary form of cohabitation; ...that no form of cohabitation is superior to another; and... that the child's needs ought to be fulfilled irrespective of circumstances and social (family) constructs into which the child is born. (Wistrand, 1981: 18 cited in Kaplan, 1992: 68)

Thus reform in Sweden was far in advance of that in other Western European countries. This, together with the influence of the labour movement on successive Swedish governments and the ease of access to the state, may help to explain the absence of a mass feminist movement in Sweden (Ruggie, 1987; Gelb, 1989; Kaplan, 1992)

In the US, state-sponsored activities were important in shaping the political opportunity structure faced by the emergent women's movement. Thus in 1961 Kennedy established the President's Commission on the status of women (Freeman, 1975: 52). This resulted in a report which outlined the considerable disadvantages faced by American women and the setting up of commissions at state level to research and publicise the position of women. Freeman argues that these commissions had three important effects. First, they brought together many politically active women around women's issues; second, they provided evidence of women's second-class citizenship and, third, they created a climate of expectation. They also created networks among the women involved in the state-level commissions. One of the outcomes of the initial report from the President's commission was the passing of the Equal Pay Act in 1963 (Ferree and Hess, 1985). In 1964 the Civil Rights Act became law and, although the legislation was conceived as dealing primarily with racial discrimination, 'sex' was added to Title VII. This act was an outcome of the civil rights movement and Title VII outlawed discrimination 'by private employers or unions based on race, colour, religion, national origin or sex' (Bouchier, 1983: 38). As many commentators have pointed out, although the inclusion of 'sex' was lobbied for by women, the amendment was actually moved by a southern congressman in order to defeat the legislation 'on grounds other than racism' (Ferree and Hess, 1985: 52). He imagined that support for women's equality would not be forthcoming. The Equal Employment Opportunity Commission was set up under the civil rights legislation to administer Title VII.

The political opportunity structure is also shaped by pre-existing social movements. In the US the social movement which is identified as a crucial precursor of second wave feminism is the civil rights movement. Ferree and Hess argue that women active in this movement acquired resources such as a sense of personal power and the ability to make things happen; they gained organising skills, an ability to deal with the media and experience of political protest. Women involved in this movement inevitably began to apply the precept of equal rights, which was being used to counter discrimination against blacks, to themselves as women. However they were met with resistance from men within the civil rights movement which inadvertently fuelled their sense of grievance (Ferree and Hess, 1985: 46–7).

In Europe it was the students' movement and the New Left which provided similar resources and grievances for women. The student uprisings in France, Italy and West Germany were not simply 'campus revolts but uprisings against the state' (Kaplan, 1992: 12). As with the civil rights movement, women were told by socialist men that women's liberation was a diversion from the class struggle and could be attended to after the revolution. Meanwhile women should be content to service the male revolutionary leaders by making cups of tea, typing agendas and being so liberated that they would sleep with them whenever the men demanded (Coote and Campbell, 1982: 19–20). So as well as providing resources and experience, these movements also fuelled women's sense of grievance against men.

Feminist organisations were also important in providing resources and networks for the incipient women's movement and a sense of collective identity and consciousness. In both Britain and America such organisations had continuously campaigned and lobbied since their inception as part of the first wave of feminism. Thus, in America there was the National Woman's Party which had, according to Buechler, a well-defined group identity and consciousness and a set of grievances and could articulate the grievances experienced by women (Buechler, 1990). In Britain the Six Point Group and the Women's Freedom League continued to work on feminist issues until the 1960s (Wilson, 1980: 182). The former took a welfare feminist position, arguing for state support of women's maternal role, while the latter 'emphasised equality rather than women's special role' (Wilson, 1980: 3). These organisations could also provide resources for the emerging women's liberation movement.

Other social movements, such as the labour movement and the population/birth control movement, also had the potential to provide networks, organisational support and resources to the emergent feminist movement. Indeed these were an important part of the political opportunity structure and alliances were formed between these social movements and feminist social movements around specific issues such as abortion (see Staggenborg, 1991 for an account of such an alliance in the US).

Finally political opportunity structures are shaped by the forms of representation associated with different states. These affect both the form taken by women's movements and their impact on social policies. Here I look briefly at the US, Britain, Sweden, Germany and Italy.

In a comparative study of the US, Britain and Sweden, Joyce Gelb argues that the US is a society where 'strong or strongly structured pluralism prevails' while Britain and Sweden are more 'corporatist/centralist', and that these differences explain the different forms taken by second wave feminism in these societies (Gelb, 1989: 7).[2] The corporatist state is centralised and relatively closed to access by 'outsider' groups while the state in pluralist systems is open and not centralised (Gelb, 1989: 6–7). Although there are problems in using pluralism/corporatism as an explanation of the existence/non-existence of social movements (see Chapter 3 and later in this chapter), Gelb points to some important ways in which the form and direction of women's movements are influenced by the form of the state, its forms of representation and organisation. In particular she argues that it is the corporatist nature of the Swedish state that explains the lack of any large-scale, second wave feminist social movement. This is due to the fact that Swedish politics is based on consensus and there is a tendency to incorporate new political interests into the dominant social democratic party and trade union organisation. Thus there is state commitment to gender equality which is reflected in many policies and it is precisely because of this incorporation and the pre-empting of many of the demands of second wave feminism that an independent women's movement has not developed in Sweden (Ruggie, 1984; Gelb, 1989; Kaplan, 1992). Ruggie argues further that it is the influence of the labour movement on the state and the state's commitment to active labour market policies, including wage solidarity, which has resulted in women's high rates of participation in paid employment and the lack of a substantial second wave (Ruggie, 1984).

In contrast, in the US the state is weak and its formal structure is open and can readily be influenced by interest groups. This has encouraged the development of the US women's movement, even its 'younger' more radical branch (Freeman, 197w5), towards the formation of professional organisations. These focus on the provision of services and campaigning and lobbying around specific issues with the aim of bringing about policy change and or providing a range of services for women. Feminist policy networks have emerged from the movement which influence government and advise on policy formation. Additionally within the US political system political parties are relatively weak and interest groups have direct access to government. The American movement is predominantly liberal in ideology and has mobilised to a considerable extent 'around state legislation and legal change'; it has also been prepared 'to engage with political and bureaucratic forces and to seek legitimacy' (Gelb, 1989: 46). It is probable that the absence of class-based political parties and the lack of importance attached to class cleavages in the political process in the US, together with the dominance of pluralism, has contributed to the relative ease with which the issue of gender has become part of the mainstream political agenda and something which is attended to by the main political parties (Freeman, 1987). The lack of a 'respected socialist tradition and political party' (Ferree, 1989: 175) in the US partly explains the dominance of equal rights feminism and liberalism. But, as Ferree argues, in the US 'the analogy between sex and race' has been of prime importance to the discourse and practice of feminism.[3] This derives from its roots in the civil rights movement and means that women's rights are linked to those of black people via the Civil Rights Act and that both have been framed in the discourse of classic liberalism (Ferree, 1987). In a sense it is the racial cleavage which has framed the way in which women's issues are understood and their rights are fought for.

In Britain the state is not so open to interest groups, the party system remains strong and politics is still largely framed in terms of class. Gelb argues that this had led to the women's movement focusing on autonomous activity rather than attempting to influence a state which is relatively closed to external political pressure. Corporatism in Britain is based on the economic interests of labour and capital and is relatively impervious to other political interests (Gelb, 1989: 15–16). She observes that:

> The backwardness of the economy has further constrained opportunities and value change for women in the class-ridden, elitist British society, reinforcing the concept of the 'family wage', which entrenches the leading economic role of male breadwinners and limits opportunities for women in the labor force. (Gelb, 1989: 28)

This rather gloomy and patronising appraisal fails to recognize both the way in which British feminists have worked, collectively and individually, within trade unions and political parties to change the policy agenda and policies, and the impact of this activity – together with the more 'unconventional' activities of the women's movement – on policies within Britain. However she does point to the continuing salience of the cleavage between labour and capital in Britain which is represented within the political parties and within the organisations of the state and which makes it difficult for gender-based politics to have much purchase. This also explains the continuing importance of attempts to link understandings of gender oppression with class analysis in feminist theory, something which has a much weaker presence in the US.

A useful typology is also developed by Gisela Kaplan who focuses on the impact of class-based political parties on the forms taken by second wave feminism in Europe. She distinguishes four groups of countries and the forms of feminism associated with them. The first group consists of the 'progressive' Scandinavian countries where many feminist demands were incorporated into policy either before the rise of second wave feminism, thus pre-empting its emergence, or as soon as it emerged. This has resulted in the cooption of women's groups into government and their trans-formation into interest groups akin to those in the US, and in the highest representation of women in political hierarchies and govern-ment in Europe (Kaplan, 1992: 58; *Guardian*, 24/10/97).

The second group is constituted by West Germany, Switzerland, Austria and Liechtenstein which she characterises as conservative and resistant to egalitarian reforms.[4] These governments emphasise women's maternal role and make generous provisions to encourage women to have more children (Kaplan, 1992: 144–5). They also maintain class hierarchies (cf. Esping-Anderson, 1990) which mili-tates against middle-class and working-class women forming alliances. The closure of the state against interest groups of any sort contributes to the autonomy and political powerlessness of the feminist movement; although it maintains an important cultural presence.

The third group of countries is constituted by France and the Netherlands where women's movements have also been autonomous and, although small, have contributed to cultural and value change. However the response of the state to feminism in France and the Netherlands was different from that of the German state: in both cases 'the content of the grievances was quickly seen as legitimate and was adopted, albeit sometimes in watered-down versions' (Kaplan, 1992: 175). The largely cultural orientation of these autonomous feminist movements may help to explain why NSMT argues that second wave feminism is a new social movement and is almost solely concerned with cultural change. Some experi-ences in Europe might lead authors in this direction, but considering the whole range of feminist movements demonstrates that charac-terising second wave feminism in this way is totally inaccurate.

Kaplan's final group is Southern Europe where the legacy of fascism and dictatorship and the tradition of underground resistance and strong left-wing parties has led to women's movements which are orientated towards the left and which participate actively in bringing about policy change through influencing the labour move-ment and political parties. Politics in Italy for instance are domi-nated by the class paradigm and class organisation. But whereas it could be argued that in Britain and Sweden the class conflict has been 'pacified' and institutionalised and social democratic parties dominate the left, in Italy this is not the case. Thus the left, in the form of the PCI and PSI, has been strong throughout the post-war years. This has resulted in the activities of the Italian women's movement being directed towards workers' organisations and parties of the left, and feminists have either worked within them or organised externally to force them to adopt feminist practices and policies. This demonstrates the continuing relevance and power of the class-based, left–right cleavage and related political parties to the women's movement in Italy and suggests that its fortunes, as the fortunes of the peace movement, are closely tied to those of the left.

What emerges from Kaplan's analysis is that working-class organisations and political parties are highly significant to the way second wave feminism has developed. Thus, in Scandinavia issues of gender equality have been incorporated into social democracy and the trade unions, in Britain, the women's liberation movement was orientated towards the Labour Party and the trade unions as well as organising autonomously, in Italy the women's movement worked in relation to parties of the left, but in Germany and France no such alliance emerged while in the US feminism has been able to have a political impact independent of political parties. The typologies developed by mainstream analysts are not very helpful in this context as they operate at a far too general level of abstraction. Thus they group together Germany, France and Italy on the basis that they are corporatist welfare states, heavily influenced by the Catholic Church and supportive of a 'traditional' form of family, or they distinguish between them on the basis of the strength or weakness of states and whether they operate inclusive or exclusive strategies towards challengers. As we have already noted there is little agreement on these classifications and it is not helpful to dwell on them further. It is also not helpful to attempt generalisations about the pacification/institutionalisation of class conflict and whether the left is divided. Thus Kriesi *et al.* (1995) argue that pacification of the left leads to a space for the emergence of new social movements, but the contrasting examples of Sweden and Italy contradict this even though Britain and France might support it. Others argue that trade unions and left-wing political parties can provide a way of implementing feminist demands but are often hostile to feminist ideas (Klein, 1987: 410) or that the labour movement is hostile to new social movements in general (Buechler, 1995: 455). Clearly, in the case of the women's movement, these generalisations are not borne out. Pacification of class conflict does not necessarily facilitate the emergence of a women's movement and its continued vitality does not necessarily prevent its emergence. It might be argued that the inapplicability of these generalisations to the women's movement relates to the fact that women's movements are sub-cultural, identity-based movements rather than instrumental movements (Kriesi *et al.*, 1995). This, however, begs the question because, as we have seen, women's movements are neither new nor old, post-modern nor modern, and they most certainly raise issues which challenge the basic gender ordering of society. The reality of gender politics is more complex than such models would suggest and their lack of explanatory power with regard to women's movements indicates not so much that women's movements are different but that the models are seriously flawed.

These brief examples demonstrate that different political opportunity structures and different political traditions have an impact on the form taken by women's movements and their ability or inclination to affect the policy-making process. They also show that generalisations about the nature of the state and the relation between parties of the left and new social movements are not helpful in explaining the emergence of second wave feminism and the different forms it has taken in different nation states. However, what is remarkable is that in all countries of Western Europe and North America, whatever the form taken by second wave feminism, reforms have taken place in the direction of greater gender equality in the public sphere, greater control by women over their own fertility and a greater diversity and tolerance of sexual expression and living arrangements, and these reforms were accompanied by changing cultural values and patterns of employment and declining levels of fertility. In the following chapters I consider the impact of feminist social movements on these changes, focusing specifically on equal opportunities, poverty, male violence towards women, fertility control and family policy. Thus the discussion moves from issues of role equity, where greater change can be expected, to issues of role change which are likely to prove more resistant to fundamental transformation.

Chapter 5

Equal Opportunities

In this chapter I focus on the so-called equality legislation of the 1960s and 70s and the equal opportunities policies to which it gave rise. I explore the impact of the women's movement on both the formation of these policies and their implementation within the organisations of the state and the economy. The equality legislation is an interesting example of the effect of changes in the political opportunity structure on emerging social movements. As we have seen, reforming governments committed to equal pay were part of the political opportunity structure faced by feminist social movements in Britain and the US. This commitment to reform was an outcome of economic developments combined with trade union pressure and, in the case of Britain, the requirements of EC membership. And it gave the burgeoning women's movement the prospect of success in pressing for further policy change. Thus the first two demands of the movement were for equal pay and equal education and job opportunities. Moreover, an exploration of the implementation of equal opportunities policies demonstrates the difficulties faced by activists in social movements once they move into existing organisations and the compromises that are associated with processes of incorporation and institutionalisation. Thus working within bureaucratic organisations can produce changes within those organisations, but it can also meet with resistance and a transformation of feminist demands such that they bear little resemblance to their initial intentions.

The issues of equal pay and an end to discrimination based on gender appear to be examples of role equity issues. This chapter demonstrates, however, that what begins as a role equity issue may develop into one of role change and resource redistribution, hence engendering considerable resistance. As we shall see, the implementation of the long agenda of equal opportunities actually constitutes a challenge to existing gender relations in the private as well as the public domain and raises questions about the organisation of child care, domestic divisions of labour, sexuality and violence against women. These can be defined as role change issues and are explored more fully in later chapters. In this chapter I look first at the legislative changes which outlawed gender discrimination in Britain and the US and then focus on the implementation of equal opportunities policies in Britain in order to explore the effect of feminist social movements on policy implementation within organisations.

Policy formation: the 'equality' legislation

The issue of gender equality and agitation for equal pay did not originate with second wave feminism; in a sense they were the unsettled business of the first wave. Equal pay for women was an issue for British trade unions from 1888, when it had become official TUC policy, and first wave feminist organisations in both Britain and the US campaigned for equal pay throughout the 20th century. It was after the Second World War, however, with women's increasing participation in the workforce and labour shortages, that pressure from women within trade unions for equal pay gathered momentum (Banks, 1986). And during the 1960s the Democrats in the US and the Labour Party in Britain made commitments to introduce equal pay for women (see Chapter 4). It has been suggested that in the US these reforms, as well as being an outcome of pressure from organisations associated with first wave feminism and the labour movement, were also facilitated by the stirrings of the second wave and the instability of political alignments which led political parties to consider the women's vote. Thus, Anne Costain argues that even though the second wave had not emerged in 1963, the incipient movement together with pressure from organised labour and women's organisations, were enough to provoke the Kennedy administration into action on women's issues. This action, in turn, facilitated the formation of the women's movement (Freeman, 1975; Costain, 1992: 18).

In Britain similar processes were at work and have led to the suggestion that the Equal Pay Act can be seen as an outcome of trade union women's pressure and campaigning while the Sex Discrimination Act has to be understood as an important policy outcome of second wave feminism. Olive Banks argues that the equal pay legislation was passed because the climate of opinion and attitudes towards women's paid employment had changed by the 1960s and this, together with economic factors, meant that women's importance to the workforce was undisputed (Banks, 1986). Thus the pressure that had been exerted by women in trade unions since 1888 at last came to fruition. In addition, the incoming Labour government's election commitment to implement equal pay for women, and its subsequent failure to do so, acted as a spur to trade union women and women within the Labour Party to organise in support of equal pay claims (Banks, 1986; Carter, 1988). Women in government were also important. As we saw in the last chapter, it was not until the Ford women machinists' strike and Barbara Castle's intervention that the Labour government legislated on equal pay. Thus, what seems to have been crucial in getting equal pay onto the statute books in Britain was increasing pressure from women in trade unions, changing cultural attitudes, an expectation that government was willing to legislate and the support of women within the Labour Party and the Labour government (Banks, 1986; Carter, 1988). An additional factor is likely to have been the requirement of EC member states to implement equal pay for women.[1] What was not in play was the women's movement. The Sex Discrimination Act (1975) was, however, a different matter; here second wave feminism was centrally involved in policy formation.

In the US similar legislative developments took the form of the inclusion of 'sex' in the civil rights act in 1964 (see Chapter 4) and the establishment of the Equal Employment Opportunities Commission (EEOC) to administer this act (Banks, 1986: 212). These events, however, were not a response to second wave feminism. On the contrary, the emergence of the US women's movement is dated from 1966 and the formation of the National Organisation of Women (Freeman, 1975: 54). This organisation was set up as a direct response to the refusal of the EEOC to implement the measures outlawing sex discrimination enshrined in the civil rights act. It campaigned initially on equal rights issues; later widening out its concerns to include issues of sexuality, fertility control and male violence against women (Banks, 1986: 212). By definition, therefore, the US women's movement was not so much involved in formulating sex discrimination legislation as in ensuring its implementation.

In Britain, however, the women's movement was influential in policy formation. As Carter puts it:

> The pattern of the campaign to achieve a Sex Discrimination Act was a series of Private Members' Bills, backed by increasingly well-organised and visible support outside Parliament and cross-bench support inside it. (Carter, 1988: 117)

In this campaign feminist organisations dating from the first wave, supporters within Parliament and the women's liberation movement worked together both within and outside government. A series of Private Member's Bills was introduced into the Commons, supported by lobbies, attendance at debates in the House, conferences, the raising of demands, submission of evidence to a House of Lords select committee, mass lobbies of Parliament, public meetings and demonstrations in support of the bill. Many of these forms of action were reminiscent of the campaign for women's suffrage. But it was not until a Labour government was elected in 1974 that a firm commitment to legislation outlawing discrimination on grounds of sex was made. The bill became law in 1975, the same year as the Equal Pay Act and a year before the EC issued its Equal Treatment Directive which deals with discrimination in employment (Gregory, 1992: 47; Blakemore and Drake, 1996: 39). Joyce Butler, a Labour MP, pointed to the importance for the passing of the Sex Discrimination Act, of:

> The tremendous surge of public support for the idea of the Bill, the tremendous interest taken by all the established women's organisations and the newer ones that sprang up after the celebration of 50 years of women having the vote. (*Hansard*, 1972–3, vol. 849, cited in Carter, 1988: 123).

She therefore saw the formation of the women's liberation movement and the pressure it brought to bear as a factor in explaining the public support for a bill outlawing sex discrimination. This shift in attitudes was apparent in the political parties, both Labour and Conservative, in the labour movement which supported such a bill, and in the media.

Feminist organisations, old and new, were therefore crucial in getting the Sex Discrimination Act onto the statute books and operated in alliance with other social movement organisations and with women in political parties and in government (Gelb, 1989). Thus, it was both insiders and outsiders who were important in ensuring that this bill became law. Finally, it was ensured a safe passage by a Labour government led by Harold Wilson (Carter, 1988). The fact that both the Equal Pay Act and the Sex Discrimination Act were passed by Labour governments supports the hypothesis that the fortunes of the main left wing or social democratic party are crucial for the impact of social movements on policy formation (Kriesi *et al.*, 1995).

Despite these acts enshrining in law two of the demands of the women's movement, there is considerable controversy about their overall impact on gender inequalities. Far from removing or at least ameliorating gender inequalities there is some support for the view that they have become even more entrenched. Thus it is argued that the Equal Pay Act, because it had a five-year implementation period and only allowed women to claim equal pay with men if they were doing the same or broadly similar work, has actually resulted in an intensification of gender segregation within the workforce, with employers ensuring that women and men were employed on different jobs so that no direct comparison of their wages could be made (Snell, 1986). At the aggregate level, although there was some improvement in pay levels in the years immediately following its implementation, this peaked in 1977 and women's pay remains at around 70 per cent of men's (Carter, 1988). The exact disparity depends on whether hourly or weekly earnings are being considered and for what types of occupation. It is commonly stated, for instance, that women's earnings are around 80 per cent of men's having risen to that point from a low of 71 per cent in 1975 (Rees, in press: 1, citing the *New Earnings Surveys* of 1975 and 1995). However, if average gross weekly earnings for full-time employees on adult rates are compared, overall women's earnings are 73 per cent of men's (*New Earnings Survey*, 1997). The legislation has not tackled, and was not designed to tackle, the gender segregation in the workforce which underpins gender-differentiated rates of pay. This means that although the demand for equal pay appears to have been met on paper, in reality women continue to work for lower rates of pay than do men and the problem of women's low pay has not been solved. The Equal Pay Act was amended in 1984, a tangible effect of EC membership, to allow women to claim equal pay with men for work of equal value. The implications of this are explored later.

There are also problems with the Sex Discrimination Act which covers employment practice (issues of recruitment and promotion for example), policy and training and education. The concept of equality embodied in the legislation was one which assumed that discrimination in the public sphere was the only obstacle to girls' and women's equal participation and achievement in education and employment. It outlawed direct and indirect discrimination and was concerned to treat men and women equally. Underpinning it is an individual conception of the obstacles to gender equality (Ruggie, 1984: 9); the problems faced by women in employment are seen as stemming from women themselves rather than arising from social structures. The solution is therefore to improve individual women's competencies so that they may compete within the labour market as it is currently structured rather than attempting to alter the social structures which lead to gender inequalities. This however takes male work patterns as the model. Women are expected to conform to these patterns and to behave as if they are men. And, as Cynthia Cockburn points out:

> It is a law giving rights not to women, as a historically disadvantaged group, but to *both sexes*. (Cockburn, 1991: 33)

Thus men can use the law to oppose measures which are intended to right these historical disadvantages, such as the introduction by the Labour Party of quotas for women which was declared unlawful by an industrial tribunal in January 1996 (*Guardian*, 9/1/96).

In addition the legislation does not cover social security and taxation, areas which had been highlighted by the women's movement as discriminatory against women and in need of reform. Neither does it include consideration of child care arrangements or sexuality. Indeed, the 1974 Equality for Women white paper which preceded the act specified that 'the legislation does not apply to personal and intimate relationships' (cited in Edwards and McKie, 1993/4: 54). As Edwards and McKie point out, this exclusion means that all women are disadvantaged because it leaves intact domestic divisions of labour which allocate responsibility for child care and domestic labour to women. Thus men continue to be more available than are women to work full time and overtime and can spend much more time on developing their careers.

At first glance, the elimination of gender-based discrimination in the public domain, a role equity issue, can do little to tackle the deep seated roots of gender segregation in paid employment. As such the passing of this legislation has muted the feminist challenge and absorbed feminists' energies without contributing to the transformation of gender relations that the women's liberation movement was seeking. But perhaps a second glance will reveal a rather different picture, particularly if the implementation of the sex discrimination and equal pay legislation is explored. Before doing this, however, it is important to situate this legislation in the context of the changing

gender composition of the workforce, the increase in part-time
working and casual employment, permanently high levels of male
unemployment and skills shortages.

Gender divisions in the workforce

Since the 1970s the advanced capitalist world has been transformed
from one where life-long, full-time employment (for men) was an
expectation to one where both women and men are expected to
participate in paid employment (albeit in gender-specific ways) but
where there are no expectations of job security and life-long
employment is a thing of the past. Associated with these changes are
a decline in manufacturing industry, particularly heavy industries
such as mining and steel which were predominantly male preserves,
and an increase in service sector employment, including financial
services, where women predominate. This shift in the structure of
the economy has resulted in the increasing availability of part-time
jobs for women and a decrease in full-time jobs for men. Thus
women's economic activity rates have increased while men's have
fallen (Walby, 1997: 51). Although economic activity rates of
women generally are increasing, there are significant differences
between women according to ethnicity. Thus white and black-
Caribbean women have the highest rates of economic activity (73
per cent) while Pakistani and Bangladeshi women have the lowest
(22–24 per cent) (Sly *et al.*, 1997: 295). Notwithstanding these
differences, it is projected that overall women's economic activity
rates will reach 74 per cent by the year 2001 (Hakim, 1995: 431).
Until the late 1980s, however, this increase was largely accounted
for by the 'conversion of full-time to part-time jobs' (Hakim,
1995: 431). In the last decade there has been an increase in the
'volume of female employment, measured in full-time equivalent
jobs'; an increase which is observable in all OECD countries
(Hakim, 1995: 432). It has been suggested – somewhat controver-
sially – that women employees can be differentiated in terms of
their orientation to paid employment and that this orientation relates
to the type of job they have. Women are either 'committed to a
career on a continuous basis' or are committed to a 'marriage career
but have jobs on an irregular basis' (Hakim, 1995: 450). This is
reflected in a polarisation between women whose labour market
behaviour is similar to men's, usually to be found in 'higher grade
occupations', and women whose commitment to the labour market

is dependent on paid employment fitting in around the needs of children and other dependants. These are the women likely to be in lower grade occupations where 'sex differentials in labour market behaviour' are more entrenched (Hakim, 1995: 450). That polarisation between women with secure, higher level jobs and women in insecure forms of employment is occurring is not in doubt, neither is the fact that different women have different orientations to paid employment: that the latter can explain the former is, however, in dispute (see for example Crompton and Harris, 1998). Be that as it may, it is possible that the form taken by the so-called equality legislation has contributed to this polarisation, benefitting middle-class women far more than their working-class sisters (Mayo and Weir, 1993).

Before moving to a discussion of this though, there are other socio-economic and demographic changes which are important in explaining the implementation of the equality legislation. Specifically these relate to the skills shortage and the so-called demographic time bomb (Rees, 1992). During the 1980s employers were exercised by both these concerns. The growth in service class occupations and the decline in unskilled and semi-skilled manual work changes the skills that are required by employees. Traditional skills associated with heavy industry are no longer required and people need, above all, to have the skills necessary to work with information technology and be prepared to undergo retraining and re-skilling during their working lives (Cockburn, 1983; Rees, 1992). This, together with an ageing workforce, has alerted employers to the necessity of retaining their skilled women workers, particularly in sectors such as banking where women form a significant proportion of the workforce (Crompton and Le Feuvre, 1992; Savage, 1992). The implications of an ageing workforce are that there will be a relative shortage of young recruits who can be trained in the new skills required, therefore the existing workforce has to be retained and retrained, and new sources of labour, such as women returners, have to be tapped (Rees, 1992: 108–11). This situation (the demographic time bomb) renders female labour valuable rather than expendable and provides the background against which the equality legislation needs to be set.

Policy implementation: liberal feminism

The Sex Discrimination Act set up the Equal Opportunities Commission, a quango with the task of monitoring the equality legislation and promoting equality of opportunity between women and men. A brief discussion of the role it played in relation to protective legislation demonstrates the limitations of equal rights feminism and the way that feminist demands are transformed in the process of institutionalisation.

One of the first things that the EOC was charged to do was to investigate the protective legislation to establish whether it was discriminatory; a requirement put on member states by the EC (Jarman, 1991: 142, 147). In 1979 it produced a report which took a liberal feminist or equal rights position, concluding that:

> The hours of work legislation constitutes a barrier – often an artificial one – to equal opportunities for women. So long as this legislation remains as it is at present, women workers will remain disadvantaged. (EOC, 1979: 29 cited in Gregory, 1987: 17)

It recommended that the protective legislation be repealed rather than being extended to men; this latter was the position favoured by the trade unions and socialist feminists within the women's movement. Needless to say it was the employers' organisation, the Confederation of British Industry, which wholeheartedly supported the version of equality enshrined in the proposals to repeal and had insisted on this review as a condition of their support for the Equal Pay Act (Jarman, 1991: 147). Thus, in 1986 when the Sex Discrimination Act was redrafted it included measures to remove protective legislation and the 1990 Employment Act got rid of restrictions on women working underground; restrictions that had been in place since 1842. This outcome demonstrates the way in which the issue of gender equality can be used by employers to increase their freedom to exploit their workforce. In the name of gender equality, women could now choose between working permanent nights and losing their job (Charles, 1990). Indeed the repeal of the protective legislation was hailed as benefitting employers, lifting restrictions on their ability to impose unsociable hours of work on any or all of their employees and increasing their flexibility. The introduction of the equality legislation was therefore used as a justification for repealing the protective legislation in the name of equality. It is particularly significant that the material differences which gave rise to protective legislation, that is, that women are the ones who have responsibility for domestic labour and child care, were explicitly excluded from the sex discrimination legislation. This means that women will continue to be disadvantaged in the world of paid employment (Bacchi, 1990: 138–41; Jarman, 1991). The impact of this is likely to be greater on working-class than middle-class women because the latter are more likely to have access to the resources necessary to solve their child care problems thereby facilitating full-time employment. This may go some way to explaining women's different orientations to paid employment noted earlier.

Policy implementation: equal opportunities policies

The equality legislation relating to gender, which came onto the statute books in 1975, was followed in 1976 by a new Race Relations Act and preceded, in 1958, by the amended Disabled Persons (employment) Act.[2] Together this legislation provided a framework for the development of equal opportunities policies within organisations. Indeed, the EOC has a role in encouraging employers to adopt positive measures to end discrimination and publishes guidelines on implementing equal opportunities. Thus after the mid-1970s, feminists and other activists were working within a legal framework set up by the state and in the context of economic and demographic changes which meant that employers were increasingly interested in retaining and investing in their women workers. These circumstances facilitated the development of equal opportunities policies which not only covered issues of recruitment and training but also developed codes of practice on sexual and racial harassment and outlawed discrimination on grounds of sexual orientation, age and disability. However, it was not until after the defeat of Labour in 1979 and the ascendancy of the new right in the form of the first Thatcher administration, that feminists active in the now rapidly fragmenting women's movement, took up these issues at their places of work, in their trade unions and in the Labour Party (Harriss, 1989).[3] Thatcher's election in effect:

> Shifted the political focus of many on the left from the national towards the local. With central government as the adversary rather than the aspiration, people turned to the local state as a hopeful site of resistance and prefigurative development. (Cooper, 1994: 21)

Second wave feminism was no exception and turned its attention away from the central state towards the local state (Watson, 1992: 189), forming alliances with other social movement activists in the process, and directing its energies towards the implementation of equal opportunities policies at the local level. Indeed, many of those appointed to oversee the implementation of equal opportunities policies identified themselves as social movement activists and saw their equal opportunity work within organisations as an extension of their political work outside them (Cockburn, 1991; Lovenduski and Randall, 1993: 217; Lawrence and Turner, 1997). This resulted in what Cynthia Cockburn has termed an 'equality movement within organisations' which she dates from the mid-1980s (Cockburn, 1991: 37) and raises the question of 'the extent to which feminist social change can be brought about via the institutions of the state' (Halford, 1992: 155).

Feminists' involvement with the local state and with the elaboration and implementation of equal employment policies at their places of work represents a move onto a different terrain of struggle from that occupied previously. Their activity was now directed towards hierarchical and bureaucratic organisations in an attempt to change them from within, they were moving onto men's territory where equality had hitherto been defined on men's terms. This was a move away from the autonomous women's movement, which had operated largely on the basis of networks and small groups loosely integrated through the regular occurrence of national conferences, and into the state, albeit at a local rather than national level. It could be argued that this marked the first stages of the institutionalisation of feminism. But is this inevitably a one-way process? And is this not of itself an indication of social movement success? I explore these questions by focusing on the implementation of equal opportunities policies within organisations.

Working for change within bureaucratic organisations

There are both practical and theoretical issues which emerge from a consideration of equal opportunities policies. The practical issues concern the effects of equal opportunities policies on gender relations and organisational culture which result from changes in recruitment, selection and promotion procedures (the 'short agenda') and the development of a 'long agenda' of positive action for women (Cockburn, 1991). The theoretical issues relate to the nature of bureaucratic organisations and whether feminists working within them can effectively change them. Indeed, feminist political practice in the form of attempts to introduce equal opportunities policies within organisations has led to the development of a more sophisticated understanding of the ways that gender divisions and male power are maintained and an appreciation that gendered structures are supported by gendered identities in which individual social actors have a considerable investment. Bureaucratic, hierarchical organisations are constituted by a gender order which effectively transforms 'successful' women into men. I look first at the effects of equal opportunities policies on gender relations within organisations.

In a study of the implementation of equal opportunities policies in four organisations, Cynthia Cockburn distinguishes between a short and a long equal opportunities agenda, the short being consistent with liberal approaches to equal opportunities and the long being more radical (Jewson and Mason, 1986). The equal opportunities agenda includes: selection, recruitment and training; maternity leave, career breaks for women; parental leave, child care provision for employees of both sexes; sexual harassment, sexist language, sexuality and gender identity (Cockburn, 1991). In moving down the agenda from selection, recruitment and training to sexual harassment, sexist language, sexuality and gender identity there is a move from role equity to role change issues, with the latter challenging not only occupational gender divisions but also, as we shall see, class and racial divisions.

Cockburn argues that the short equal opportunities agenda is unlikely to improve the situation of women in lower paid jobs, where working-class and ethnic minority women are concentrated. Thus, in the capitalist enterprise included in her study, most of the positive action initiatives to do with training, promotion and retention of female staff were confined to women at management level; maternity leave, for instance, was introduced for career positions only. This had resulted in an increase in the number of women in lower management posts. Similarly, in the state bureaucracy, even though measures such as maternity leave and career breaks had been adopted to retain women staff, these measures reinforced existing gender divisions because it was overwhelmingly women rather than men who took career breaks. So although such measures facilitate women's return to paid employment after having children and allow them to combine paid employment with responsibilities for child care, they also serve to reinforce women's disadvantaged position within the workforce because they are often only available to women. And even if they are also available to men, men are reluctant to take advantage of them precisely because of their career implications (Cockburn, 1991). This is also the case in Sweden where, despite the universal availability of parental leave it is overwhelmingly women who take it (Blakemore and Drake, 1996: 92).

As long as equal opportunities are perceived in terms of women's having to change in order to fit in with the existing demands of paid employment within the organisation women are likely to remain disadvantaged. Equal opportunities policies, particularly the short agenda, do not aim to change the rules. This raises the issue of organisational cultures and their gendered nature which dictate that, in order to succeed, women have to play by the rules. Thus Sophie Watson comments that femocrats in Australia have to 'play the boys' games'. Women are incorporated into organisations on male terms and deny the 'lived experience of a female body in their public lives' (Watson, 1992: 200). As a result of this most are without dependants and:

> Rarely in conventional marital relationships. Drinking after work and working at weekends is an unspoken prerequisite for high-level positions. Forms of masculine dominance are the ascribed norm. (Watson, 1992: 196)

Women who are unable to fit this male profile do not succeed in bureaucratic organisations nor does the equal opportunities legislation benefit them (Bacchi, 1990: 169). Thus the women who do benefit are either unencumbered with dependants or the demands of conventional heterosexual relationships, or have access to enough resources to enable them to employ other women to take over their domestic responsibilities rather in the way that successful men have hitherto been able to rely on their wives (Wajcman, 1996; Dunne, 1997). This points up the class dimensions of the short agenda for equal opportunities, it may help middle-class, career women compete successfully with men but it is unlikely to have any effect on working-class and ethnic minority women in low paid and/or part-time jobs (Cockburn, 1991).

There is considerable evidence that men in managerial positions cultivate a specific work culture which involves long hours of work and is predicated on their having partners at home to take care of their domestic arrangements and their children (French, 1995; Itzin, 1995). The long hours that are expected and the difficulty of combining these with domestic responsibilities and child care deter many women from seeking promotion and, conversely, women are not seen as suitable for such jobs because assumptions are made about the difficulties they would have with such a commitment (French, 1995). However, women who are in senior jobs share their male colleagues' commitment to a culture of long working hours, it is seen as something that goes with the job, the price of promotion and power (Wajcman, 1996). Power, however, also poses problems for women because, as Cockburn argues, it is defined as masculine (Cockburn, 1991). This association of power with masculinity disqualifies women from holding positions of power, their gender makes them unsuitable candidates and if they do aspire to such positions they become honorary men (as Margaret Thatcher), adopting stereotypically male attributes. They then forfeit men's approval and are condemned for being either too authoritarian or not being authoritative enough. Thus women's relation to power is problematised in ways that men's is not. As Ramsay and Parker put it:

> The separation of the public and private spheres, the association of women with the latter and the higher status accorded to what men do in the public sphere has left its legacy in the association of masculinity with prestige and status. (Ramsay and Parker, 1992: 260)

Indeed evidence suggests that with the feminisation of certain jobs power shifts, and although women may get better jobs, they still do not have access to power and authority within the organisation (Cockburn, 1991). This appears to be a widespread phenomenon. Thus women move into managerial positions involving skill and expertise rather than those associated with power and authority. Mike Savage argues that:

> The influx of women into professional and managerial jobs indicate [sic] not that women are moving into positions of power and authority, but rather that these positions are being redefined and restricted... [and] senior management remains overwhelmingly male. (Savage, 1992: 148)

So although equal opportunities policies may result in an increase of women in managerial positions, the gender order of organisations, whereby men monopolise positions of power and authority, is maintained.

The issue of organisational culture and its relation to gender identity is also explored in other studies (see for example Cockburn, 1983; Collinson *et al.*, 1990). Thus Collinson *et al.* (1990) explore the implementation of the short agenda in 45 companies. Their study focuses on recruitment and selection procedures in firms which define themselves as equal opportunities employers. They found extensive discrimination against women but discriminatory practices were not monopolised by men. Thus women personnel managers were sometimes instrumental in maintaining a rigidly gender-divided workforce. For instance, a mail order firm had developed a 'people bank' consisting of reliable women who could be called on at periods of peak demand to work and who could be laid off when demand fell – men were excluded from consideration for these jobs because the work was defined as 'women's' work (Collinson *et al.*, 1990: 114). Collinson *et al.* argue that women collude in these processes of discrimination in order to protect their own careers.

This need to fit in with the culture of the organisation in order to be effective creates specific problems for feminists, particularly when their feminism encompasses a profound critique of masculinist organisational cultures. Women working within state organisations experience these tensions which often result in compromise (Watson, 1992). Thus femocrats can be effective in bringing about change within state bureaucracies, such as ensuring funding for refuges, but these changes may not take the form that the feminist movement initially wanted. This points up the dilemma of working within an organisation but, at the same time, having allegiances and loyalties to a wider constituency represented by the feminist movement (Franzway *et al.*, 1989).

Resistance to change in organisations in the direction of positive policies for women has been identified in many studies, some of which attribute it to the gendered nature of bureaucratic organisations (Halford, 1992) while others argue that it stems from the ways in which gender and sexual identities are constructed within organisations (Collinson *et al.*, 1990). Thus Collinson *et al.* conceptualise resistance to the changes involved in implementing equal opportunities policies in terms of identity. Men and women fear change because it threatens their identity, whether this is their gender identity or their professional identity. For instance, women who challenge gender divisions of labour by doing so-called men's jobs are likely to have their femininity and sexuality called into question, whereas if they become a secretary or work on an assembly line with other women this will not happen (Dunne, 1997). And women themselves invest in their feminine identity. A similar situation arises for men who become secretaries or stay at home and look after their children; their gender identity becomes problematic because part of the construction of gender identity is through the sorts of activities we engage in (Morris, 1990). Similarly, line managers' identity as 'good' managers might be threatened by taking the risk of employing a woman instead of a man in a job normally associated with men; a personnel manager's identification with the job, the firm and the promotion ladder may also be threatened by insisting on strict adherence to equal opportunities policies which could undermine the ability of the organisation to function.

These contradictions become more obvious the further down the equal opportunities agenda you go. Thus feminists working within capitalist organisations may be constrained in their attempts to extend the equal opportunities agenda by the costs of its implementation (Cockburn, 1991). Indeed there is a significant difference between the public and private sectors in terms of formal commitment to equal opportunities. For instance, by 1991, 75 per cent of local authorities had equal opportunities policies relating to employment and some had them relating to service delivery (Itzin, 1995: 133). But a British Institute of Management Survey in 1988 showed that of its 350 member organisations half had a commitment to equal opportunities but only a third were taking active steps to implement their policies (Colgan and Ledwith, 1996: 3). Banks (and the finance sector more generally), where large numbers of women are employed, are the only private sector organisation to be significantly involved in providing such things as career breaks and child care for their women employees. These provisions can be seen as a response to the need to retain skilled women employees after child bearing and maternity leave as can policy initiatives like Opportunity 2000. This was launched in 1991 by Business in the Community and was specifically designed to improve women's representation in senior positions in employment. By 1994 278 employers had affiliated to it, including the NHS and several universities, representing 25 per cent of the workforce.

It is significant that the employers most likely to be providing workplace nurseries are in the public sector and/or state organisations. Thus in a survey of 2,000 employers only 2 per cent were found to have workplace nurseries and, at the end of the 1980s, there was a total of about 100 in the UK; 80 per cent of these were in the public sector, mostly in local authorities and some in civil service departments (Rees, 1992: 119). This difference between the public and private sectors is perhaps not surprising given the fact that many social movement activists are employed in the public sector and have been influential in pressing for the adoption and implementation of equal opportunities policies. Indeed, it is a measure of the effect of social movements in terms of policy implementation.

Also important in a consideration of organisational culture is the issue of sexuality and attempts by feminists to transform the sexual regime within organisations through equal opportunities policies (Halford, 1992). Sexual harassment was put on the political agenda by the feminist movement. The term was coined in the early 1970s in the US and is now recognized as a major problem for women in education and paid employment. Although the measures for positive action did not originally encompass sexual harassment, codes of practice have subsequently been developed by feminists working within organisations. Sexual harassment is notoriously difficult to define but is centrally concerned with the abuse of power. It is something which is overwhelmingly perpetrated by men against women and has been defined as follows:

> Any sexual advance, request for sexual favours, comment, look or physical contact of a sexual nature when:
> a) It is unsolicited, repeated, or unwelcome; or
> b) Submission to such conduct is made explicitly or implicitly a term or condition of the individual's employment, academic assessment, or promotion; or
> c) Submission to or rejection of such conduct by an individual is used as the basis for employment, academic assessment, or promotion for that individual; or
> d) Such conduct has the purpose or effect of unreasonably interfering with an individual's work or academic performance, or of creating an intimidating, hostile, or offensive working or academic environment. (LA/2665a. May 1985)

Cockburn explores the sexual regime of organisations and the ways in which sexual harassment, sexual jokes and sexist language are used to keep women out of 'men's' jobs. She analyses these processes as a way of men retaining their power and argues that it is part of the masculinist culture of most organisations which sexualises women and makes them feel out of place. Sexual orientation is another issue which has been introduced by gay movement activists into equal opportunities policies (Cooper, 1994). Lesbians and gay men are similarly made to feel out of place and are discriminated against by the dominant male, heterosexist culture of organisations (Cockburn, 1991). In order to deal with this many keep their sexuality hidden (Dunne, 1997). Women's sexuality and perceived vulnerability to sexual violence can also be used to justify their exclusion from jobs. Thus in a study conducted by Collinson *et al.*, women were seen as unsuitable for becoming insurance 'salesmen' and the arguments supporting this view cited the dangers involved in visiting prospective customers alone after dark in their homes. Here an ideology of paternalism is apparent with men ostensibly protecting women. But its effect is to maintain men's monopoly on a job which is identified with an aggressive masculinity (Collinson, *et al.*, 1990).

Transforming the gender order within organisations involves struggles over meaning. Thus what a woman defines and experiences as sexual harassment may be seen by a man as a bit of fun or a joke. And if women allow themselves to be upset about it they are simply demonstrating their unsuitability for the job. Thus attempts to implement the long agenda involve transformations in ways of seeing the world which challenge gendered power relations and the gender identities which support them; they therefore provoke considerable resistance.

As we have seen, women working within capitalist organisations are constrained from attempting to implement the long agenda of equal opportunities by its costs to their employers. Cockburn found that it was in the local authority and trade union that the equal opportunities agenda had gone furthest. Recruitment, selection and promotion had been overhauled, maternity leave and career breaks introduced, child care provision in the form of workplace nurseries and creches provided, and issues of sexual and racial harassment and equal value claims had been taken up. These are significantly organisations which are political rather than economic. The local authority was a left-wing Labour authority and feminist influence within the Labour Party led to the active pursuance of equal opportunities policies by many Labour-led authorities after 1979. The Trade Union is a social movement organisation which organised low-paid women workers; trade unions were also a target of socialist feminist activists during the 1970s and 80s. Their influence is reflected in the way the equal opportunities agenda has been implemented, particularly when the situation of working-class and ethnic minority women is considered.

As a result of the amendment of the Equal Pay Act in 1984, women can claim equal pay with men if they are doing work of equal value. In Cockburn's study she found that this had been taken up by the trade union and, in the Northern Ireland division where the chief divisional officer was a woman, sustained attempts had been made to support equal value claims. There were also efforts to democratise the union and decision-making processes within it and to increase the participation of union members, most of whom were women (Cockburn, 1991). Research in the US shows that women's organising around the issue of comparable worth (an issue which is analogous to equal value claims) at their places of work has resulted in improvements in their pay (Blum, 1992). Improving conditions and pay for the low paid always has the effect of reducing gender differentials because women are so overrepresented among low paid workers. Thus equal value and comparable worth cases are a way of improving pay and conditions of low paid women workers particularly. However, as Cockburn points out, implementing equal value claims has serious resource implications for employers and prevents them from using women and other low paid workers as a source of cheap and flexible labour, that is, it reduces their power to dictate their employees' conditions (Cockburn, 1991). This dimension of the equal opportunities agenda is therefore unlikely to be implemented unless women organise collectively within their organisations (Hastings, 1992). And although the legislation provides a framework, its implementation, particularly when it involves the redistribution of resources, is likely to be resisted by men and by employers (Cockburn, 1991). In contrast, what many firms are doing in the name of equal opportunities is providing women with part-time, 'flexible' hours of work and time off during the school holidays (all at very low rates of pay with no job security) and calling this taking account of women's needs. This is how equal opportunities are translated into reality for most working-class and ethnic minority women.

The imperatives of capitalist production therefore make it likely that, despite the best efforts of feminists, equal opportunities will be implemented in such a way as to benefit women in so-called career posts. If they also benefitted working-class women they would threaten the supply of a cheap and flexible workforce on which capitalist production depends. In addition to the constraints of capitalist production, Cockburn argues that men resist women's equality in organisations because existing gender divisions benefit them. Because of the 'equality' legislation their resistance can no longer take the form of overt discrimination. Thus the gender order is maintained by shifting power away from where women are located and gendered boundaries are reinforced through the use of sexual jokes and sexual harassment which continually remind women that they do not belong. In order to minimise men's resistance and to legitimate change the feminist orientation of the equal opportunities agenda has been disguised. Thus equal opportunities is now supported by arguments about wasting resources and skills shortages and the case for equal opportunities is put in terms of efficiency; this makes it compatible with market forces and individualism (Colgan and Ledwith, 1996: 19). Indeed, the liberal approach to equal opportunities is much more acceptable to the business community as it confines itself to eliminating discriminatory practices thereby allowing women and ethnic minorities to 'play the white man' rather than changing the nature of the playing field (Webb and Liff, 1988). As we have seen, this is likely to benefit women in middle-class jobs who either have no dependants or have enough resources to be able to pay others to look after them. Radical equal opportunities policies, or the long agenda, are much more likely to be found in some types of organisation than others, that is, in those which are committed ideologically and politically to equality such as Labour-led local authorities and trade unions. Here it is possible to gain the support of the organisation in initiating a process of organisational and cultural change (Itzin, 1995).

Many of the measures introduced to increase women's employment opportunities, such as Opportunity 2000, the development of family-friendly policies within organisations and the recognition that women's 'softer' styles of management are increasingly needed in the world of business (Colgan and Ledwith, 1996: 2), are mostly aimed at retaining highly skilled, professional women and ensuring that their skills are not lost to the workforce. Similar processes are at work in Europe, the US, Canada and Australia. However, as Joyce Outshoorn asks in an article of the same title, 'Is this what we wanted?' And although her focus is on the development of equal opportunities legislation and policies in Holland her conclusions are more widely applicable. She relates the demands of the women's movement to actual policy development and traces the way in which issues are put on the political agenda and are then taken up by political parties and policy makers in a transformed form. When they eventually get implemented they do not reflect the original demands and may have quite opposite effects from those intended, like the advancement of the careers of middle-class women and the reinforcing of individualistic and competitive ideologies. As the author puts it:

> Without sufficient child-care facilities, jobs, a decent incomes policy including women's own right to social security benefits, further implementation of policy on sexual violence, reduction of working hours so that men may at

last start sharing housework and child care, and effective legislation on
equal treatment, positive action in its current definition is a palliative. It
does not contribute to the redistribution of paid work and housework, one of
the oldest demands of the women's movement, it does not make for a redi-
vision of the 'roles' of men and women. In addition, it is a demand which
only aids women already employed (except in the case of hiring policy) and
in practice it is only meaningful to the better educated at the higher echelons
of the job pyramid. (Outshoorn, 1991: 118)

Career advancement for middle-class women was not the aim of
feminist social movements when they raised the demands for equal
pay and equal education and job opportunities in the 1970s.

It seems clear that whatever the outcome of the equality legislation of the 1970s and equal opportunities policies in the 1980s,
feminists working within the feminist movement, and within other
organisations such as political parties, trade unions and firms, have
been influential in affecting both the formulation of policy and its
implementation. Feminist activity within organisations has largely
been in alliance with organisations of the labour movement and
other social movement activists on issues of 'race'/ethnicity,
disability, sexuality and so on.

These alliances show how political opportunity structures affect
the form of feminist organising. Reforms in the 1970s provided the
opportunity for feminists to press for further-reaching changes in
the direction of gender equality within organisations. In addition the
way into the local state and access to political power is via the
labour movement and it has largely been socialist feminists who
have taken this route. However, working within organisations also
poses problems, primarily because they are structured by the very
relations of power and domination which feminists are seeking to
challenge. Thus feminists find themselves having to play according
to the rules which they wish to change. In this process feminist
goals tend to be modified so as to fit in with the, often conflicting,
goals of the organisation. This can result in unintended outcomes,
one of which is clearly the way equal opportunities policies have
been used by employers to attract and retain skilled women at a time
of skills shortages. Equal opportunities policies are applied differentially within workforces so that women whose jobs are low paid
and unskilled, mainly working-class and ethnic minority women,
have benefitted least. Thus class relations and the imperatives of
capitalist production ensure that it is middle-class women who
benefit most from equal opportunities policies. This points to the

difficulties of implementing any aspect of the equal opportunities agenda that involves a redistribution of resources.

Attempts to transform the way things are done within organisations is met by resistance, particularly from those who feel their positions and identities threatened. And changing the way things are done by implementing equal opportunities policies involves changing organisational cultures. Cultural change in the form of shifting values also preceded the emergence of second wave feminism and contributed to the passage of the 'equality' legislation; it is therefore both cause and consequence of feminist social movements.

Finally, there appears to have been more progress in implementing the long agenda within public sector organisations, the very areas of employment where social movement activists are located. Within capitalist enterprises equal opportunities are only implemented as long as they are congruent with the requirements of capitalist production and are likely to apply differentially to different sectors of the workforce. The problems associated with implementing equal opportunities policies, even the short agenda, highlight the continuum between role equity and role change issues. In order to achieve genuine equality of opportunity for women and other minority groups it is necessary to challenge the relations of inequality that underpin unequal opportunities and which render the short agenda unachievable without more profound changes in the class, gender, racial and sexual structuring of society.

Chapter 6

Poverty

It seems clear from the experience of attempting to implement equal opportunities policies that it is the short agenda, the role equity issues which do not challenge the structures of capitalism, which are most likely to be implemented. Indeed it could be argued that all that equal opportunities policies are likely to achieve is the integration of women into the capitalist labour market on the same terms as men. In Ruth Levitas' words:

> It is salutary to remember that even if women, ethnic minorities and disabled people achieve equal opportunities within the labour market, it will still be the case that what 'integration' means is participation in a capitalist economy driven by profit and based upon exploitation. (Levitas, 1996: 18)

This sort of integration is unlikely to alleviate poverty because women, ethnic minorities and disabled people are overwhelmingly concentrated in the low paid sectors of the workforce and access to low and insecure wages is one of the problems which feminist researchers have identified as contributing to women's vulnerability to poverty. Thus, although equal opportunities policies may be of benefit to a small sector of the female workforce, those who are in middle-class, professional, full-time jobs, they are much less likely to improve the lot of working-class and ethnic minority women whose integration into the workforce depends precisely on the fact that they provide a source of cheap and flexible labour. As we have seen, equal opportunities policies which challenge this, such as those attempting to implement the 'long agenda', are likely to meet with considerable resistance. If this is the case then such policies are unlikely to affect the unequal distribution of resources which lies at the heart of gender inequalities.

This issue has been highlighted by feminist research on poverty which shows that the world's resources are unevenly distributed between women and men and that, as a result, poverty is much more

116

likely to be experienced by women and children than by men. Thus women do two thirds of the world's work (paid and unpaid) and receive 10 per cent of the world's income (Scott, 1984: x). These figures were published in a UN report on the status of women in 1979, itself a testimony to the influence of feminists working within that organisation, and refer only to income. However, there has been much subsequent research which shows that women's access to all forms of resources, within the labour market, the household and in the form of welfare, is less than that of men and results in their overrepresentation among those living in poverty. This research, and the making visible of women's poverty, is a direct result of second wave feminism and the activities of feminists within social policy networks and the academy. Feminists have undertaken research into the gender dimensions of poverty which has high-lighted the way in which women's financial dependence on men renders them vulnerable to poverty. They have also been active in the so-called poverty lobby and in political parties in attempting to influence policy. This chapter focuses on the research findings and assesses their impact on mainstream poverty research and the formation and implementation of social policy. I concentrate partic-ularly on the way this has developed in Britain, drawing on the experiences of other countries where appropriate.

Joyce Gelb, in her analysis of the impact of second wave femi-nism on social policy in the US, Britain and Sweden, argues that it is in the US that feminists have had the greatest impact on policy because of the development of feminist policy networks. Indeed, she argues that it is policy networks through which pressure group interests are fed into the policy-making process and that this is 'without parallel in the UK' (Gelb, 1989: 22). In the US, feminist organisations, such as the Center for Women Policy Studies and the Institute for Women's Policy Research, are 'tradi-tional interest group[s] organised as a hierarchical structure with staff dominance' (Gelb, 1989: 185). They are the bureaucratic organisations identified by RMT as being essential for social move-ments to have a political impact. In Britain such organisations have tended not to develop from second wave feminism, instead femi-nists have attempted to influence policy by developing non-hierar-chical forms of organisation and working within existing organisations, whether these be the local state, universities, 'think tanks', political parties or other 'interest group organisations' such as the Child Poverty Action Group or the National Council for Civil Liberties (Gelb, 1989: 37, 42). As we have seen, working within non-feminist organisations is problematic in terms of pursuing feminist goals. However, it is through this type of involvement that feminists in Britain have gained access to the networks that are drawn upon, informally, by political parties in order to develop policy, and that feminist research on poverty has begun to influence the policy agenda.

Women's dependence

The fifth demand of the women's movement called for financial and legal independence and was adopted in 1975. The immediate targets of this demand were the inability of married women to get mortgages independently of their husbands and the notorious cohabitation rule which stipulated that if a woman was sharing food and sex with a man she was deemed to be financially supported by him, thereby losing all independent entitlement to welfare benefits. Underpinning this was the assumption, built into the British social security system since Beveridge, that married women were financially dependent on their husbands, the main breadwinner, who supported them by means of a wage when in work, and by his entitlement to social insurance or benefit when out of work. Thus most married women had no independent access to resources, either in the form of a full-time wage or in the form of independent entitlement to benefits. Their relation to the labour market and to the welfare state was mediated by their relationship to a man. The whole system of social security in Britain was based on this assumption and, in many ways, ensured that the option of dependence on a man was more attractive than the option of independence via (low) paid employment or dependence on the state, particularly when children were involved. Entitlement to benefit was assessed on the basis of the family unit, thus the resources of a heterosexual couple were aggregated rather than the adults in the household having their resources and entitlements assessed on an individual basis; this was also true of the tax system. Disaggregation was an aim of feminist campaigning in the 1970s (McIntosh, 1981).

Since the British women's movement raised the issue of women's financial and legal dependence on men, feminist researchers have demonstrated that such dependence, far from protecting women from the vicissitudes of the labour market and the risks of poverty, increases their vulnerability to poverty (Millar and Glendinning, 1987). The unequal treatment of women and men within the social security system was not included in the remit of the Sex Discrimination Act and has only been undermined piecemeal by successive directives from the EC and successful actions taken by British women to the European Commissioners (Whitting, 1992: 71–2; Millar, 1996: 59). Although the tax system was reformed so that married couples were taxed separately in 1990, the financial dependence of women and the idea of a male breadwinner on which such dependence rests still underpins the British social security system and, as we shall see, renders women vulnerable to poverty.

The feminisation of poverty?

There are two main strands to feminist arguments that poverty is gendered. First there is the debate about the feminisation of poverty, which largely emanates from the US (see, for example, Goldberg and Kremen, 1990a) and second there is the documenting of women's lesser access to resources in comparison with men. The debate about the feminisation of poverty centres around whether women are, in fact, falling into poverty in ever greater numbers or whether it is simply that poor women are losing their invisibility (Millar and Glendinning, 1987). I shall explore this debate briefly before looking more closely at feminist research on the gendered distribution of resources.

Support for the feminisation of poverty thesis comes from the increasing numbers of woman-headed households counted in the ranks of the poor (Scott, 1984: vii; Zopf, 1989; Goldberg and Kremen, 1990b). Scott defines the feminisation of poverty as a phrase 'used to describe the fact that a growing proportion of families below the official poverty line are headed by women alone' (Scott, 1984: vii; see also Goldberg and Kremen, 1990b). Thus it has been argued that the feminisation of poverty is associated with increasing numbers of lone mothers. This suggests that it has something to do with increasing rates of family breakdown, that is, the breakdown of dependency, and assumes that where dependency works women are protected from poverty. It also appears to contradict the feminist argument that women's vulnerability to poverty arises precisely because of this dependence. Indeed, in societies such as Sweden which do not assume women's economic dependence on men, there is no feminisation of poverty taking place (Rosenthal, 1990). Similarly, the point that women's overrepresentation among the ranks of the poor is a new phenomenon is not supported by historical evidence. Indeed, as Lewis and Piachaud point out, at the beginning of this century in Britain '61% of adults on all forms of poor relief were women... Today 60% of adults for whom supplementary benefit is paid are women' (Lewis and Piachaud, 1987: 28). What has changed is the causes of female poverty and its visibility. In the early years of this century married women whose partners were low paid and who had large families predominated among women living in poverty and were closely followed by widows and older women. Now, however, 'female poverty is concentrated among lone women, especially among the elderly' (Lewis and Piachaud, 1987: 50). Thus women's poverty is increasingly visible due to demographic changes, particularly the ageing populations of advanced capitalist societies and increasing levels of divorce, both of which result in woman-headed households. Older women are heads of household because of their longevity in relation to men, younger women because they are bringing up children alone. The former are in poverty because of their dependence on inadequate pensions and means-tested benefits and lone mothers because of their dependence on state benefits (Millar and Glendinning, 1987; Glendinning and Millar, 1991: 24). Vulnerability to poverty is also greater among ethnic minority women. Thus, in the US:

> Black and Hispanic single mothers suffer poverty rates 50 per cent greater than their white counterparts, and black women are three times as likely as white women to be in the economically vulnerable position of single motherhood. Three-fifths of poor, single-mother families in the US... are women of color and their children. (Goldberg and Kremen, 1990b: 4)

Similarly in Britain ethnic minority women are overrepresented among low paid workers, they are far more likely than their white counterparts to be unemployed and less likely to take up all the benefits to which they are entitled, and black households are generally worse off than white households (Cook and Watt, 1992; Sly *et al.*, 1997).

The overrepresentation of women and ethnic minorities in poverty has been apparent from poverty studies for some time (Townsend, 1979). Thus in the late 1960s Peter Townsend found that at all ages except under 15 women were more likely than men to be living in households with incomes below the Supplementary Benefit level (Townsend 1979: 285).[1] Such studies did not, however, explore the way gender affected access to resources within households and it was assumed that poverty was equally shared by all household members. There is evidence, however, that women cushion men from the full effects of poverty. Thus studies earlier this century showed how women managing on a low male wage would go without food for themselves in order to ensure that the male breadwinner and their children had enough to eat (Spring Rice, [1939] 1981: 157; Pember Reeves, ([1913] 1984): a study published in 1997 reiterates these findings (Middleton *et al.*, nd). What these studies point to is that poverty is experienced differently by women and men, even by those living in the same household. Indeed, it may be that in some households women are experiencing poverty while men are not. This calls into question not only the basis of most conventional poverty studies but also the way official statistics on poverty are constructed which is always on the basis of households or some other collective unit (Millar, 1996). This obscures not only the number of women who are in poverty but also the different levels of living that may be experienced by individuals living under the same roof.

Access to resources

The feminisation of poverty also refers to the fact that many women 'would be poor if they had to support themselves' (Goldberg and Kremen, 1990b: 2). This raises the issue of women's lesser access to resources which is legitimated by an 'ideology of dependency' (Millar and Glendinning, 1987: 25). This has been documented in three spheres: the labour market, the family-household and the welfare state (Millar and Glendinning, 1987). I look at each in turn.

Despite the advent of equal pay, women continue to be paid less than men. They are overrepresented among the ranks of low paid workers and segregated into the less-skilled and secure sectors of capitalist labour markets (see, for example, Walby, 1997). Women's low wages are not seen as a problem by policy makers because women supposedly also have access to a man's wage. This is not, however, the case. In Britain, for instance, less than a fifth of women are wholly dependent upon a male breadwinner. Thus 'the financial dependence of *some* women' is used 'to justify ignoring the lower resources of *most* women' (Millar and Glendinning, 1987: 11). In addition, even when a woman has a male partner whose income is adequate to support a wife and children there is no guarantee that it will be equally distributed among family members

(Graham, 1987; Pahl, 1989). Thus Hilary Graham's research on lone mothers revealed that many of them felt better off without their partners than they had with them, even though the income coming into the household was much lower. She argues that this is because when they were with their partners they had no control over how the money was being spent and items of consumption ostensibly for all the family, such as a car, might in fact take up a large share of the resources and be of limited benefit for the woman and her children. Similarly there is no guarantee that increases in men's wages will be passed on to women and children. This brings me on to the second dimension of women's lesser access to resources and that is the distribution of resources within households.

It is by now a truism that conventional social policy and economic research does not enquire into what happens within households. Resources enter households and, because of the difficulties surrounding the operationalisation of any other assumption, household members are assumed to have equal access to those resources. Feminist research has demonstrated that this assumption is not valid. This is true not only of money, whether in the form of wages or benefits, but also in the form of food, leisure and the resources that are available from the welfare state such as help with caring for disabled or older dependants (Land, 1983; Walker, 1983: 122; Brannen and Wilson, 1987; Charles and Kerr, 1988; Pahl, 1989; Green *et al.*, 1990). Initially feminist research was small scale and qualitative and as such open to accusations of unrepresentativeness (Jenkins, 1991). But latterly its findings have been supported by large-scale, quantitative studies which have shown not only that women's access to resources within families is circumscribed, particularly if they are not in full-time paid employment, but also that women's poverty, if minimal reallocation of income between partners is assumed, is significantly higher than men's (Davies and Joshi, 1994; Vogler, 1994). This research invalidates the assumption that poverty (or wealth for that matter) is shared equally within households and means that estimates of the numbers of women and children in poverty are likely to be inaccurate. In addition qualitative research has shown that it is women who bear the brunt of managing household budgets on limited incomes (Pahl, 1989; Vogler, 1994). This, together with the fact that women's access to resources is most unequal in households where female-managed systems of money allocation operate, suggests that significantly higher numbers of women than men are in poverty, even in households which are in aggregate terms above the poverty line (Vogler, 1994).

Feminists have also explored the importance of women's independent access to resources for the welfare of children. They argue that women are more likely than men to spend any income they have on their children (Pahl, 1989: 171) and women's wages, even though they are often low, are crucial for keeping families out of poverty. Thus in 1989–91, 18 per cent of all families containing a woman of working age were in poverty but if none of these women had been in work then 36 per cent of all families would have been poor (Harkness *et al.*, 1995: 28). The difficulties faced by women in combining paid employment (which is often low paid) with the care of young children goes a long way towards explaining the high numbers of children in poverty in Britain. Thus 1 in 20 families solely dependent on a male wage were in poverty in 1989–91 compared with 1 in 100 families where there were 2 earners. Conversely, 1 in 3 families headed by a female breadwinner were in poverty during the same period demonstrating that dependence on a female wage is even more precarious than dependence on a male wage (Harkness *et al.*, 1995: 26).

Women not only have less access to resources within households than men but their responsibility for domestic labour and child care enhances men's earning power. Thus women's unpaid labour in the home helps to free their partners from caring and domestic activities enabling them to engage in wage labour and to increase their wages and/or career prospects (Millar and Glendinning, 1987). This means that men on low wages are 'free' to work excessive amounts of overtime in order to earn a living wage. For men higher up the income scale there are more benefits. They do not have to reduce their earnings by paying for someone else to look after their children, this is taken on unpaid by their partners or, if their partner is also in paid employment, is taken out of her wage rather than his (Brannen and Moss, 1987). This domestic division of labour and responsibilities enhances men's position within the labour market and, as we have seen, is assumed by many bureaucratic organisations in the hours they expect their senior personnel to work and the hours of work they demand and wage rates they offer to their lower paid staff.

In the third sphere, that of the welfare state, women have access to fewer resources than do men because of the assumptions of female dependency that are built into the system and the way that eligibility for benefits is tied to male patterns of employment. It is this which has led feminists like Carol Pateman to argue that women are denied full citizenship rights because these rights are earned through participation in full-time, lifelong employment, a pattern which, until recently, characterised men's but not women's working lives. Recently, however, feminists have argued that entitlements are not only tied to citizens as workers but are also linked to care work within the domestic sphere. The extent to which this is the case varies in different welfare states and, it has been argued, relates to the prevalence of the breadwinner model of social policy. Thus, in Sweden care work is recognized as a basis of entitlement and mothers receive benefits as mothers as well as workers. In Britain, the US and the Netherlands, in contrast, their entitlement tends to be through the male breadwinner or in their own right as workers (Sainsbury, 1994). These differences have implications for women's vulnerability to poverty. Thus, in the US if women are on their own with children they are entitled to virtually no support from the state and are likely to become welfare claimants, whereas, in Sweden, they are entitled to financial and other support and their continuing participation in the workforce is facilitated. This is reflected in the fact that Sweden has very low rates of poverty among lone mothers while in the US the rates of poverty are high (Hobson, 1994: 177–8). This suggests that the extent of poverty among lone mothers depends on the basis of entitlement. If entitlement is solely through paid employment and linked to contributions then lone mothers are likely to experience greater poverty than where entitlement is also linked to motherhood, that is, care work. However, there is a difference in the extent to which mothers are expected to participate in the workforce. Thus, in Sweden they are expected to, and state support facilitates this, while in the Netherlands and Britain (until recently) there is no such expectation (Hobson, 1994: 184). These differences perhaps explain why the feminisation of poverty argument has emanated so forcibly from the US where lone mothers receive virtually no state support, either to enable them to care for their children full time or to combine child care with paid employment. As one commentator puts it:

> The high rates of poverty of American women should come as no surprise after the discussion of adverse labour market conditions, the failure to mount and sustain a vigorous campaign to reduce gender and racial inequality in employment, and the very limited antipoverty effects of social welfare programmes. (Goldberg, 1990: 45)

State support for lone mothers which enables them to combine mothering with paid employment, together with care work as a basis of individual entitlement, reduces their vulnerability to poverty and also reduces their dependence on a male breadwinner. Conversely, it is women's alleged dependence on a male breadwinner that justifies their being paid 'pin money'; this is despite the decline of the male breadwinner and the increasing importance of women's earnings to the well-being of families (Harkness *et al.*, 1995; Machin and Waldfogel, 1994).

Conceptualising poverty

There are two ways of conceptualising poverty which underlie feminist arguments and which are often linked. One relates poverty to access to material resources and the other conceptualises it as an inability to participate fully in the society to which an individual belongs. Differential access to resources is conceptualised as structured by relations of power based on gender, 'race' and class. This derives from a Marxist-inspired definition of poverty which sees it as 'a material relationship' and as 'about access to and control over the material conditions of life' (Novak, 1995: 67). This is the definition used by feminists such as Glendinning and Millar who talk about 'women's unequal access to material resources and... inequalities in their power to determine how those resources are consumed' (Millar and Glendinning, 1987: 5). Access to resources can also determine an individual's ability to participate in society, that is, the ability to be a full and active citizen. Inadequate resources force individuals to withdraw from the normal activities associated with membership of society. In Townsend's words:

> Poverty may best be understood as applying... to those whose resources do not allow them to fulfil the elaborate social demands and customs which have been placed on citizens of that society. (Townsend, 1993: 36)

This echoes Marshall's definition of social citizenship as the right to a 'modicum of economic welfare and security' and to 'share to the full in the social heritage and to live the life of a civilised being according to the standards prevailing in the society' (Marshall, 1950: 11). Thus a lack of resources is associated with an inability to participate to the full in society, that is, it results in social exclusion and an inability to exercise all the rights associated with citizenship.[2] For instance, during the anti-poll tax campaign opponents of the poll tax disenfranchised themselves by excluding themselves from the electoral register so that they would not be liable for the tax and many poor people and ethnic minorities continue to avoid community charges in this way. Similarly children who go to school too hungry to attend to their lessons are argued to be deprived of their rights as citizens. Thus social exclusion prevents citizens from participating to the full in the life of the nation; they are unable to *exercise* their citizenship rights. Poverty diminishes the status of citizenship and because women, along with other minority groups, have access to less resources than men, they are more vulnerable to poverty and to a reduction in the status of citizenship. Many feminists argue, however, that it is not poverty which reduces the status of citizenship for women but the gendering of citizenship rights which renders women vulnerable to poverty. Thus access to the social rights of citizenship are based on male patterns of employment in the public sphere, women's and men's social rights of citizenship are therefore different because their patterns of employment and location in the paid workforce are different and, as a result, women have access to less resources. In order to combat women's poverty, according to this argument, it is necessary to redefine citizenship such that rights and entitlements are based on unpaid work in the private sphere as well as paid work in the public sphere.

Feminist policy proposals

The policy proposals emanating from feminist research aim at reducing women's dependence on men and increasing their independent access to resources, whether by means of paid employment or through transfer payments on the basis of motherhood. Primarily feminists argue that policies must move away from assumptions of a male breadwinner and must assume that women and men are 'breadwinners of equal status' (Glendinning and Millar, 1991: 34). Equal opportunities policies are seen as one way of improving women's pay and this, together with better access to training, could contribute to undermining the vertical and horizontal segregation which characterises the workforces of advanced industrial societies. In Mayo and Weir's words, feminists wish to widen 'women's opportunities for training and better paid employment to enable women to achieve economic independence, *above* rather than *below* the poverty line' (Mayo and Weir, 1993: 40). However, there also needs to be an increase in the wages of the low paid which is an extremely effective way of reducing both gender inequalities in pay and women's vulnerability to poverty. Gender divisions of labour within households also need to be transformed such that men as well as women participate in caring and domestic work. We have already seen evidence of men's resistance to these sorts of reforms and, despite women's increasing participation in the workforces of advanced industrial societies, changes in domestic divisions of labour appear to be minimal. Indeed, it has been suggested that what is happening is a polarisation between women who model themselves on male employment patterns, who benefit from equal opportunities policies and have access to sufficient resources to guarantee their independence, and those who adhere to the traditional male breadwinner, female dependent model whose labour market participation takes second place to their domestic commitments and who, as a consequence, remain vulnerable to poverty and dependence (Mayo and Weir, 1993; Hakim, 1995). Feminists also argue for disaggregation, that is, that women's and men's resources should be treated independently and that all adults should be enabled 'to support themselves without relying upon others' (Millar and Glendinning, 1992: 9). To facilitate this women, even when they are caring for young children, should be enabled to participate in wage labour and, if they choose not to do so, should be supported by the state on the basis of citizenship rather than on the basis of need (Hobson, 1994). However, as Hobson asks, is it realistic to expect welfare states to provide support for women to continue in paid employment when they have young children and, at the same time, enable them to maintain an independent income if they choose to become full-time mothers (Hobson, 1994: 186)? It may not be 'realistic' but it is precisely what some feminists prescribe (Lister, 1997) thus valuing women both as worker–citizens and as mother–citizens. Arguably this choice should also be made available to men through entitlements to parental leave in order to facilitate the breakdown of domestic gender divisions of labour.

It is evident that feminist research has put the idea of women's greater vulnerability to poverty on the policy agenda. But what has been the response? Has it been to argue that it is a result of the breakdown of women's dependence on men and that this dependence should be restored? Or has it been to accept that women's dependence is precisely the problem? And, if there has been an impact on policy formation as well as the policy agenda, has this impact been confined to role equity rather than role change issues?

The impact of feminist research

There seems to have been relatively little impact of feminist ideas on mainstream research into poverty and into the way poverty is measured. Thus in the Rowntree report *Income and Wealth* published in 1995 there was little attention to the gender dimensions of poverty:

> There is virtually no gender analysis in the main report, other than in rela-
> tion to employment trends; thus it fails to bring out the extent and ways in
> which poverty is gendered, and ignores the gender dimension in its discus-
> sion of pensioners' incomes. The report has little to say on disability, and
> age, ethnicity and disability are primarily discussed only with reference to
> employment. (Beresford and Green, 1996: 96)

In contrast, gender and ethnicity are mentioned as important dimensions of poverty, inequality and social exclusion in an exploration of
the research agenda published in 1996 (Millar and Bradshaw, 1996).
It is not insignificant that the section of the report dealing with
poverty was written by two feminists and that a leading researcher
into the gender dimensions of poverty was one of the editors. Similarly, theoretical and analytical approaches to poverty, while
normally mentioning gender, do not fully incorporate it into their
analyses (for example, Townsend, 1993 and Jordan, 1996) and some
do not mention it at all (Scott, 1994). In studies of poverty which
rely on official statistics this lack of attention to gender is perhaps
understandable given the difficulties of disaggregating and
reanalysing household-based data which have already been collected
(Jenkins, 1991), although whether it is excusable is another matter,
particularly in light of studies that have done precisely this (Davies
and Joshi, 1994; Machin and Waldfogel, 1994; Harkness *et al.*,
1995). It is still the case that the extent of poverty among women in
the EC is not known simply because statistics are not collected in an
appropriate way (Whitting, 1992: 65).

As well as being involved in social policy research within acade-
mia, feminists are involved in the poverty lobby, working in organisations such as the Child Poverty Action Group and the Low Pay
Unit, independent think tanks, such as the Policy Studies Institute,

the Institute for Public Policy Research, Demos and the Institute for Welsh Affairs. Together these organisations constitute a powerful policy network with influence on the political parties, particularly those which are left of centre. In Britain there is also an influential right-wing think tank, the Institute of Economic Affairs, which argues for the retention and restoration of the male breadwinner family and against equal opportunities (Quest, 1992, 1994). Thus parties of the left and right consult these policy networks which thereby have an influence (albeit informal) on policy formation.

An example of this process is provided by the report of the Commission for Social Justice which was published in 1994. This Commission was set up by the then leader of the Labour Party, John Smith, in 1992 and was explicitly hailed as the equivalent of the 1942 Beveridge Report. Its remit was to 'carry out an independent inquiry into social and economic reform in the UK' (Social Justice, 1994). Among the seven women members of the sixteen-person commission were Ruth Lister, a feminist academic and activist who had previously been director of the Child Poverty Action Group; Eithne McLaughlin, a feminist social policy expert and academic; Patricia Hewitt, a feminist who had run the National Council for Civil Liberties for many years and who was deputy director of the Institute of Public Policy Research; Emma MacLennan, vice-chair of the Low Pay Unit, Anita Bhalla from the Asian Resource Centre in Birmingham and Margaret Wheeler from UNISON. Thus feminist researchers, academics, members of think tanks, activists and trade unionists were included in the membership of the Commission. Indeed Lister and McLaughlin have researched and published in the field of gender and poverty. The report of the Commission suggests that feminist thinking on these issues has had an impact but, as we shall see, this impact is more apparent on role equity than role change issues and the influence of the new right is also evident.

The report recommends a 'mixed economy of welfare' and argues that the aim of social security is to 'promote social cohesion' (Social Justice, 1994: 225). It is concerned with preventing social exclusion and the main way of achieving this is through the integration of the population, women as well as men, into paid employment. Care work is acknowledged to be a legitimate and socially useful activity which, ideally, should be more equally distributed between women and men. The Commission recommends a national minimum wage, mentioning that women form the majority of the low paid but not drawing out the implication of this (ibid.: 202). A national minimum wage would affect women and ethnic minority workers to a much greater extent than other categories of workers because of their concentration in low paid employment. The report also recommends that equal opportunities be available to all. This is primarily framed in terms of 'race' but gender, age and disability are also mentioned (ibid.: 195–7). Indeed, discrimination is defined as one of the five evils in society that need to be overcome. There is recognition of a social revolution 'of women's life chances, of family structures and of demography' (ibid.: 77) which has resulted, among other things, in high rates of family breakdown 'through which women and children most often fall into poverty' (ibid.: 79). However, the 'real victims are the older men who have been made redundant from old industries, and the young men with little education and few skills who have never had the chance to enter industry' (ibid.: 79). Thus family breakdown is identified as the cause of women's and children's poverty but it is unemployed men who are the 'real victims' of social and economic change. This emphasis illustrates the influence of the new right rather than feminism on the Commission's thinking.

The solutions offered by the Commission are more flexible working patterns for women and men, greater support for parenting by both women and men, and greater social acceptance of men as carers. Thus there is an acknowledgment that the gender divisions of paid and unpaid work are in need of change (ibid.: 223). However, the difficulties involved in implementing such change are not discussed. There is also recognition that 'paid work for a fair wage is the most secure route out of poverty' (ibid.: 223). This leads to proposals that labour discipline be extended to lone mothers once their children are over a certain age and that child care provision should be expanded (ibid.: 240); proposals that are being implemented by the Labour government elected in 1997. The report accepts that entitlements should be individually based for women and men (ibid.: 227) and that a social insurance programme should 'provide for people looking after very young children or caring for disabled adults' (ibid.: 229). However, there are no proposals to disaggregate the resources of women and men deemed to be a couple for means-tested benefits (ibid.: 231) even though the report acknowledges that 'the more the benefits system recognises women as individuals, the more it will... tackle poverty' (ibid.: 249).

The influence of feminist ideas can be seen in parts of this report and in some of its recommendations. Thus unpaid care work is recognized as a basis to entitlement within the social security system, access to an independent and adequate income is acknowledged as an important means of avoiding poverty and recognition is given to the need to involve men in unpaid work. In addition women's participation in paid work is accepted as something which is here to stay. Indeed, many of the report's recommendations are moving towards an individual model of social policy rather than a breadwinner model. However, what the report embodies is a commitment to role equity issues rather than role change issues which would involve a more fundamental redistribution of resources. Thus, women as well as men are to be integrated into the workforce and, through provision of support for parenting, enabled to participate on a more equal basis. There is also some recognition of the importance of unpaid work within the home and an attempt to minimise any disadvantages that may arise from this for women's paid work. But although lip service is paid to the need for greater sharing of domestic tasks between women and men there is no indication of how this is to be achieved. And it is precisely within the household that a reduction of gender inequalities in access to resources would require a significant degree of role change and where resistance to change appears to be greatest (Morris, 1990). The main strategy of the report is to increase women's access to resources through integration into wage labour backed up by an individually based entitlement to social insurance payments. And underpinning it is a functionalist if not Durkheimian view of society and the welfare state, which sees social integration as resulting from participation in the division of labour (defining labour as labour in the public sphere of the market rather than in the private sphere) and argues that inequalities that are too great will lead to disintegration and social breakdown (Levitas, 1996).

Although the influence of feminist research into poverty is discernible in this particular report, it has been incorporated in such a way as to facilitate women's integration into the public world of paid employment on men's terms, while reducing the obstacles placed in the way of this integration associated with women's domestic labour. However, domestic labour, despite all the talk about parental responsibilities and sharing care work, remains very firmly women's work; men's involvement in reproductive activities is not tackled although the state is prepared to take over some of these tasks from women. This is the situation which pertains in Sweden and before ending this discussion it is instructive to look briefly at the experience of Swedish women.

Much is made of women's increasing participation in the work-force throughout the western world. However, this increase is

Feminism, the State and Social Policy

largely in part-time employment and Sweden is no exception (Gelb, 1989; Kaplan, 1992; Hakim, 1995). Indeed Britain and Sweden have the highest rates of female part-time employment in the EC and large numbers of part timers are employed in the public sector (Kaplan, 1992: 96). It is important to note, however, that women in Sweden work 'long' part time compared with women in Britain who work 'short' part time. Until recently this meant that women in Sweden were eligible for all the benefits associated with paid employment while the latter were not (Lewis, 1993: 10).[3] Despite women in Sweden having an hourly income 98 per cent that of men's (1985 figures) and an 80 per cent participation rate, Sweden has the most highly gender-segregated workforce in Western Europe (Kaplan, 1992: 70). And despite universal provision for parenthood, generous maternity allowances which facilitate women's high participation rates and a recognition of care work in the bases of entitlement, women are still the ones who undertake the bulk of that care work and who take the bulk of parental leave (Gelb, 1989: 209–10; Dominelli, 1991: 172). This coexists with a recognition of the importance of changing gender roles which led to the minister for Equal Opportunity setting up a working party to investigate men's roles in the early 1980s. In Kaplan's words:

> These developments in Scandinavian countries should indicate to us that neither part-time work nor work in the public sector alone will suffice to give women the same job security and chance of economic independence as men. As long as women have not infiltrated all levels of the labour market and have not obtained firm job security they can be made to vanish from the labour market at a moment's notice. (Kaplan, 1992: 97)

The persistence of gender divisions of labour within the home and women's part-time employment are unlikely to be changed in Britain if they have not so far altered in Sweden and suggest that 'traditional sex role attitudes' (Hakim, 1995: 434) are resistant to change and structure women's greater vulnerability to poverty. Indeed, as Hakim suggests, what may be happening is a polarisation among women such that some give priority to marriage and child rearing while others prioritise employment (Hakim, 1995: 438). This is reflected in patterns of allocation of money within marriage (Vogler, 1994), in patterns of labour market participation and in the differential impact of equal opportunities policies on women; those who benefit most are those whose work patterns most closely approximate to men's.

The policy recommendations embodied in the report of the Commission on Social Justice are part and parcel of a European strategy for combatting social exclusion and integrating women into the workforce (Whitting, 1992; Levitas, 1996). This attention can be seen as an outcome of feminist input into the policy-making process but, overall, the policies being developed derive from social democracy. The impact of the women's movement in this policy area, although limited, has been via feminist research and feminist activism in organisations making up the poverty lobby and policy networks, rather than through specifically feminist policy networks as in the US (Spalter-Roth and Schreiber, 1995).

The experience of Britain also demonstrates the importance of left-of-centre political parties to the formation and implementation of policies advocated by progressive social movements. Thus during the 18 years of Conservative government from 1979 to 1997 feminists had very little impact on the development of anti-poverty policies; on the contrary the influence of the new right was much more significant. A similar pattern can be observed in the US and Australia. In the US, feminist influence on policy was substantial prior to the election of Republican President Reagan in 1980. This ushered in a period of right-wing assault on feminist policy gains and only ended with the election of a Democratic President, Clinton, in 1992 (Spalter-Roth and Schreiber, 1995). In Australia the Labour government of Whitlam was elected in 1972 and incorporated femocrats into the state bureaucracy; this resulted in a significant number of feminist policy initiatives (Eisenstein, 1995: 71) which came to an end in 1975 when the right-wing Fraser government was elected (Franzway *et al.*, 1989: 74).

Between 1979 and 1997 the policy of successive Tory administrations in Britain seemed to be to make the poor poorer and the rich richer (Townsend, 1993: 14–16; Social Justice, 1994: 28–32), and to reinforce women's dependence on men. This was attempted through such measures as the Child Support Act, which forced women into financial dependence on the absent fathers of their children rather than depending on the state, and the rules governing payment of income support, which make it financially unviable for women married to unemployed men to continue in employment. In addition, child benefit was frozen for most of the 1980s, thus reducing women's independent access to resources (Millar, 1996). Feminist influence on British social policy during these 18 years has been minimal, but during that time feminists have influenced the policy agenda and policy formation through participation in policy networks and, indirectly, through the EC. The influence, however, seems stronger on role equity than role change issues and it seems particularly difficult to move gender divisions of labour within families from the research onto the policy agenda.

In this chapter I have focused on the way in which feminist research on poverty and involvement in policy networks has influenced the policy agenda and fed into processes of policy formation. I have thereby concentrated on only one dimension of the influence of feminist social movements on social policies, their impact through the incorporation of relatively elite women into the policy-making process.

It is important to note, however, that poor women and organisations which represent them have also influenced policy and, perhaps more importantly, have begun to empower women by increasing their access to resources. I am thinking specifically of the initiatives of community-based social movement organisations and their involvement in obtaining funding for setting up training programmes to enable unemployed women, often lone parents, ethnic minority and disabled women, to gain the skills necessary to find paid employment. Such women's groups can often be found in areas of high male unemployment, such as South Wales, and are testimony to the organising skills and abilities of poor women themselves. Thus the South Glamorgan Women's Workshop was set up in 1984 'with support from the European Social Fund and South Glamorgan County Council' (Rees, 1992: 62). It targets women who are disadvantaged in the labour market, providing child care for trainees and offering training in electronics and computing. There is a similar women's training centre, known as the DOVE, in the Dulais valley in South Wales which developed in the wake of the 1984–85 miners' strike and was spearheaded by the women's support group (Jones, 1997). Such community-based organisations, in which women predominate as activists, can have the effect of increasing women's access to resources and/or providing alternative forms of welfare where the welfare state fails to provide (de Leonardis, 1993; Lustiger-Thaler and Shragge, 1993; Jordan, 1996: 185). Such organisations often have their roots in social movements and, through increasing women's access to resources, may contribute to a reduction in their vulnerability to poverty. In the next chapter I focus on this type of organisation in order to explore their interaction with the state and their impact on state policies relating to male violence against women.

Chapter 7

Violence

The last two chapters have focused on feminists working within existing organisations as a strategy for change. In this chapter I turn to feminist organising outside the state, focusing particularly on alternative service provision such as women's refuges and rape crisis centres. These two strategies, that of working within existing organisations or maintaining a distance from them, are often seen as emanating from different types of feminism and their theoretical understanding of the state. Liberal feminism views the state as gender neutral and therefore open to influence in the direction of greater gender equality while socialist and radical feminism analyse the state as embodying repressive class and gender relations and, in their political practice, tend to maintain a critical distance from it (Watson, 1992; Reinelt, 1995: 87). Thus, in Australia and the US where liberal feminism is relatively strong, feminists are to be found in significant numbers within state bureaucracies, hence the term femocrat, whereas in Britain where socialist and radical feminism have predominated, the phenomenon is not so widespread. As we have seen, however, this characterisation is not altogether accurate as both socialist and radical feminists have engaged with the state, the former via local authorities and the latter through such organisations as refuge groups. The difference is that socialist feminists have engaged with the state on its own terrain while radical feminists have engaged with it from an autonomous organisational base. The different strategies adopted are also affected by the nature of the state, whether it is open to pressure from interest groups and how rapidly it moves to incorporate unrepresented interests. Thus the US state is open to the formation and influence of interest groups, the Australian state tends towards rapid incorporation of social movements (McGregor and Hopkins, 1991: 28) while the British state is more closed, centralised and secretive. This has led to the characterisation of US feminism as interest group feminism, and British feminism as ideological or left-wing feminism which 'lacks national political presence and impact' (Gelb, 1989: 4). It has also been claimed that 'in the US the scope and significance of legislation on domestic violence has been greater than in Britain, largely owing to the existence of a feminist lobby and a newly created policy network focusing on wife abuse' (Gelb, 1989: 126). During the course of this chapter this verdict will be shown to be wide of the mark, particularly where the issue of male violence towards women is concerned.

Second wave feminism put male violence against women on the political agenda in the late 1960s and early 1970s and, since then, there have been significant shifts in related areas of social policy. Thus in Britain domestic violence has been recognized as a legitimate cause of homelessness, police practice towards victims of male violence has changed, sexual harassment has been named and accepted as a legal concept (initially in the US) and there is an ongoing public debate about date rape. These changes are clearly the result of feminist organising. This chapter explores the nature of this organising with particular reference to the anti-rape movement in the US and the refuge movement in Britain and its effects in terms of policy developments and cultural change. I explore, first, the way the problem of male violence was redefined by the women's movement and the challenges this poses to the separation of the public and private. I then look at the alternative forms of service provision that were set up by activists and their impact on policy development and implementation. Finally, I discuss the effect of engaging with the state on feminist organisations and political practice and assess their impact in terms of political and cultural change.

Redefining male violence

In the early 1970s male violence was taken up as an issue by the feminist movement. Women's groups began to discuss male violence against women, redefining it in terms of gendered power relations and organising to do something about it. They were concerned to change people's ideas about rape, to 'redefine publicly the experience of rape from the victim's point of view, rather than from the perspective of the rapist or law enforcement officials' (Matthews, 1994: 13). Thus rape was defined as a crime of violence and its sexual nature was de-emphasised. Feminists challenged the culturally accepted view of women as asking for it by wearing provocative clothing or being out too late at night unescorted and hence provoking men's uncontrollable sexual urges. Similarly the idea that women say no when they mean yes was attacked, as was the idea that rape is an impulsive act (Schechter, 1982). As Susan Schechter puts it:

> The anti-rape movement articulated that violence is a particular form of domination based on social relationships of unequal power. Through the efforts of the anti-rape movement, it became clear that violence is one mechanism for female social control. Today this sounds obvious; ten years ago it was a revelation. (Schechter, 1982: 34)

Male violence was defined not as aberrant actions of deviant and probably mentally unbalanced individuals, but as something which benefitted all men and which all men were capable of. Hence the slogan 'All men are potential rapists' and, from the point of view of a woman walking home alone in the dark, this is undoubtedly the case.

The organising took the form of Reclaim the Night marches, street theatre to raise awareness of the issue, and setting up alternative forms of welfare provision such as refuges and rape crisis centres. This provision was not seen as an end in itself but as a way of providing women with an escape from violent men and a means of understanding their predicament; not as something that they had brought upon themselves but as something which had social roots and could be collectively challenged and transformed. In other words these alternative forms of provision were envisaged as a means of empowerment for women and a challenge to male domination.

The first rape crisis centres were established in the US in 1972 (Matthews, 1994) and by 1976 there were 'approximately 1500 separate projects – task forces, study groups, crisis centers, "doing something about rape"' (Schechter, 1982: 39). In Britain the first refuge opened in 1971 (Pizzey, 1974) and a significant amount of legislation giving rights to women experiencing domestic violence was passed during the 1970s (Charles, 1995; Dobash and Dobash, 1992).[1] Thus male violence against women was being defined as a political concern by second wave feminism on both sides of the Atlantic at about the same time, although the focus of organising, at least initially, was different. Both, however, challenged men's control of women through violence and men's right to unlimited sexual access to 'their' women; a right which was enshrined in law in so far as there was no offence of marital rape in Britain until 1991 (Lees, 1997). The women's movement also exposed the reluctance of the police to intervene in 'domestics' which was justified by a respect for the privacy of the home (Faragher, 1985). Feminists showed this so-called privacy to be a myth; arguing that sexual relations and marriage are regulated by the state and this regulation includes a tolerance of men's violence towards the women with whom they have intimate relations. Feminists questioned the reluctance of the state to intervene on behalf of women and argued for the protection of the law to be extended to the so-called private realm of the family. In a sense they were calling for increased state intervention in the private sphere to limit men's 'freedom' to abuse the women and children with whom they lived, thereby questioning the separation between public and private that underpins the liberal democratic state and the sexual ordering on which it is based (Buechler, 1990: 197). They 'attempted to challenge the hegemonic ideology that the family was a private sphere, not subject to state interests or action, and that the state had no interest in the family' (Bush, 1992: 599).

The redefinition of male violence and its political importance for gender relations, together with the setting up of rape crisis centres and refuges/shelters for women and children experiencing domestic violence, meant that women's groups were involved not only in political activity but also in the provision of services; they were providing feminist forms of welfare run by women for women.

Policy response

During the 1970s, despite the ambivalence of the women's movement towards the state, feminists campaigned for improvements in women's social rights and for changes in the law. In both areas there have been significant developments many of which can be attributed directly to the feminist movement. Here I focus initially on legal reforms in Britain and the way domestic violence was defined as a housing issue. Then I look at parallel developments in the US where the issue of male violence towards women has been defined as a criminal justice issue. I relate these differences to the nature of the state and the resulting different tactical choices available to women's groups.

In Britain the refuge movement seems to have had a considerable impact on the development of state policy which has resulted in an expansion of women's rights and a potential increase in women's access to those resources which would enable them to challenge domestic violence. In 1975 the National Women's Aid Federation was formed in order to campaign around the issue of male violence against women within the home and to coordinate the work of the growing number of refuge groups in Britain (Hanmer, 1977: 95). The Federation gave evidence to the Parliamentary Select Committee on Violence within Marriage which reported in 1975. Several recommendations emerged from this committee. First, it recognized the importance of the work that refuge groups were doing and recommended that the network of refuges be expanded. It also defined domestic violence as a housing issue and recommended that refuges should be resourced by local authorities, that is, through the local state rather than receiving funding centrally. Third, it recommended that legislation should be introduced 'clarifying the responsibility of local authorities' towards women and children who become homeless as a result of domestic violence and giving women legal protection from abusive partners (Dobash and Dobash, 1992: 124). These recommendations were rapidly implemented. In the following year, after lobbying by the National Women's Aid Federation, Jo Richardson, a woman and a Labour MP, introduced a private member's bill which became the Domestic Violence and Matrimonial Proceedings Act 1976 and came into force in 1977 (Barron, 1990: 15). This bill enabled women who were married or cohabiting to apply for a non-molestation or exclusion order against their abusing partner. In 1977 the Housing (Homeless Persons) Act was passed which, for the first time, recognized that women who became homeless as a result of domestic violence, and who were defined as being in priority need, had a right to be permanently rehoused by a local authority.[2] And in 1978 the Domestic Proceedings and Magistrates' Courts Act enabled women who were married to an abusing partner to apply to a magistrates' court for an injunction to prevent further abuse. All this legislation conferred rights on women which had not been theirs previously and, in theory, gave them some redress in law against an abusing partner.

In the US, as in Britain, there was considerable attention given to the way the police reacted to domestic violence and women's groups argued that women experiencing domestic violence should have the same legal rights as any other victim of crime. Their actions resulted in 'innovative criminal justice programmes and new law enforcement legislation' (Dobash and Dobash, 1992: 167) but in 1983 it was still 'only seventeen states [that] provided protection orders... that enabled courts to refrain men from abusing, harassing and assaulting the women with whom they live' (Dobash and Dobash, 1992: 168). Similar legal reforms giving rights to women were enacted in Australia in the 1980s (McGregor and Hopkins, 1991: xix). The shortcomings of legal remedies have been well documented (Barron, 1990; Mama, 1989); it is one thing to enshrine rights in law and quite another to ensure that they are translated into practice for all women.

Rape crisis centres in the US targeted the way women were treated by state institutions. Thus attempts were made to raise awareness of violence against women among the police and in hospitals and to change the way they treated women who had been raped (Matthews, 1994: 11). In 1973 the National Organisation for Women set up a Rape Task Force and began to work towards reforming the rape laws such that the rape victim was no longer held responsible for being raped (Matthews, 1994: 13, 1995: 293). Official concern was reflected in the establishment of the National Center for the Prevention and Control of Rape in 1975 and in the availability of funding, initially through Social Services but later through the Office of Criminal Justice Planning for, among other things, rape crisis centres (Matthews, 1994: 13, 1995: 292).

The refuge movement in the US also had an impact on legislation although it was not as immediate as in Britain. Although the National Coalition against Domestic Violence was formed in 1977 (Schechter, 1982: 137), it was not until 1984 that legislation was passed providing funding for refuges and then it was as an amendment to the Child Abuse Act (Dobash and Dobash, 1992: 140). Thus funding was eventually won for women as 'victims' of 'family violence' in the context of concern with the rights of victims of crime and a focus on law and order. Domestic violence was to be policed and funded in the context of victim support and associated police practice rather than in the context of access to resources, such as housing and social security, which would enable women to be independent of their abuser: the latter was the approach taken in Britain.

In Australia funding initially (1975) was to states (and hence to refuges) through the Community Health Program and was greatly facilitated by the support of the 'fledgling femocracy' installed by the Labor administration after 1972 (McGregor and Hopkins, 1991: 36–7). Indeed it has been argued that the support of the femocrats for the refuge movement was essential at both federal and state level in securing funding, legal reform and the continuing influence of feminist analyses of male violence in the response of the state to such violence. Thus in the US and Australia, but not in Britain, funding for refuges was secured at a national level for disbursement at state level. In Britain, funding was a matter for the local state. Both forms of funding permitted considerable variation and necessitated state or local level organising to ensure that individual groups received some of the money which was available.

Accounts of the way legislation is enacted and policies changed show that sympathetic individuals within the system, along with pressure from movement activists and organisations, are important in bringing about change (see, for example, Abrar, 1996; Mackay, 1996). This is illustrated in the case of the anti-rape movement in California whose attempts to gain funding were supported and, in some cases, initiated by women who were strategically placed within the funding agencies (Matthews, 1994: 106, 108). In addition, legislative success depends crucially on the complexion of government. Thus the initial legislative changes in Britain were introduced by a Labour government while in the US the election of Reagan stymied the attempts of the movement to introduce federal legislation for refuge funding and ensured, when it finally did reach the statute books, that it was under the control of the criminal justice system. Similarly, in Australia, the political complexion of federal and state governments has been crucial in both securing legislative change and funding (McGregor and Hopkins, 1991).

From rights to reality

Of course, legislation which recognizes domestic violence as a problem has to be implemented and, 'if tangible benefits are to follow from legal symbols, organisation and collective action are necessary' (Meehan, 1985: 160). Legal reforms and rights have to be translated into reality and it is here that the feminist politics of refuge and anti-rape groups is so important. In order to illustrate this issue I wish to concentrate on the problems associated with translating the social rights enshrined in the British housing legislation into measures which have a real impact on the way in which women live their daily lives. I draw on two research projects I conducted in association with Welsh Women's Aid in the late 1980s and early 1990s (see Charles, 1994a, 1994b, 1995 for details).

In Britain refuge groups are reliant on the state for three types of resources: funding, refuge premises and housing. The relationship,

however, is not all one way. Local authorities have a statutory oblig-
ation to provide permanent accommodation for women and children
who are homeless as a result of domestic violence and who are in
priority need. And until such time as they are able to provide permanent housing they are required to provide temporary shelter which
often takes the form of the local women's refuge. It is now recognized that refuges provide much more suitable accommodation and
support for women and children in this situation than other forms of
temporary accommodation are able to. It is in recognition of this,
and of the fact that refuges assist local authorities in discharging
their statutory responsibilities, that refuges receive funding from
local authorities. In effect, refuges are operating as part of the
welfare state.

Through providing refuge accommodation, representing the interests of women and children escaping domestic violence, campaigning around the issue and producing evidence of a legitimate social
need through commissioning research, the refuge movement in
Wales has effectively increased the resources available to women
and children escaping domestic violence. Since 1975, when the first
Welsh refuge was opened in Cardiff, the number of refuge groups
has grown considerably as has the funding they receive from local
authorities and other housing providers (Charles, 1991). Thus in the
early 1990s there were 35 refuges and thirteen information centres
run by 31 refuge groups (Welsh Women's Aid, 1992). Access to
permanent housing is also seen as a key issue for women fleeing
domestic violence (Pahl, 1985). Most women and children in Welsh
refuges have become homeless as a result of domestic violence and
are therefore entitled to be rehoused permanently under existing
legislation (Charles, 1994a, 1994b). If there is a risk of continued
violence in their home area they are entitled to be rehoused in a
completely different area. There is, however, considerable variation
in the way the legislation is implemented (Charles, 1994a; see also
Malos and Hague, 1993) and some local authorities are reluctant to
provide permanent accommodation to women who cannot demonstrate a local connection; thus even though women have rights in
law, implementing them at local level can be problematic. Welsh
Women's Aid (the umbrella organisation which represents the interests and coordinates the work of refuge groups in Wales) has
supported refuge groups in their attempts to persuade local authorities that women, even from outside the area, have a legitimate claim
to housing resources if they are homeless due to domestic violence
and, in several cases, this pressure has had tangible results.

Welsh Women's Aid has consistently argued the case for an increase in move-on accommodation for women and children leaving refuges (J. Taylor, 1989; Welsh Women's Aid, nd) and pointed out that existing housing resources are inadequate to meet the needs of women and children who are homeless due to domestic violence (Charles with Jones, 1993). They have backed up their case by commissioning research,[3] much of which has resulted in policy changes.

As far as housing is concerned, then, feminist political activity, in the form of the refuge movement and Welsh Women's Aid, has been effective in altering the distribution of housing resources in favour of women and children escaping domestic violence. It has also been effective in increasing the levels of funding available to refuge groups. This means that increasing numbers of women are able to leave an abusing partner and no longer have to tolerate circumstances in which they feel powerless and oppressed. In 1978, for example, 432 women and 600 children were given refuge whereas by 1990–91 these figures had more than trebled, with 1,302 women and 2,112 children staying in Welsh refuges (Welsh Women's Aid, 1990). In this sense feminist political practice, in engaging with the state, is empowering women.

The effectiveness of Welsh Women's Aid as a campaigning organisation which seeks to influence policy and the distribution of resources and which has contributed to the legitimation of feminist forms of organisation is not unconnected to its unity and coordination. It is significant that in Wales almost all refuge groups are affiliated to Welsh Women's Aid. This means that the organisation can legitimately claim to represent the interests of all Welsh refuge groups and this is bound to strengthen its negotiating position.

The skills and expertise of refuge groups and Welsh Women's Aid are recognized by local housing departments and social services and by the Welsh Office. This suggests that consistent campaigning and educational work by refuge groups locally and by Welsh Women's Aid nationally has had the effect of legitimating feminist forms of organisation and welfare provision and the attempts of Welsh Women's Aid to influence policy. Refuges are seen to provide a much-needed service: feminist welfare provision works. And it works to empower women, enabling them to change their own lives and to challenge male domination within the home. This has been achieved with support, albeit limited, from the state while, at the same time, retaining autonomy from the state.

In Britain, feminist-run refuges are part of the voluntary sector of the welfare state. This sector has become increasingly important in providing services which have been cut back under successive Tory administrations and, arguably, allows greater flexibility and autonomy than engagement with those parts of the state more concerned with control and coercion such as the criminal justice system.

State funding

Dependence on the state for funding presents dangers of cooption, an issue which has been of concern to activists from the early days of the movement. Here I compare the experience of refuge groups in Wales with that of rape crisis centres in the US in order to highlight the variable impact of different branches of the state on feminist service provision.

In Wales, the organisational autonomy and feminist principles of refuges are jealously guarded by refuge groups. Indeed this autonomy is seen as vital in enabling groups to support women in their attempts to resist male violence. It may be the case that the preservation of autonomy has been facilitated by the fact that refuges are funded by local authorities and are seen as part of the voluntary sector of the state. Control over their operations and practices is therefore relatively loose and they have been free to develop woman-centred forms of support. Workers in statutory state agencies, however, are constrained by legal requirements to make the family their first priority rather than the woman. In the refuge movement in Wales, working outside the state but engaging with it, feminists have been able to retain the initiative and to set the terms under which they are prepared to work. It could, of course, be argued that the price of this autonomy is that the refuge movement in Wales and the rest of Britain is very poorly funded despite repeated calls for a national funding strategy. And although in a discussion document published in 1995 the Labour Party committed itself to 'a national strategy to tackle domestic violence' (Labour Party, 1995), it did not mention funding and the current trend is towards increasing investment in victim support services. This is likely to have the effect of tightening the control of the state, redefining the problem of male violence as one of individual pathology and marginalising feminist refuges and rape crisis lines (Foley, 1994; Gillespie, 1994; Lupton, 1994; Kelly, 1995/6). As one activist put it:

> Many women in and around the refuge movement are not fooled by the apparently benevolent nature of VSS [Victim Support Services]. Like many others, I believe that they have been set up to provide an 'establishment' alternative to women's organisations such as Rape Crisis and Women's Aid and to eventually contribute to the demise of these initiatives. (Maguire, 1988: 43)

Her concern is echoed by others and may not be unfounded, particularly if we bear in mind the experience of these movements in the US.

In the US, funding for rape crisis centres and refuges comes mainly through the criminal justice system (Dobash and Dobash 1992; Matthews, 1994). In an analysis of the anti-rape movement in California, Nancy Matthews documents the problems associated with this; similar problems were also experienced by the US refuge movement (Schechter, 1982; Bush, 1992).

In 1979 legislation was passed which established 'a regular source of funding for rape crisis centers through the California Office of Criminal Justice Planning (OCJP)' (Matthews, 1994: 105). This created a dilemma for many radical groups who took an oppositional stance to the state, particularly the law enforcement branch of it, and who were reluctant to compromise their principles by being indebted to it for funding (Matthews, 1994, 1995). As Matthews puts it:

> Law enforcement represented the most obviously repressive arm of the state, and the LEAA [Law Enforcement Assistance Administration] requirement that victims report their rapes to the police conflicted with RCC's [Rape Crisis Centre] principle of empowering women by allowing them to decide for themselves whether to use the criminal justice system. (Matthews, 1995: 297)

The movement, however, as well as containing radical groups also included more moderate, social service agency orientated groups. Matthews argues that the absorption of these more moderate, mainstream feminists into the state agencies dealing with funding rape crisis centres led to state agencies adopting a less sympathetic approach to the more radical groups. An example is provided by the requirement of the OCJP that rape crisis centres collect statistics on the women who approached them. Some groups resisted this, arguing that they were not part of the state bureaucracy and there was no statutory requirement on them to do the data collection work of the state. Refusal, however, could and did result in withdrawal of funding while groups who behaved in the required way received generous funding (Matthews, 1994: 116, 119). Through this selective funding, the social service definition of rape crisis work was institutionalised and 'the feminist political agenda of relating violence against women to women's oppression was marginalised, ridiculed, and suppressed by various means' (Matthews, 1994: 126). The incorporation of moderate feminists into the state made those who were left outside seem unreasonable and discredited their criticisms of the programmes.

On the other hand Matthews also documents the way in which the state can be involved in setting up rape crisis centres. She argues that groups that originated in this way did not have strong links to contemporary feminism, were more bureaucratic and were more influenced by criminal justice definitions of rape (Matthews, 1994: 137–8). Rather than emerging from the feminist movement with a strong commitment to feminist politics and a feminist analysis of rape, they were set up in the context of an emphasis on victims' rights and a discourse of therapy (Matthews, 1994: 143). Thus women who had been raped or violently attacked by men needed therapy to help them overcome the 'individual psychological trauma' (Matthews, 1994: 159). Rape had been redefined as an individual problem for which individual rather than political solutions are necessary. In Matthews' words:

> The OCJP was willing to address rape as a crime problem and as a problem for the individual victim, but not as a reflection of problematic gender relations. The social service aspects of the movement's work were more amenable to adoption by state agencies than the feminist political agenda... Victim services mediated through state programs have a social control aspect aimed not so much at individual women, but at feminist attempts to change gendered power relations. (Matthews, 1994: 165)

A similar process has taken place within the US refuge movement. Thus Diane Bush argues that its association with the criminal justice and/or mental health system has resulted in the state 'providing special protection for women':

> Protection measures may formally, bureaucratically meet SMO [Social Movement Organisation] demands without facilitating empowerment for individual women nor producing social change in the structure within and between family, state, and economy as institutions. (Bush, 1992: 591)

And this has been achieved by separating service provision from the feminist political analysis of domestic violence. Thus the state has supported the provision of services to women survivors of male violence, but in the process has redefined and depoliticised the problem, something that Schechter warned about in persuasive terms:

> [I]t is essential that services and politics not be separated from each other. Small feminist and grassroots shelters offer not only safety and caring, but also the courage needed by women to rebuild their lives. They actively demonstrate a model of cooperation, a possibility people in this society, especially those of different races and classes, rarely experience together. As institutions, they convey a radically different explanation to battered women and to the society of why women are beaten and what social conditions must be changed to end violence. (Schechter, 1982: 250–1)

This evidence suggests that state funding comes with strings attached and, in accepting it, feminist organisations lose their ability to define the problem and their own goals, that is, they lose their autonomy. This interpretation is supported by comparing the experience of refuge groups in Britain with those in the US. In Britain, refuge groups have managed to retain their autonomy and the fusion of service provision and feminist politics, while this has been more difficult in the US (Charles, 1995). It seems that the crucial variable is the state agency through which funding is channelled and the resultant positioning of refuge groups within the state.

Thus funding for rape crisis and refuge work in Britain is neither tightly controlled by the state nor very generous. In the 1970s domestic violence was seen as giving rise to problems of homelessness to which local authorities, in partnership with housing associations, have a statutory duty to respond. Refuges receive funding from the local state in recognition of their role in providing accommodation for women and children who are homeless as a result of domestic violence, they are not funded through the criminal justice system. In contrast, in the US it is the criminal justice system which funds this type of work and, because of their interest in crime prevention and detection and, arguably, the repressive nature of this part of the state, groups in receipt of funding are subject to much tighter control. They have also been incorporated into crisis intervention and victim support work in the US and Australia, a move which is only just beginning in Britain, and often this involves a redefinition of male violence against women in individual terms. It has been argued that this results in the cooptation and institutionalisation of feminist organisations and their incorporation into a non-feminist state agenda of control and management of male violence rather than its elimination. It can also be seen as issue perversion; something which I discuss more fully in the next chapter. Here I wish to situate this discussion in the context of the debate on the nature of feminist organisations and the relation between feminist politics and bureaucratic forms of organisation.

Feminist organisations and the state

It has been argued that the muting of the feminist challenge is achieved in capitalist societies by the transformation of feminist organisations into bureaucracies and that this is brought about through engaging with the state (Ferguson, 1984 cited in Bush, 1992: 590). This contrasts with the RMT argument that it is only bureaucratic organisations that are able to bring about policy change. Here I wish to explore the forms of organisation character-ising the refuge and anti-rape movements and evaluate the effects on these organisations of engagement with the state.

Refuge groups emerged from the local, autonomous groups of the women's movement in the late 1960s and early 1970s. They have a collective form of organisation, generally eschewing hierarchy and specialisation and not having any formalised structure or positions of leadership. The early refuge groups in Wales, as elsewhere, grew out of local women's liberation groups with an explicitly feminist ideology. The women who set them up were active in feminist poli-tics and saw refuge work as part of their political activity and their form of organisation as prefiguring the movement's 'vision of the ideal society' (Arnold, 1995: 277). Most of the groups were organ-ised on a collective, democratic basis with no specialisation of tasks and a commitment to skill sharing and decision making by consen-sus (Hanmer, 1977: 96). Thus recruitment into a refuge group was based on a commitment to feminism and/or having experienced some form of male violence rather than any formal skills or creden-tials. This enabled many refuge residents to become involved in refuge work after leaving a refuge. This form of organisation was widespread in Britain, Australia, the US and Canada and marks these early feminist organisations off from the hierarchical, specialised, bureaucratic forms of organisation which characterise state organisations (Rodriguez, 1988; Ristock, 1990; McGregor and Hopkins, 1991; Halford, 1992; Witz and Savage, 1992).

Such organisations have been conceptualised as counter or neo-bureaucracies; a form of organisation said to typify so-called new social movements. Frequently this form of organisation has been defined as quintessentially feminist, any other form being a deviation from the norm and betraying a move away from feminist politics.

Problems have, however, been identified with this form of organisation. Thus, Jo Freeman has argued that although it represented an attempt to avoid a concentration of power in the hands of a few leaders at the top of a hierarchy, what in effect happened in many groups was that particularly charismatic or confident women, often supported by friendship networks, were able to impose their views on the rest of the group. This resulted in a 'tyranny of structure-lessness' no less antithetical to democracy and participation than the hierarchical, bureaucratic organisations of which these groups were critical (Freeman, 1975). Indeed, their reliance on group soli-darity and a sense of collective identity to hold group members together often made these groups exclusive and positively unwel-coming to outsiders or rendered them unstable. In addition, the importance of maintaining the group's identity as a means of ensur-ing its survival tends to suppress difference and create an imperme-able group boundary (Rodriguez, 1988). Some groups attempted to overcome these problems by instituting caucuses whereby the inter-ests of 'minority' groups could be represented within the collective. This is a recognition not only of differences between women of different ethnicities, sexualities and so on but also of the power relations which structure even the most informally structured organisation (Ristock, 1990; Leidner, 1991). There is, however, evidence that collective identity is not only important in holding together small groups but also in enabling them to interact effec-tively with outside agencies, particularly where refuge groups operate in the context of overlapping social movement communi-ties (Charles and Davies, 1997).

It has been suggested that such groups are good at innovation but that their survival is problematic, consequently a lot of energy goes into group maintenance (Freeman, 1975: 145–6). In contrast, more formally organised and centralised groups are more stable and better able to put innovations into practice (Staggenborg, 1995: 344). Indeed Freeman argued that what was needed for 'movement survival' was a balance between both forms of organisation and it seems that this is what has emerged in the refuge and anti-rape movements (Matthews, 1994: 75). For instance, in a study of the refuge movement in Australia, the authors argue that movement organisations can be characterised:

> As having a 'hybrid organisational form', part collective and part hierarchy, and... that such a form is particularly appropriate for organisations seeking the type of social change pursued by the movement against domestic violence. (McGregor and Hopkins, 1991: xxii)

There is evidence of this within the refuge movement in Britain. Thus in Wales some refuge groups have begun to employ specialist workers but there is disagreement as to the optimum balance between non-specialisation and skill sharing and the need for specialist skills. This has become more acute since refuges have been more closely involved with quasi-state organisations, such as housing associations, for funding as the amount of paper work has increased enormously (Charles, 1995). Filling in complicated funding applications has, in some groups, become a specialised activity while, in others, it remains a task which everyone knows how to do. Thus engagement with the state and the requirement to be accountable to other organisations could be seen as posing a threat to the non-hierarchical, non-specialist, democratic form of organisation which has been a hallmark of the refuge movement. Most groups have moved towards some specialisation of tasks while adopting measures to ensure that this specialisation does not involve power (McGregor and Hopkins, 1991: 65). Thus all workers are paid the same and, even programme coordinators or directors, are subject to control by the collective. This, however, does not address the differences that can develop between paid and unpaid workers or volunteers who are often doing the same work.

Thus in practice, in order to be effective, small groups with no formal structure seem to have evolved into groups which are more formalised and centralised but are not bureaucratic and hierarchical. They are therefore characterised as hybrids or counter-bureaucracies. But how does their form of organisation relate to feminist politics? Do groups become less feminist as they adopt more formal structures? Is it possible to retain feminist values and political principles with a variety of forms of organisation? Do different feminist ideologies result in different forms of organisation? And are different forms of organisation more or less effective in terms of achieving the goal of a transformation in gender relations?

In the US, professionalisation seems to have gone furthest. Schechter notes that in 1976, which she defines as the heyday of the anti-rape movement, there were something like 400 'autonomous feminist rape crisis centers' but now 'it is impossible to estimate the number of feminist rape crisis centers because as funding became available, professionals increasingly became involved in providing services' (Schechter, 1982: 39). Indeed, in comparison with Britain where almost all groups are affiliated to the Women's Aid Federations and there is considerable homogeneity in ideology and practice, in the US there is a much greater diversity of groups providing refuge and other crisis services (Dobash and Dobash, 1992; Matthews, 1994). This variation in the ideology and politics of groups is often translated into their organisational structures (Schechter, 1982; Staggenborg, 1995). Thus Matthews distinguishes between feminist groups and social service groups (see also Rodriguez, 1988; Arnold, 1995; Hyde, 1995) while Dobash and Dobash identify philanthropic, organisational/bureaucratic, therapeutic and activist groups; most refuges being run by activists (Dobash and Dobash, 1992: 76, 90).

Finally, the refuge movement has a national presence in Britain, the Women's Aid Federations of England, Wales and Scotland, which focus on campaigning work, pursue policy initiatives, provide training and develop codes of practice in consultation with affiliated refuges. This type of umbrella organisation is also common in the US and Australia where there are state-based coalitions (Schechter, 1982; McGregor and Hopkins, 1991). In both the US and Australia there are also organisations operating at the national level which are either part of the state, having been set up by the federal government as in Australia, or operate as pressure groups or coalitions with or without significant government funding, such as the Washington-based National Coalition Against Domestic Violence and the Center for Women Policy Studies in the US. The latter receives government funding via the Family Violence Programme (Spalter-Roth and Schreiber, 1995). These organisations press for legislative reform and policy change and may also adopt a coordinating role.

It seems then that the refuge and anti-rape movements are characterised by various organisational forms, ranging from small collectives with minimal structure to bureaucratic organisations which are sometimes part of the state. There are two questions which are important here. One relates to whether all these forms of organisation can be considered feminist and the other relates to their effectiveness. With regard to the first point and in opposition to the view that a truly feminist organisation is characterised by a particu-

lar organisational form, Martin has argued that feminist organisations take many forms and that 'No other social movement of the
1960s, or later, has produced such a rich variety of organisations'
(Martin, 1990: 183). She suggests that an organisation is feminist if
it is 'pro-woman, political, and socially transformational' (Martin,
1990: 184) and that there are five criteria which can determine this.
These are whether an organisation:

> (a) has feminist ideology; (b) feminist guiding values; (c) has feminist goals;
> (d) produces feminist outcomes; (e) was founded during the women's move-
> ment as part of the women's movement. (Martin, 1990: 185)

Martin also points out that while radical feminists tend to view
collective forms of organisation as the only form that is feminist,
liberal feminists do not see hierarchy and bureaucracy as inherently
non-feminist. There is a suggestion here that different feminist
ideologies are associated with different forms of organisation and
this might help to explain the greater professionalisation and
bureaucratisation characterising the US movement. In addition, and
as we have seen from the refuge and anti-rape movements, most
feminist organisations are neither hierarchical and bureaucratic nor
purely collectivist; this questions the utility of such a distinction.
Indeed Martin argues that a particular organisational structure is not
a defining feature of feminist organisations and that most combine
features of democracy and bureaucracy (Martin, 1990: 188). There
is therefore little evidence to support the view either that only one
form of organisation can be regarded as feminist or that bureaucratisation necessarily compromises the radical aims of an organisation (Staggenborg, 1995: 343). There is no doubt, however, that
engagement with the state, particularly an acceptance of state
funding, can lead to greater specialisation and professionalisation.
But whether this mutes the feminist challenge or allows feminist
organisations to be more effective in bringing about significant
social change is a moot point.

The experience of the refuge and anti-rape movements and the
effect they have had on policy and practice in the sphere of violence
against women[4] is itself testimony to the fact that organisations do
not have to be bureaucratic to succeed in influencing policy, particularly in view of the commitment of most feminist organisations to
time-consuming, participatory democracy (Leidner, 1991: 267;
Staggenborg, 1995: 339). Indeed, more formal organisation may
serve to make feminist organisations more effective service

providers but this does not necessarily need to negate the political framework of feminism and women's empowerment within which alternative feminist services are offered. The political edge has been taken off some refuge and anti-rape groups by engaging with particularly repressive and controlling parts of the state, this engagement also appears to encourage bureaucratisation. This suggests that the cooption of the anti-rape movement by the state and the depoliticisation of male violence noted in the US is an outcome, not so much of changing forms of organisation, but of dependence on the state for funding. State control can thereby be exercised over the organisation, legitimating some forms of organisation and feminist practice and delegitimating and marginalising others. It may also be a result of control being exercised by part of the repressive state apparatus as opposed to the less coercive local state as in Britain.

Before leaving the issue of male violence I want to return to definitions of male violence and explore briefly the cultural changes associated with feminist political activity in this area.

Conflicting definitions

It seems clear that second wave feminism has had an enormous impact on the visibility of male violence against women and the way that it is thought about. Thus, in 1996, the UN declared that women who have been subject to male violence are entitled to refugee status if they leave their country (*Guardian*, 24/2/96); the EC recognizes violence as a denial of women's citizenship rights and a form of social exclusion; and UNICEF, in its annual Progress of Nations report published in 1997 includes in its definition of progress 'the degree of protection women have against discrimination and violence' (Coward, 1997). Violence against women is a topic included in soap operas. Thus in May 1992 *Brookside*, a soap on British television, featured the killing of an abusive man by his wife and daughter and their subsequent treatment by the judicial system. This was at a time when there was considerable public debate about the way the law treats women who are driven to kill abusing men after years of tolerance of horrific violence (Lees, 1997). And in 1997 the *Archers* on BBC Radio 4 featured a middle-class business man violently assaulting his girlfriend and her subsequent decision to report him to the police. This soap also highlighted the unsatisfactory way in which these cases are dealt with once they reach court. The 1980s film *The Accused* featured the gang rape of a woman which bore an uncanny resemblance to the gang rape described in an article in *Gender and Society* (Chancer, 1987: 239), again demonstrating the difficulties women have in bringing a successful prosecution for rape. And acquaintance or date rape has been the subject of much debate with some widely publicised cases problematising the issue of consent and highlighting the different interpretations that can be put on it (Lees, 1997: 67–8). What appears to be in progress is a struggle to redefine consent from a woman's rather than a man's perspective and a shift in cultural attitudes towards rape in the direction of accepting the feminist claim that yes means yes and no means no. How far this still has to go is indicated by a judge's summing up in a rape case in Britain in 1990: 'As gentlemen of the jury will understand, when a woman says "No" she doesn't always mean "No"' (Lees, 1997: 75). Notwithstanding the difficulty of changing the British judiciary and the law, the presentation of a feminist perspective on male violence in the media (not only in fictional accounts but also in seeking the views of feminist organisations when cases involving violence are reported) is an indication of the impact of feminism in the cultural domain and the increasing legitimacy afforded to feminist analyses and explanations of male violence. These shifts are important in themselves, but also have an indirect effect on policy change because of their impact on the way such issues are understood by individuals, particularly women, involved in the policy-making process (Mueller, 1987). And we have seen that women 'on the inside' are important for introducing legislative change.

This chapter has shown that feminist social movements have had an impact not only on policy formation but also on its implementation. This impact has relied on pressure from an autonomous women's movement together with sympathetic individuals within the state in order to facilitate the progress of legislation or policy change through formal channels. It has also explored the way in which involvement with the state, while necessary because the state has the resources which women's groups need to provide alternative services and pursue their political goals, may have the effect of increasing women's access to resources and/or services, something which is essential for women to become independent of men, while, at the same time, subverting the feminist goals of transforming gender relations. Thus incorporation is a double-edged sword in that it improves the material circumstances of ordinary women while blunting the transformational goals of the women's movement.

These effects of incorporation are more marked when the repressive arm of the state is involved in providing funds for this sort of work. It has also shown that incorporation and state redefinition of the problem (or issue perversion) can reinstate women as part of the family and redefine the issue of male violence against women as a problem of family violence, thus presenting it in gender neutral terms and robbing the issue of its capacity to challenge oppressive gender relations (Bush, 1992; Kelly, 1995/6). Thus the refuge and anti-rape movements are involved in a struggle over definitions and meaning. Or, to use other language, what began as a role change issue is redefined such that it no longer threatens the gender order. At the same time, however, incorporation is an indication that the issue of violence towards women is no longer invisible and that the state accepts a responsibility to be seen to be doing something about it, albeit on its own terms. Finally, the nature of the refuge and anti-rape movements demonstrates that feminist organisations take many forms and that it is not only bureaucratic organisations which can be effective at the level of policy change.

Chapter 8

Abortion

The emergence of second wave feminism is associated with the liberalisation of abortion laws, the widespread availability of contraception and increasing sexual freedom. Indeed, one of the central demands of the movement was that women should be able to control their own fertility. In Britain this took the form of the third demand for free contraception and abortion on demand raised in 1971. In the 1980s, and in response to criticisms of the ethnocentrism of the abortion campaign, women's ability to control their own fertility was defined more broadly. Attention was given to opposing population control strategies based on forced sterilisation and the need to create conditions under which women would be able to decide whether and when to have children rather than simply enabling women to prevent or terminate pregnancy. Thus the Campaign for Reproductive Rights was formed in Britain in 1983 and there were similar developments in the US (Staggenborg, 1991). Here I focus specifically on the policy debate surrounding abortion which continues to be a major issue for feminists, particularly in the context of a virulent anti-abortion lobby in the US and the attacks on women's reproductive rights in former communist societies (Einhorn, 1993).

A close examination of the way in which abortion law reform came about reveals that feminist social movements have hardly ever been solely responsible for putting the issue of legalisation of abortion on the policy agenda. Subsequently, however, they have been active in defence of the limited rights to abortion enshrined in law. In the process their energies have been absorbed in the legislative and parliamentary arena rather than in providing alternative feminist abortion services or in broadening out the campaign to encompass the whole range of women's reproductive rights. This has meant that although women's rights to abortion, under specific circumstances, are enshrined in law, the movement has only had a limited impact on turning these rights into reality. This is partly due to the emergence of an anti-abortion counter-movement which has succeeded in restricting further the already limited rights to abortion that characterised the initial stages of legalisation. This is particularly acute in the US where legalisation arguably went further than in many other societies and where the counter-movement has, as a result, been stronger. This counter-movement sees women's reproductive rights as undermining 'the family' and motherhood, suggesting that this is a role change rather than a role equity issue (Gelb and Palley, 1982: 125).

In assessing the effect of feminist social movements on abortion policy formation a distinction has to be made between the issue attaining agenda status, the way the issue is defined and the way it is translated into law. In this chapter I look at the ways in which abortion reached the political agenda in different countries and the alliances which were formed in the course of this process. I discuss the legalisation of abortion and assess the part played in this by feminist social movements; this includes a consideration of alternative ways of framing the issue and the ways in which feminist demands and definitions have been perverted in the course of legalisation. I then turn to the problems associated with defining a right to abortion solely in terms of individual rights, the defensive nature of much subsequent social movement activity, its limited effect on women's access to fertility control and, finally, to the symbolic nature of the abortion controversy.

Abortion law reform

Despite the importance of abortion and women's reproductive rights to second wave feminism, there is little agreement among feminists as to the effectivity of the women's movement in securing the legalisation of abortion. Thus Drude Dahlerup claims that:

> The issue of abortion on demand was to the new women's movement of the 1970s what the suffrage issue had been to the feminist movement around the turn of the century. (Dahlerup, 1986: 10)

While Karen Coleman observes that the liberalisation of abortion legislation is often attributed to the women's liberation movement by feminists and anti-feminists alike, but that:

> Analysis of the period of liberalization in the late sixties and very early seventies shows however, that in large part, changes crucial to the liberalization of abortion practices in Australia *pre-dated* the emergence of Women's Liberation. (Coleman, 1988: 76)

Rosalind Petchesky takes a similar position when she says that the re-legalisation of abortion:

> Had little connection to women's right to legal abortion, either in theory or in practice. It was spearheaded by a coalition of private and family planning organisations, foundations, and corporate interests organised around the population issue. (Petchesky, 1986: 117)

To be sure, these authors are all discussing different countries and the significant variations in the timing of abortion law reform means that in some countries the women's movement had a greater impact on the process of legalisation than in others. Thus, in the USSR and Sweden abortion was legalised in 1920 and 1937 respectively. In Britain it was legalised in 1967, before the emergence of second wave feminism, while in France and Italy abortion law reform occurred during the 1970s in the presence of strong women's movements (Kaplan, 1992). Gisela Kaplan compares the experience of Scandinavia with other Western European countries:

> The issue of abortion was decided earlier and usually with far less public uproar than in other countries. The change occurred almost quietly and, in Sweden, even without much debate... Thus abortion never became the catalyst for women's movements, as has been the case in other western European nations... Iceland, Sweden and Denmark liberalised their abortion laws in the interwar period (1918–1939), Finland in 1951 and Norway in 1965. Abortion on demand was introduced in Denmark in 1973 and in Sweden in 1975. (Kaplan, 1992: 64)

These differences go some way towards explaining the contradictory statements regarding the impact of feminist social movements on the abortion issue and its significance for women's mobilisation. They also show that the legalisation of abortion is not dependent on the existence of feminist social movement activity. Similarly, access to abortion on demand is not a feature of most abortion legislation, even if its passage was campaigned for by an active feminist movement (Ketting and Van Praag, 1986).[1] Almost everywhere the right of women to control their fertility through access to abortion is to be exercised under the control of the medical profession, within a specified time period and, in the case of minors, with parental consent.

Thus although abortion was, and is, of central importance to second wave feminism, the impact of the movement on abortion legislation appears to be limited. If this is the case it is important to examine the forces that led to the liberalisation of abortion legislation and the part played by feminist social movements in this process. I look first at Britain and the US, where abortion law reform pre-dated or coincided with the emergence of second wave feminism. I then discuss developments in Western Europe where, in some countries, the abortion issue functioned as a catalyst for the emergence of feminist social movements in a way analogous to the issue of equality discussed in Chapter 5.

In most countries abortion laws were reformed in response to political pressure – from a variety of sources – and a failure of existing legislation to succeed in regulating women's abortion practices in the context of the changing demographic and employment patterns we have already explored (see Chapter 4; Luker, 1984; Petchesky, 1986). As Petchesky puts it:

> Shifts in state policies regarding abortion or fertility have usually been responses to, rather than determinants of, changes in the economic and social conditions that structure women's work and marital patterns and birth control practices. These conditions give rise to movements and organisations that put pressure on the state to change its policies, but out of 'distinct or opposed reasons'. (Petchesky, 1986: 102)

It is the movements and organisations involved in putting pressure on the state that vary and it is the extent to which organised feminism is a part of these alliances which is of interest here.

In Britain abortion was legalised in 1967. The main organisation campaigning for reform was the Abortion Law Reform Association, founded in 1930, which drew together the family planning (population) movement and women's organisations such as the Women's Cooperative Guild which was concerned with the protection of maternal health (Llewelyn Davies, 1978). The medical profession recognized that some reform was inevitable in order to regain its state-sanctioned professional jurisdiction over whether and when to perform an abortion which was being undermined in practice (Lovenduski, 1986b: 52). The majority of abortions were carried out illegally by back street abortionists resulting in high rates of maternal injury and often death. Thus part of the pressure towards liberalising the abortion laws came from the unworkability of existing legislation, which did not prevent abortions but forced women into

illegal abortions which were not regulated by the state. The Thalidomide episode in the early 1960s strengthened the case for therapeutic abortions in the case of severe foetal abnormality. In addition, the
atmosphere of liberalisation in sexual and moral issues during the
same decade favoured relaxation of the abortion legislation. In
response to these pressures, abortion law was reformed such that 'it
expanded the category of those eligible for an abortion' (Cohan,
1986: 37) but a woman had to seek the consent of two doctors in
order to have an abortion and there were very specific grounds on
which this was granted. It did not allow abortion on demand; far
from it. Whether or not a woman was allowed an abortion was the
doctor's decision and this was often determined by moral judgments
about what category of woman was fit to be a mother and whether
or not 'promiscuous' women should be made to pay for their sexual
freedom by being forced to go through with their pregnancy (Doyal,
1981: 233–4). It was very often young, white women who had to
pay by having the baby, and black and poor women who may
already have had a number of children who had to pay by being
forcibly sterilised or by submitting to medically administered
contraception such as the injectable contraceptive Depo-Provera
(Bryan *et al.*, 1985: 103; Petchesky, 1986). Thus the maintenance of
medical control over access to abortion ensured that the state regulated motherhood and sexuality and defined which groups of
women should be allowed to reproduce; abortion was not a right to
which all women were equally entitled.

Whatever the limitations of the legislation, it was an advance on
previous practice, and since 1967 the women's movement has been
active in defending the abortion act against repeated attempts to
restrict it, primarily by reducing the upper time limit for abortions
(Lovenduski, 1986b). This struggle for women's reproductive rights
and in defence of the 1967 act has been taken into the labour movement by the National Abortion Campaign and, in 1979, the TUC
supported a demonstration opposing a private member's bill which
would have restricted women's access to abortion by reducing the
upper time limit. In 1990, with the passage of the Human Fertilisation and Embryology Act, the upper time limit was reduced from 28
to 24 weeks but was completely removed in some circumstances.
These changes reflected the views of the medical profession,
together with the belief that it is better to abort a disabled foetus
than to carry it to term (Morris, 1991: 66). The removal of the upper
time limit on abortion was precisely to cater for those cases where

potential disabilities were not discovered until later on in pregnancy. In Jenny Morris' words:

> The effect of the legislation is that, if a foetus has been diagnosed as having a physical or learning disability, termination of the pregnancy is now legal right up until the moment of birth. (Morris, 1991: 67)

Thus medical definitions of abortion, together with eugenicist arguments about the lesser value of people with disabilities, are enshrined in the legislation rather than feminist definitions of abortion as a woman's right.

In the US there was considerable agitation for reform of state abortion laws before the legalisation of abortion nationwide in 1973; some of which involved the emergent feminist movement. There is agreement that the feminist movement was not instrumental in putting the issue on the policy agenda, however commentators disagree about the extent to which the movement succeeded in reframing the issue as one of women's reproductive freedom and the right to control their own bodies. Thus Kristin Luker argues that abortion ceased to be defined as a medical issue and came to be seen in terms of women's right to control their own bodies (Luker, 1984: 94). Her evidence comes from a study of the abortion law reform movement in California which consisted of 'small, well-defined groups of elite professionals: public health officials, crusading attorneys, and prominent physicians' and feminists who were in favour of repeal rather than reform and regarded abortion as a woman's right (Luker, 1984: 66). The professionals were mobilised behind the cause of abortion law reform for similar reasons as in Britain. In 1967 legislation was passed in California which enabled abortions to be performed in order to prevent damage to a woman's mental or physical health, the likelihood of which was to be determined by a hospital's therapeutic abortion board. It did not allow abortion on grounds of possible foetal abnormality, although this was widely practised under the rubric that raising a handicapped child would create physical and mental health risks for the mother (Luker, 1984), and it did not enshrine a woman's right to abortion on demand. Abortion was still defined as a medical issue and access to it was controlled by the medical profession.

In the wake of this legislation Luker argues that abortion on demand became a reality and it was no longer defined in medical terms but in terms of women's reproductive rights. Thus in 4 years the number of abortions carried out in California increased by 2,000 per cent (Luker, 1984: 94) and, by 1970, 99.2 per cent of women seeking abortions had them. She uses these statistics to argue that, *de facto*, medical control of access to abortions had become a legal fiction. 'By 1971, women in California had abortions because they wanted them, not because physicians agreed that they could have them' (Luker, 1984: 94). This demonstrates that 'a substantial number of citizens agreed, at least in practice, that women, not doctors, should decide when an abortion is necessary' (Luker, 1984: 94). In her view the emergent women's movement had succeeded in radicalising a sector of the abortion law reform movement in support of the idea that a woman had the right to control her own body. This does not, however, necessarily indicate that abortion was no longer defined as a medical issue and that it had been redefined in terms of women's reproductive rights.

In contrast to Luker, Rosalind Petchesky argues that the women's movement did not succeed in redefining abortion as a rights issue. She demonstrates that pressure for change came from an alliance of the population movement, the medical profession and the women's movement (see also Staggenborg, 1991: 18). The main arguments used in favour of reform were that the law could not be enforced and that this was bringing it into disrepute and that abortions should be performed in hospitals on medical grounds under the control of doctors. In Petchesky's words:

> Abortion had to be legalized because the pressure of popular practice on doctors, health facilities, and finally the state had become irresistible... the population controllers' and physicians' participation in the abortion repeal campaign was an accommodative response to a trend they could not stop; their commitment was one not of principle but of pragmatism. (Petchesky, 1986: 123)

The medical and family planning professionals were also moving towards a reform position by the late 1960s, facilitated by the commitment to continued medical control of abortion provision and, Petchesky argues, the eugenicist overtones of the population control movement (Petchesky, 1986: 124).

Petchesky argues that the pressure emanating from the women's movement and women's determination to have abortions in increasing numbers meant that a set of principles on which to legalise abortion without conceding abortion on demand had to be found, and this was provided in the notion of therapeutic abortions. This is the idea that an abortion is justifiable in order to preserve a woman's health and that it is only medics who are qualified to make this judgment (Petchesky, 1986: 125). Feminists however wanted repeal of the abortion laws such that 'medical authorities could no longer be moral gatekeepers' (Petchesky, 1986: 126; Staggenborg, 1991).

Before the legalisation of abortion in 1973, women's groups set up alternative services, 'an abortion "underground" that provided counseling and referrals to safe, reliable practitioners; and eventually, a national network of freestanding abortion clinics' (Luker, 1984: 100; Petchesky, 1986: 128; Staggenborg, 1991). As with refuges these alternative services were not only about the provision of services but were also politically engaged and aimed to empower women in their practice and organisation (Hyde, 1995; Morgen, 1995). One of the most well known of these was set up in 1968 by feminist activists in Chicago. It became known as Jane and although it was initially a referral agency the women involved in it began to carry out abortions themselves. This was a direct challenge to medical control of abortion and a demonstration that alternative, non-hierarchical ways of delivering health care worked (Petchesky, 1986: 128; Staggenborg, 1991: 49). The women's movement was also involved in direct action, which attracted media attention, and in providing information, such as *Our Bodies Ourselves* produced by the Boston Women's Health Collective, and courses on women's health issues (Staggenborg, 1991: 43–4). This information was aimed at empowering women in relation to the medical profession by giving them the knowledge that would enable them to make informed decisions about their bodies. Together they represented a powerful critique of the hierarchical and disempowering ways in which reproductive health care was organised and delivered.

Petchesky argues that this sort of feminist activity precipitated the 1973 decision of the Supreme Court which legalised abortion; indeed it could be argued that the decision was framed the way it was in an attempt to delegitimate the feminist challenge to the state's and the medical profession's control of access to abortion and to avert the threat posed to the medical profession's monopoly of abortion techniques. However, in contrast to Luker, Petchesky asserts that 'On the level of public discourse – policy, law, media representation – the feminist voice on the abortion question was and remains barely audible' (Petchesky, 1986: 131). This is despite the fact that:

> The militant organizing of feminists and the threat of 'alternative services' –
> were crucial political influences toward loosening population establishment

and medical abortion policy. The role of feminist activists as 'shock troops' – doing underground abortion referrals and counseling, conducting speakouts, sit-ins, and demonstrations – was critical for the timing of the Supreme Court decision and earlier decriminalization statutes in several states... the impact of feminist *ideas* about birth control and abortion was less clear. (Petchesky, 1986: 129)

She suggests that this was partly because of divisions within the movement. Two important issues were the ways in which poor and ethnic minority women's reproduction was policed and their access to fertility control regulated, and divisions between the liberal and radical wings of the movement. Increased availability of contraception and abortion was associated in the lives and experiences of black and ethnic minority women with forced sterilisations and contraceptive use, that is, coercive population control measures designed to limit the reproduction of ethnic minority and poor women, rather than with increasing women's ability to control their own fertility. As we have already seen, this critique of white feminism and the narrow focus of the abortion campaign led to the broadening of the campaign to include all reproductive rights issues, not only the means of preventing pregnancy. This included an emphasis on the provision of health care to women in ways that met their needs and was not dependent on the ability to pay; a position that was part of the radical feminist approach to the abortion campaign. Radical feminists recognized that framing a woman's reproductive rights simply in terms of her legal right to choose was limited as it ignored the material circumstances of women's lives. Many women, particularly poor and ethnic minority women, were unable to avail themselves of their right to choose and were constrained by their circumstances from being able to make a meaningful choice (Himmelweit, 1988). This highlights the problem with abstract rights that are not translated into reality by social provision available to all women. They leave the whole issue of the resources needed to make these rights a reality out of account and, in addition, define abortion in individual terms, seeing it as an individual problem capable of individual solution. Again this detracts from a recognition of the social circumstances that prevent many women from making meaningful reproductive choices and which are in need of transformation (Fletcher, 1995). Additionally, framing the issue in this way opens the door to opposing one set of rights against another, as in the opposition of women's rights to foetal rights; a way of framing the debate that sets up an irreconcilable and seemingly evenly balanced conflict.

Thus for Petchesky state policy changed in response to the population movement, the women's movement and social need coming together at a particular historical moment. However, in order for feminist definitions of the issue to have been translated into legal rights and into the practical provision of reproductive health care there would have to have been a popular feminist ideology, something which the women's movement recognized as important in its attempts at consciousness raising but which did not become hegemonic. Indeed, in the popular imagination medical and neo-Malthusian ideas about abortion prevail rather than feminist ideas (Petchesky, 1986: 131).

Petchesky's verdict on the hegemony of non-feminist definitions of abortion is supported by data on public opinion provided by Suzanne Staggenborg. She concludes that after the Supreme Court decision in 1973 'there was substantial support for legal abortion, but no public consensus on "women's right to choose" abortion for any reason' (Staggenborg, 1991: 58). Thus although a majority (68 per cent) of the US public approved of legal abortion for all reasons, there was a marked difference in the proportion approving it for 'soft' as opposed to 'hard' reasons. 'Hard' reasons include 'danger to maternal health, rape, incest, and fetal deformity' while 'soft' reasons are 'economic, unmarried woman, and personal choice' (Staggenborg, 1991: 191, fn3). While a majority approved abortion for 'hard' reasons support hovered at around 50 per cent for 'soft' reasons (Staggenborg, 1991: 58). In addition, public opinion researchers have argued that 'although there is public support for legal abortion, there is not public support for the entire pro-choice platform, including the rights to Medicaid funding, abortion without parental or spousal consent, and second-trimester abortion' (Staggenborg, 1991: 202, fn5). This evidence seems to lend weight to Petchesky's view of the limited impact of feminist definitions of abortion as a woman's right to control her own body; this right is supported, but only in certain, very specific circumstances.

As in the British legislation, medical definitions of abortion predominate. Thus the decision of the Supreme Court in 1973 which legalised abortion did not embody a woman's right to choose. As Petchesky puts it, 'the feminist concept of abortion as rooted in women's right/need to control their bodies was never accorded legitimacy by the state' (Petchesky, 1986: 288). She argues that the decision was framed in terms of medical necessity and an abstract right to privacy, a right that many cannot exercise due to a lack of resources. Thus the decision to have an abortion is a medical decision and the right to privacy 'does not entail "an unlimited right to do with one's body as one pleases", or "abortion on demand"' (Petchesky, 1986: 290). Thus the Court ruled that during the first trimester of pregnancy the abortion decision should be arrived at by a woman in consultation with her doctor and that interference by the state was unconstitutional. However, during the second trimester the state could intervene on the grounds of protecting the woman's health and, in the third trimester, on the grounds of its 'interest in potential life'. This reflects the importance of motherhood and biological reproduction to processes of social reproduction and their definition as a legitimate area of state intervention and control. Indeed Petchesky argues that the state is involved in regulating women's access to fertility control for two reasons. The first is its interest in the reproduction and composition of its population and the second is its concern to regulate women and sexuality. The Supreme Court's decision 'established the legality and legitimacy of abortion... within a normative framework that emphasized women's health, very broadly defined, rather than abstract moralism or "fetal rights"' (Petchesky, 1986: 292). This represents issue perversion from the perspective of the demands of the women's movement for a woman's right to control her own body (Wiik, 1986: 145). Thus medical control of abortion, both in terms of arriving at the decision and in terms of delivering care, was reasserted by the Supreme Court. However, in terms of provision of health care services abortion is not really defined as a health issue. This is clear in subsequent decisions, such as the 1980 decision to legitimate the removal of Medicaid funding from non-therapeutic abortions. In effect this denied women who were dependent on Medicaid for their health care the means of exercising their constitutional right. And an inability to get an abortion often has severe health implications, particularly for women living in poverty.

Other bases for attacks on women's access to abortion were the introduction of parental consent requirements for under-age women seeking abortions and requirements that women be made aware of the nature of the decision they were taking before being granted an abortion. Petchesky argues that the parental consent issue was about controlling the sexuality of young women and reasserting parental, particularly paternal, control within the family. However the Supreme Court, in a 1976 decision, upheld neither parental nor spousal consent which had previously been enacted in some states.

It upheld only 'relatively benign informed consent' (Halva-Neubauer, 1993: 169) and according to Petchesky was ambivalent about upholding parental consent. Subsequently, however, it reaffirmed the desirability of minors obtaining the consent of both parents but, exceptionally, permits them to go to court where a judgment is reached as to whether they are mature enough to make the decision about abortion for themselves (Petchesky, 1986: 306). This withdraws from young unmarried women the limited right to abortion enshrined in the constitution and also effectively puts obstacles in their way. It also enables states to decide that parental consent is required in cases that come before them, thus reinforcing parental control over the sexual behaviour of young women. With respect to women without the material resources to pay for an abortion and the expenses that may be associated with getting one, the 'punishment' of pregnancy and childbirth for engaging in heterosexual sex has been effectively reinforced (Schnell, 1993: 26). Indeed, Petchesky argues that although population concerns were at the forefront of the debate when abortion was legalised in the US, subsequently a concern to reassert control over women's sexuality, which was perceived as being dramatically weakened by the way abortion had been legalised, shaped Supreme Court decisions.

Of course, the way in which Supreme Court decisions affect state legislation varies from state to state. Some retain more liberal practices with regard to funding and parental consent than others (Goggin, 1993). However, it allows less liberal states to place significant restrictions in the way of young and poor women in their access to abortion. Petchesky argues that this is to do with the importance of controlling women's sexual behaviour and reinforcing the link between heterosexual sex and motherhood which a woman's right to choose is in danger of completely severing.

Thus in the US and Britain liberalisation of the abortion laws was a response to the increasing difficulty of enforcing a prohibition on abortion together with pressure from those concerned with population and family planning issues. The women's movement was also an actor in the US but did not succeed in getting its definition of abortion as a woman's right to control her own body enshrined in law. Abortion in both countries remains under the control of the medical profession and the decision is in their hands not those of the woman involved. Subsequently, in both countries, even these limited rights have come under severe attack. This has meant that the feminist movement has been involved in a defensive struggle in the realm of institutional politics. In effect this has contained the feminist challenge and maintained a definition of a woman's right to choose as an individual civil right. In contrast, the feminist claim that women have the right to control their own bodies involves a recognition that reproductive rights are social and are a prerequisite for women's full participation in the public sphere. Reproductive rights involve not only a right in law, which women do not yet have, but also provision that enables those rights to be translated into reality. The defensiveness of the abortion struggle has meant that the women's movement has been unable to maintain alternative forms of provision in the way that it has in response to male violence. According to Petchesky, access to abortion should be a social right if women 'are to function as full persons in the public domain' (1986: xiv). Arguably, however, this is precisely what the forces opposed to abortion are trying to prevent. This will be returned to later. Here I wish briefly to consider the impact of second wave feminism on the legalisation of abortion in those countries where it took place during the 1970s when the women's movement was in full swing.

Western Europe

In many Western European countries the legalisation of abortion took place during the 1970s (Ketting and Van Praag, 1986: 159). However, in most cases the influence of second wave feminism, in terms of putting the issue on the policy agenda, defining it as an issue of women's rights and affecting the form taken by the legislation was limited. Thus Joyce Outshoorn argues that in the Netherlands abortion was put on the agenda prior to the emergence of the women's movement. It emerged as a political problem in the mid-1960s, being taken up by the medical profession in the light of the Thalidomide disaster and a German Measles epidemic (Outshoorn, 1986a: 17). Initially the political parties were reluctant to intervene in what was defined as a medical issue (Outshoorn, 1986a: 18). This position was, however, untenable in the light of increasing public pressure for reform and the need to decide on who it is who takes the abortion decision, a woman or her doctor. During this time abortion practice in effect instituted abortion on demand and the women's movement, in the form of Dolle Mina, put forward the idea that women had the right to control their own bodies. They were crucial in challenging the way the issue was defined and in bringing pressure to bear for legislative change:

> Prior to 1972, abortion had been seen as a medical or ethical problem to be judged by experts; later, it became a woman's issue on which most people felt they were competent to judge. (Outshoorn, 1986b: 68)

It has been suggested that widening an issue out is a tactic used by social movements in order to mobilise support to their cause (Goggin, 1993: 9). Thus the fact that many people feel qualified to judge on the issue of abortion does not necessarily mean that they accept the definition of it as a woman's rather than a medical issue. Rather it means that there is conflict over the issue in which each side has attempted to mobilise public opinion. Indeed, there were anti-reform groups who were active on this question in the Netherlands but, despite their pressure, the political parties reached agreement that legislation was needed in order to depoliticise the conflict and to allow politics to return to more easily controlled issues (Outshoorn, 1986a: 23). Kaplan claims that 'Dutch society in reality has introduced abortion on demand as a free health service' (Kaplan, 1992: 175). This may be so in practice, which in many countries is more liberal than the legislation which governs it. But in the Netherlands legislation liberalising abortion coexists with the 'prohibition of abortion in penal law' (Ketting and Van Praag, 1986: 158). This is also the case in Britain. Thus Ketting and Van Praag argue that:

> Most disingenuous in this respect is the Dutch Abortion Act of 1981. By virtue of this Act, the woman decides, but the acting physician is obliged to determine whether she took her decision freely and whether she has taken into account all the interests involved... Thus, depending on religious and political affiliation, there are three interpretations possible: the woman decides, the physician decides and woman and physician decide together in mutual accord. (Ketting and Van Praag, 1986;159)

This clearly falls short of a legal embodiment of the feminist demand for women to have control of their own bodies. Similarly, in some countries abortion legislation contains statements about protecting human life from conception and the desirability of motherhood. This is the case in the Italian and French legislation and seems to encourage women, at least in law, to make the morally acceptable decision to proceed with the pregnancy but allows her, in closely specified circumstances and in consultation with a doctor, to choose abortion (Ketting and Van Praag, 1986: 158–9). Thus in none of this legislation do women have an unambiguous right to make their own decision about whether or not to continue with a pregnancy. It could be argued that this way of framing the issue was necessary in order to appease those who are opposed to abortion while, in practice, women are actually able to take this decision for themselves. This may be particularly important in societies where religion is a major social cleavage. However, it means that the feminist demand that women have the right to control their own bodies is not written into abortion legislation and, according to Outshoorn, demonstrates a process of issue perversion.

In France and Italy the issue of abortion acted as a catalyst to feminist mobilisation. In France the population movement and the medical profession put abortion on the political agenda. This mobilised the women's movement which adopted similar tactics to those used by women in the US (Batiot, 1986: 97). In 1971 the *Manifeste des 343* was published, this was a list of 343 well-known women who had had abortions including Simone de Beauvoir and Giselle Halimi, thus demonstrating the unworkability of existing law. Similar tactics were used in West Germany but without comparable success (Kaplan, 1992). In addition the movement arranged for women to go abroad to have abortions and practised abortions themselves (Jenson, 1987: 83). Anne Batiot claims that feminist discourse 'hegemonised the discursive terrain regarding abortion' (Batiot, 1986: 100). Jane Jenson takes a more nuanced position arguing that, due to the activities of the women's movement and, particularly to a celebrated legal case brought under the law criminalising abortion and defended by a feminist lawyer, the idea that abortion was a woman's issue became part of the universe of discourse surrounding abortion. Indeed, 'themes of women's right to control their own bodies were part of the legislative debate, as were discussions of equity, fairness, and family planning' (Jenson, 1987: 84). So also were fears about the declining birth rate and the need to encourage women to have more children rather than facilitating their avoidance of motherhood (Mossuz-Lavau, 1986). Thus pro-natalist sentiments entered into the debate in France, as they had in the former Eastern bloc and the USSR, in an attempt to legitimate women's restricted access to abortion (Rai *et al.*, 1992). In 1973 it was announced that the law would be reformed in order to embody a woman's right to choose and abortion would be paid for out of the public purse (Jenson, 1987: 84). Opposition from pro-natalists and the Catholic Church meant, however, that much more restrictive legislation eventually reached the statute books (Jenson, 1987: 85). In 1975 a bill legalising abortion was passed which ensured 'medical control over its practice and ma[d]e it medically safe and legally restricted' (Batiot, 1986: 98). Thus the women's movement had defined the issue in feminist terms and this definition had been taken up by certain actors within the political process, it was however in competition with other definitions and was not enshrined in the law. In France, therefore, the issue had acted as a catalyst for the women's movement rather than being put on the policy agenda by it. And although the movement managed to affect the 'universe of discourse' its demands were perverted by the process of legislating on abortion.

Similarly in Italy the women's movement was crucial in bringing a feminist definition of abortion into the public domain and was itself galvanised into action by the abortion issue (Pisciotta, 1986: 26). It was, however, powerless 'to carry through what women of the movement wanted' (ibid.: 26). In Italy, unlike the other cases considered, it was the women's movement that put the issue of abortion on the political agenda. Like the French women's movement, Italian feminists carried out an 'action of self-denunciation' in 1971 which failed to raise the profile of the issue. This is despite the fact that between one and 3 million Italian women were having abortions annually even though fascist legislation criminalising abortion remained on the statute books (Pisciotta, 1986: 34). In Italy there were divisions within the women's movement over whether existing legislation should be reformed or repealed. Women's organisations attached to the parties of the left were critical of the fascist law but were not in favour of the complete repeal of legislation on abortion. The autonomous groups, on the contrary, favoured repeal and argued that the decision was one to be taken by the woman alone (ibid.: 35). In the early 1970s, once the issue had been taken up by the media and become a topic of public debate, a situation of confrontation between the Catholic Church, in the person of the Pope, and the women's movement rapidly developed. The Pope made statements denouncing abortion and supporting 'severe punishment for abortion' (ibid.: 35) six times during 1972; the state responded by arresting women in Trient in large numbers for having had abortions and closing down an illegal abortion clinic in Florence (Kaplan, 1992: 246). This had the effect of mobilising many thousands of women who took to the streets in favour of abortion law reform and in support of a woman's right to choose (Pisciotta, 1986: 39).

The issue was taken up by the parties of the left, all of which supported women's demands, but in the process of translating them into policy the parties altered them in such a way that the resulting bills were no longer feminist (Beckwith, 1987: 166). Thus feminists were instrumental in getting the issue on the political agenda and taken up by the political parties, but they then lost control of it. This eventually resulted in a new law in 1978 which represented a compromise between the political parties, the women's movement and the Catholic Church (Pisciotta, 1986: 41). This compromise is apparent in the conditions surrounding women's access to abortion and the right of doctors to refuse to perform abortions on grounds of conscientious objection. This means that in practice in Italy the number of illegal abortions remains high (Pisciotta, 1986: 42) and particularly affected are women under the age of 18 and those living in non-communist-controlled regions.

What is interesting about the Italian experience is that there have been two referenda on the abortion law since its passage; the first was put forward by the Pro-Life movement and was supported by the Catholic Church, it resulted in a 67.9 per cent vote in favour of maintaining the new legislation. The second was a referendum on whether the law should be repealed, that is, that there be no regulation of abortion. This too was rejected with an 88.5 per cent vote in favour of maintaining the existing law (Pisciotta, 1986: 43). This indicates that in Italy, as in the US, abortion is approved of but only under clearly specified circumstances. This suggests that although the women's movement was instrumental in getting the issue onto the policy agenda, its subsequent adoption by the political parties and the resulting process of compromise which took place, while not embodying the feminist demand for women's right to control their bodies, may have been a closer reflection of Italian public opinion.

Pisciotta comments that the effect of the women's movement, in terms both of legislation and cultural change has been significant. Thus without the movement, particularly the autonomous groups, the issue would neither have achieved agenda status nor would it have been taken up by the political parties. However, the influence of party women's organisations rather than the autonomous women's movement is more apparent in the final form of the legislation. This issue perversion has led the autonomous movement to move away from an engagement with the formal political process, an engagement that they were forced into in the early part of the decade because of the need for legislative reform but which led to an increasing disillusionment with the ability of parliament to deliver the goods. This resulted in the withdrawal of the feminist movement from the abortion debate and their lack of impact on the provision of services, so necessary to make paper rights meaningful (Pisciotta, 1986: 46). Conversely, Pisciotta argues that the women's movement contributed to a cultural revolution in Italy which shifted the attitudes of women towards sexuality, motherhood and women's social roles away from 'traditionally ascribed roles as housekeeper, wife and mother' (Pisciotta, 1986: 45) and that it was the issue of abortion and the ramifications of the feminist insistence on a woman's right to control her own body that made this possible. This suggests that the struggle over abortion may, at one and the same time, reflect the value shift that is said to be occurring in advanced industrial societies and contribute towards it. Thus social movements such as the feminist movement may be both product of and contribution towards this underlying process of value change of which attitudes towards abortion are an important measure.

Abortion as sign

In reaching this conclusion Pisciotta is pointing to the symbolic significance of the abortion issue, a significance which has been highlighted by others. Luker, for instance, sees abortion as symbolising the conflict between two world views, one which defines biology as destiny and motherhood as the primary role of women and the other which regards motherhood as only one option available to women and one that should be freely entered into. The former is associated with a belief in God and the nation and a commitment to 'traditional' family values while the latter comes out of the humanist tradition and shares the values of rationality and individual self-determination associated with the enlightenment. She says that 'this round of the abortion debate is so passionate and hard-fought *because it is a referendum on the place and meaning of motherhood*' (Luker, 1984: 193). In somewhat different language Petchesky comments that 'abortion is the fulcrum of a much broader ideological struggle in which the very meanings of the family, the state, motherhood, and young women's sexuality are contested' (Petchesky, 1986: vii). If these authors are right this explains the vigour and persistence of the anti-abortion movement and its influence, not only in trying to limit women's access to abortion, as in Britain and the US, but in framing the conflict in terms of foetal rights. If we accept this framework, women, in asserting their right to abortion are denying the right of the foetus to life. This way of defining the conflict, as a rights issue, must be seen as a response

to the feminist definition of abortion as a woman's right. It is therefore an indication of the success of the movement in changing the
cognitive framework within which abortion is understood and challenging the underlying values which support an anti-abortion position (Luker, 1984; Schnell, 1993: 37).

There are two observations that I wish to make at this point. The
first is that feminist social movements question the public/private
boundary on which liberal democratic states rest and, indeed, the
abortion issue questions the sexual contract on which they are
based. Women, in demanding reproductive rights, are challenging
the control over their sexuality and fertility vested in men by the
state. They are also challenging the right of the state, via the church
or the medical profession, to limit their ability to control their
bodies, specifically their sexuality and reproductive behaviour, in
the interests of the nation or other collectivity. The state encourages
and discourages reproduction differentially, for instance encouraging women of the upper and middle classes to reproduce while
discouraging motherhood among poor, ethnic minority, disabled
women and lesbians, thereby pursuing pro- and anti-natal policies
at the same time (Petchesky, 1986). Feminists challenge the practices which embody these policies, policies which are often justified
by recourse to notions of racial purity and/or national interest.
Feminists argue that decisions about whether and when to have children should be made by women in a context which enables them to
act on their decision, rather than by men or by the state. Reproductive rights are defined as an aspect of social citizenship without
which women are unable to participate fully in the public sphere
(Einhorn, 1993).

My second observation is that if we accept Luker's proposition
that the struggle over abortion rights is a struggle between two
world views, then what is being played out on the terrain of
women's bodies is a struggle between reason and faith, modernity
and tradition, emancipation and reaction. Putting it in these terms
stresses the links between women's liberation and the modernist
project, a link which was apparent in the Bolsheviks' commitment
to women's emancipation and their legalisation of abortion after the
1917 Revolution. One of their aims was to undermine the patriarchal peasant household and free women to participate in the workforce; giving women reproductive freedom was an essential
prerequisite to breaking male control not only of their reproductive
and sexual capacities but also of their labour. And, as Petchesky
points out, when women are required in the workforce, as is the case

in advanced, industrial societies, the state is more likely to support women's access to fertility control.

Liberalisation of the abortion laws has taken place in most western industrial societies since the late 1960s with or without an input from second wave feminism. As we have seen, despite the importance of fertility control to feminist social movements, their impact on this legislation has been variable and dependent on the way in which the issue is framed, the alliance of forces supporting reform and the way political parties take up the issue, that is it is affected by the political opportunity structure. In most societies, with the exception of the Scandinavian countries, abortion legislation does not include a commitment to providing the facilities which would make legal rights a reality (Lovenduski, 1986b: 4; Wiik, 1986).

Opposition to reform

Despite the limited nature of much of this reform it has spawned significant opposition, not only where abortion reform has taken place but also where it has not. Much of this opposition is spearheaded by the Catholic Church and has been particularly successful in countries where women's labour force participation is relatively low and where Catholicism is strong. Thus, in the Republic of Ireland, a strongly Catholic country with low formal participation of women in the workforce, the pro-life forces went onto the offensive after the legalisation of contraception in 1980 (Barry, 1988: 58). They campaigned for an amendment to the Irish Constitution to protect the right to life of the unborn child. This amendment was the subject of a referendum in 1983 and is now enshrined in the constitution (Randall, 1986). As Barry remarks, the wording of the amendment owes a great deal to the American pro-life movement and their framing of the issue in terms of foetal rights (Barry, 1988: 59). Indeed she suggests that this amendment is part of an international counter-movement on the part of anti-abortion forces. This counter-movement, however, received a setback in 1992 when a 14-year-old girl was prevented from travelling to Britain for an abortion after being raped by a family friend (*The Economist*, 22/2/92). Outrage over this case resulted in a referendum in November 1992 which 'passed two constitutional amendments affirming the right to travel and the right to information on abortion services' (Fletcher, 1995: 64fn). It also rejected an amendment which would have made abortion illegal unless a woman's life was in danger. This led to an abortion information bill being passed in the Dail in 1995 which allows provision of information on abortions, something which had previously been illegal (*Guardian*, 11/3/95). Needless to say the Catholic Church was totally opposed even to this limited concession.

The influence of the American pro-life movement has also been felt in Poland where American pro-life organisations have been funding anti-abortion activities (Hadley, 1994: 98; see also Buechler, 1990: 188–9). Even the notorious Operation Rescue which has been involved in violent picketing of abortion clinics in the US and has murdered at least one doctor involved in carrying out abortions (Morgen, 1995: 238–9) has blockaded clinics in Poland (Hadley, 1994: 98). This example raises the question of the fate of women's reproductive rights in former communist countries. In common with many countries of the former Soviet bloc, abortion was legal in Poland and, from 1959, easy to obtain; indeed it was the main method of contraception. It is now under attack from the powerful Catholic Church, women are being urged to leave the workforce in the face of mass unemployment and the religious hierarchy has defined abortion as 'a mortal threat to the "biological substance of the nation"' (Hadley, 1994: 97). Thus women's duty is to have children to ensure the continuance of the nation rather than to be in paid employment, and abortion, previously facilitated by a foreign occupier and associated with communism, is understood as a threat to the continuance of the nation. In 1993 a law was introduced in Poland which permits abortion only if the woman's life or health is threatened by the pregnancy, if the pregnancy is a result of rape or incest, or if there is a serious danger of foetal abnormality (*Guardian*, 3/4/95). In neither Poland nor the Irish republic is there a strong women's movement although in both there are women organising against the restrictions on abortion (Randall, 1986; Fuszara, 1991: 225). Both countries are also marked by an association of Catholicism with national identity, consequently they tend to prioritise women's maternal role over any other (Randall, 1986: 80). This is facilitated by a lack of demand for women in the workforce, in Ireland because of its predominantly rural nature and in Poland because of high rates of unemployment.

Clearly women's reproductive rights are seen not only as threatening patriarchal control within the family but also the continued existence of the nation. This perception has led to the adoption of pro-natalist policies on the part of the state and the denial of women's reproductive rights. During the communist period this conflict, between the need for women in the workforce and the need for them to have children, between anti-natalist and pro-natalist policies, was also apparent in the shifting fortunes of reproductive rights in the USSR (Davin, 1992). Thus the legalisation of abortion can and has occurred for reasons other than a commitment to a woman's right to control her own body. It is only in societies where abortion reform has taken place during the 1960s and 70s that this feminist definition of the problem has entered into the debate and this is totally due to feminist social movements. Thus although abortion legislation would probably have been liberalised without an input from second wave feminism, and in some cases was, the contribution of second wave feminism is to have framed the issue in a new way, a way that stresses women's reproductive rights and their necessity to be able to control their own bodies. This claim, and women's limited rights to abortion, symbolise a challenge to the power of men and the state to control female sexuality and reproduction. Its importance is demonstrated by the strength of the counter-movement it has spawned and by ongoing debates about reproductive technology and fertility control. These conflicts relate to ideas about families, children, parenting and sexuality and will be explored more fully in the next chapter.

Before leaving this discussion there are two important points to make about the feminist struggle for abortion on demand. Feminists have been forced to engage with the state on the terrain of the law. The legal apparatus is a core part of the repressive state apparatus and as such it is much more difficult for feminism to have an impact here than it is in the more peripheral areas such as the voluntary sector of the welfare state. It is a more masculinised part of the state and is likely to be more resistant to feminist discourse and language. As we have seen, this resistance is also apparent in the legal response to rape. As Petchesky puts it:

> Feminists and radicals do not control the courts. Except in rare instances, their language does not become the courts' language nor their reasons the courts' reasons. This is not an argument for abandoning the courts as an area for political struggle in a progressive cause. But it does say that feminist ideas and the feminist movement must find a louder, stronger voice in popular culture and consciousness before they can have a lasting impact on state power. (Petchesky, 1986: 319)

In other words the feminist concern with transforming consciousness is crucial for struggles waged on the legal terrain of the state.

The fact that feminists have been forced onto the defensive with regard to the issue of abortion and that they have had to take their struggle into the institutional realm of political parties and the law has meant that the feminist definition of the issue is not legally sanctioned. In all countries there are important limitations put in the way of women seeking abortions. Thus there are strictures about parental consent for minors, waiting periods, time limits and so on. In addition this defensive struggle has taken away from the need for adequate and accessible provision for all women which does not exist in many countries despite liberal abortion laws. So in confronting the issue of abortion the women's movement is confronting a core part of the state apparatus, and in some countries has drawn down the full repressive force of the state on women seeking abortions or assisting other women in getting abortions. And second, the women's movement is challenging a set of values which are associated with religion, a repressive sexual morality and women's confinement to the home. There is evidence that these values are changing and, as we have seen, it is argued that we are moving towards a post-materialist society (Inglehart, 1990). The evidence we have explored in this chapter suggests that in the struggle for a woman's right to control her own body, feminist social movements are, at one and the same time, responding to value change that has already occurred and contributing to further change in the direction of self-determination and individual freedom for women. In this they are challenging the public/private divide and the sexual contract on which liberal democracies rest.

Chapter 9

The Family

As Chapter 8 demonstrates, second wave feminism, together with the socio-economic and demographic changes which are associated with it, pose a profound challenge to the idea that motherhood is the only meaningful occupation available to adult women. This has been interpreted by the new right as an onslaught on the family which must be resisted if society is not to experience irretrievable breakdown. It is true that feminism has developed a critique of 'the family', arguing that it ensures women's dependency on men and their ideological confinement to the domestic sphere and that it institutionalises heterosexuality and defines other forms of sexuality as deviant. In this chapter I explore these analyses and their relation to the political practice of second wave feminism, focusing particularly on the issue of child care. I then look at the relation between feminist demands and policy developments at national and local level, including an exploration of the counter-movement which was spawned in response to the early successes of second wave feminism. Finally, I discuss the impact of both these movements and socio-economic and demographic developments on state policies in the area of child care, comparing the responses of social democratic and liberal welfare state regimes. I argue that the issue of child care has been defined as an issue of women's employment within socialism and by labour movements influenced by socialist ideologies, and that where these have been incorporated into state policy-making processes the result has been an acceptance of collective responsibility for child care. Where this has not been the case, however, responsibility for children is defined in individual terms and states are reluctant to intervene in the so-called private realm of the family.

Feminism and the family

It is possible to argue that all the demands of the women's movement have implications for the social arrangements within which
biological reproduction take place. However, there are two demands
which are particularly important. They are the demand for free, 24-
hour nurseries and the demand for an end to all discrimination
against lesbians and a woman's right to define her own sexuality.
The first demand was one of the original four raised by the British
Women's Movement in 1971 and the second was added as the sixth
demand in 1976. These demands relate to different analyses of the
nature of women's oppression emanating from Marxist and radical
feminism. Marxist feminists, following Engels, argued that
women's subordination could be explained by their dependence on
men within the domestic sphere and their exclusion from public
production. The allocation of paid work to men and unpaid work to
women within the household, including the work of bearing and
rearing children, was defined as the problem. The solution lay in the
socialisation of domestic work and child care so that it too became
a collective activity which was the responsibility of society rather
than individual women in isolated households. Thus state provision
of child care available to all women was seen as the main way of
liberating women from their oppressive situation within the family
and enabling them to participate equally with men in the public
sphere (Barrett, 1980). This was, of course, the classic Marxist
analysis of women's oppression and was reflected in measures to
implement women's emancipation which had been enacted in the
USSR in 1917 and subsequently in other socialist societies (Charles,
1993). These measures, however, were widely perceived as not
having led to women's liberation and a major problem with such
policies was that, although they enabled women to enter the world
of paid work on the same terms as men, they did nothing to address
the gendered division of labour within families. This was recognized within the women's movement and from the outset feminists
were concerned to involve men in the caring work associated with
young children and to break down the gender stereotypes which
were imparted to children through child-rearing practices (Dartmouth Park Hill, 1982; Rowbotham, 1989; Lovenduski and
Randall, 1993; Randall, 1996).

   Radical feminists, on the other hand, were more concerned with
issues of sexuality and power and domination within sexual relationships. In contrast to the view that having children disadvantaged

women in relation to men and was therefore something to be avoided, it was argued that motherhood was a positive experience for women and that it was its confinement within institutionalised heterosexuality which rendered it an isolating and negative experience. This institutionalisation meant that if mothers were not white, middle class, heterosexual and married their motherhood was regarded as deviant (Richardson, 1993). Thus lesbian mothers, lone mothers, poor mothers and black mothers were stigmatised because their very existence challenged the normative assumption that the proper place for motherhood was the white, middle-class, heterosexual family. One of the aims of second wave feminism was to remove this stigmatisation and to legitimise motherhood outside of heterosexual relations.

The stigmatisation of non-heterosexual motherhood is apparent in the problems faced by lesbian mothers in fighting custody cases which was an issue taken up by the women's movement in the 1970s. Whereas it was normal practice for heterosexual mothers to be awarded custody by the courts when their marriages broke down, if lesbian mothers made their sexuality public this was sufficient to ensure that custody was awarded to their male partner. As a writer in *Spare Rib* put it in 1976:

> The judge will only separate children from their mother if there are over-riding factors like the mother's health or actual neglect or cruelty. Such considerations are obviously relevant to the children's welfare.

> The mother's sexual orientation is taken to be just such a factor, and no other evidence has to be produced to disqualify her from bringing up her children. (Stephens, 1982: 91)

Awarding custody to a lesbian mother would be tantamount to approving of homosexuality, which would mean 'the decay of society as we know it and could only corrupt others' (Stephens, 1982: 91). Lesbian mothers are therefore less likely than heterosexual mothers to win custody of children because being brought up by a lesbian mother is seen as potentially harmful for a child (Richardson, 1993). And if a lesbian mother is awarded custody then conditions are often attached in an attempt to ensure that she does all she can to prevent her children from growing up gay; this is in the absence of any evidence that children raised by lesbian mothers are any more or less likely than other children to be heterosexual. Diane Richardson reports that:

In one case a mother was asked to sign a formal undertaking that she would not sleep with her lover while her son was staying with them, would hide any literature on homosexuality, and would never mention the subject in her son's presence. (Richardson, 1993: 80)

Thus where individual men have failed to control women's sexuality the state steps in via the courts and constrains them to pretend heterosexuality on pain of losing their child. In this way they attempt to make lesbian motherhood invisible and to legitimate heterosexual motherhood. I return to the issue of state control of women's sexuality below, here I focus on the ways in which feminists in Britain organised around the issue of child care.

Child care as a feminist issue

During the 1970s there was considerable feminist activity around the issue of child care, particularly on the part of socialist feminists. The demand for free, 24-hour nurseries was directed at the state (Franzway *et al.*, 1989: 60). Its aim was that state-provided nurseries be made available so that the child care needs of working women would be met. They had to be available 24 hours a day in order to meet the needs of women working shifts and 'so that children might be left in the evening, or at more flexible times than nine to five' (Rowbotham, 1989: 129). The demand for state provision of child care was not wholeheartedly supported within the movement, however, because of a suspicion of state-provided services and the ways in which they might indoctrinate children into capitalist and sexist values (Lovenduski and Randall, 1993). Many feminists voiced a conviction that day care should be prefigurative and should 'overcome the isolation of mothers' by providing collective rather than individual, privatised care. But at the same time it needed to enable women to participate in paid employment if they so wished (Rowbotham, 1989: 132). Sheila Rowbotham argues that these two strands were difficult to reconcile. Indeed the provision of day care in order to facilitate women's employment is a demand associated more directly with the labour movement while the prefigurative forms of child care advocated by many women's groups can be seen as owing more to the libertarian tradition within the women's movement.

The demand for 24-hour nurseries 'proved unrealistic and unworkable' (Dartmouth Park Hill, 1982: 112) and what emerged in

Britain was a variety of local campaigns aimed at setting up community-based nurseries. In Britain it is local authorities which have the statutory responsibility for day care provision, it was therefore to the local rather than the national state that women's groups directed their attention in attempts to get funding and/or premises for community run nurseries. Accounts of these show varying degrees of success (see, for example, Hughes *et al.*, 1980; Dartmouth Park Hill, 1982). For instance, Camden Women's Group in London set up the Dartmouth Park Children's Community Centre in 1972. It was funded by the local authority but run by the parents who, along with one full-time worker, staffed it on a rota basis (Rowbotham, 1989: 134). It provided 'an example of "community-run, non-sexist and anti-authoritarian day care" ' (Spare Rib collective 1976 cited in Rowbotham 1989: 134), an alternative to the limited state-provided day care which existed only for dysfunctional families (Moss, 1991). Here I provide a brief account of a nursery campaign run by North Staffs Women's Action Group (NSWAG), a group which aligned itself with the Working Women's Charter[1] and in which I was involved during the 1970s. This account highlights many of the difficulties encountered by women's groups in attempting to set up and run nurseries as alternative, feminist forms of provision.

The campaign for a day nursery on a large, council estate in the Potteries area in North Staffs was launched in November 1975.[2] Initially the demand for a nursery was aimed at the local council. This tactic had been successful in London where demonstrations, pickets, and sit-ins-cum-creches in council buildings had forced local authorities to prioritise nursery provision. However, mobilising support for this sort of activity on a working-class housing estate in the Potteries proved to be more difficult despite the hundreds of signatures on a petition supporting nursery provision. The need for a nursery, which everyone recognized, was not reflected in active support for the nursery campaign. This was because the group was trying to mobilise the very women for whom activity outside the home was severely restricted by their child care responsibilities; the beneficiary adherents as RMT would have it. It became clear that mobilisation for direct action was out of the question given the resources of the campaign and the narrow sector of the population that the issue directly affected at any one time. The group therefore changed tactics and decided to organise a community day nursery which would be run by and for the women involved in the campaign.

Because of the decision to set up a community-based nursery the emphasis of the campaign changed. Rather than needing to recruit activists, the priority was to identify volunteers to run the nursery and a nursery nurse who would be employed full time. Thus the nursery group was being absorbed into the voluntary sector of the state and working within the constraints of existing forms of organisation and power relations. In order to attract volunteers and to interest parents in placing their children in the nursery, there was extensive publicity and the group carried out a house-to-house survey. Significantly most of the women who eventually became involved as voluntary workers came from a neighbouring estate. They were at home full time with small children and were not intending to return to paid employment until their children started school. They were thus available to undertake voluntary work precisely because of their situation as full-time housewives.

The nursery's existence was precarious for a while as it had to be financially viable and when it opened there were not enough children to make this possible. Gradually, however, the number of children attending increased and, with fund-raising activities, it eventually managed to overcome its financial teething problems and succeeded in becoming a viable project. The involvement of the women's group, which had dwindled to the activism of two women who were committed socialist feminists, ceased at the end of the first year of the nursery's existence as it had become a viable entity in its own right.

Several points emerge from this account. First, because the women whom the nursery group was trying to reach were those with young children at home, the problems of mobilising their support for a nursery campaign were enormous. Forms of organisation had to be evolved which took their situation into account, such as daytime meetings in the women's homes where the children could come along. It was also difficult to keep up interest in the campaign. Those who thought a nursery was important because it would enable them to go out to work often needed an immediate solution to their child care needs. Thus, although the women's group could see the day nursery in a long-term perspective, for most of the women on the estate it was a much-needed facility now. And in the event of its non-existence alternative solutions were found. Second, the group found that it had to work within the constraints of the social relations it was attempting to transform. Thus to staff the nursery it had to rely on women who were happy to look after their own and other people's children in order to free other women to go out to work. Thus the very relations which were the point of attack of the women's group in the end determined the form that the day nursery would take. Third, engagement with the state almost proved to be the death knell of the campaign. Subsequently it operated as part of the voluntary sector of the welfare state. The practical difficulties of setting up and running a day nursery absorbed all the energies of the activists and the process of attrition, which reduced the active involvement of members of the NSWAG and of women on the estate, meant that although a day nursery was established, the extent to which it represented a feminist form of service provision is questionable.

Unlike the refuge movement and the abortion campaign, these struggles for nurseries remained largely local. In the 1970s there was no national organisation to coordinate them, to present their demands for policy change to national government and, perhaps most importantly, to challenge hegemonic definitions of child care. Several groups, including the one described here, were loosely linked to the network of groups organising around the Working Women's Charter; a network which defined nursery provision as strategically important in enabling women to take up paid employment (that is, as an employment issue) and orientated itself towards working within the labour movement and with working-class women (Rowbotham, 1989: 135). In London a nursery campaign was established in 1977 as an outcome of this loose coordination but it was not until 1980, a year after the election of the first Thatcher administration, that a National Child Care Campaign was set up in a very hostile political environment (Rowbotham, 1989: 136; Lovenduski and Randall, 1993; Randall, 1996: 488, 495).

Several commentators have asked why it was that a feminist-inspired nursery campaign failed to get off the ground during the 1970s and have sought part of the answer in ambivalence within the women's movement over issues of motherhood, child care and paid employment (Franzway *et al.*, 1989; Randall, 1996). We have already noted that feminists were ambivalent about state-provided child care facilities but this ambivalence also expresses itself in the contradictory experience of motherhood. Thus, as Franzway *et al.* put it:

> The contradictions of motherhood as a source of oppression and of identity for women, and the risks that state provision of child care opened up a space for state control of mother's lives, tended to obfuscate the politics of child care. (Franzway *et al.*, 1989: 73)

And in the more libertarian wing of the women's movement, there was also ambivalence about the desirability of capitalist paid employment which was seen as exploitative and to be avoided (Randall, 1996: 501). According to Vicky Randall, state-funded child care was seen as being important for working-class women but was not something that women in the feminist movement necessarily wanted for themselves (Randall, 1996: 502). This antipathy towards the establishment, whether it be the 'bourgeois' family, capitalist employment or the state, and a predisposition to set up alternatives rather than engaging with dominant institutional forms has been seen as characteristic of the British women's movement (Gelb, 1989; Randall, 1996). This, however, cannot provide the whole explanation for the relative lack of feminist activity around child care as this lack also marks women's movements in other western countries such as Australia where such antipathy is less noticeable (see, for example, Franzway *et al.*, 1989).

Another factor is the association of nursery campaigns with socialist feminists and those orientated towards the labour movement. This contrasts strongly with the association of radical feminism with the successful setting up and running of alternative feminist forms of provision such as refuges and rape crisis centres. As Franzway *et al.* put it, 'it is striking that feminist child-care centres were not established in the same way that refuges, rape crisis and women's health centres were' (Franzway *et al.*, 1989: 65). The association of the demand for child care with socialist feminists meant that it was taken into the labour movement and local authorities at the end of the 1970s and its autonomous organisational existence in the form of alternative provision to all intents and purposes vanished. Radical feminists retained their autonomy and their visibility outside the organisations of the state while socialist feminists, by moving onto the terrain of the state, lost their visibility as part of an autonomous women's movement. The difficulty experienced by women's groups in establishing and maintaining alternative child care provision may also have to do with the mass of regulations surrounding day care for young children. Day care provision was already regulated and controlled by the state whereas provision for women threatened with or experiencing violence was not, precisely because no provision existed and it was not seen as an issue at all. Thus acceptable forms of day care were prescribed and hemmed about with bureaucracy and red tape with which nursery groups had to conform. This meant that the opportunities for autonomous organisation were limited from the start and that the local state effectively stifled autonomous feminist organisation which, to a considerable extent, depended on spontaneity and enthusiasm. Thus as one woman put it, 'This group negotiated with the council for eighteen long and disheartening months. How long can a pre-school child wait?' (Dartmouth Park Hill, 1982: 113).

In the 1980s the initiative on child care passed to the local state and employers through the development of equal opportunities policies and because of feminist activism within trade unions and political parties. It was also in the early 1980s that national campaigns for increased child care provision were established in Britain. Initially organisations such as the National Childcare Campaign defined child care as a feminist issue and aimed to 'build a mass national child care campaign around the demand for comprehensive, flexible, free, democratically controlled child care facilities funded by the state' (Randall, 1996: 488). Later, however, they redefined it as a private issue which necessitated individual solutions. Given the political context within which they were working, particularly the public expenditure cuts and the ascendancy of the new right, this move is hardly surprising. And it seems that what kept the issue alive during the 1980s and 1990s was not so much the women's movement (although women working within organisations to implement equal opportunities policies were important) but the requirements of the economy for female labour and, towards the end of the decade, the threat of the demographic time bomb and the resulting skills shortage. Before considering this, however, it is important to explore the impact of the new right on the policy domain and the way in which it related to the feminist movement.

The pro-family counter-movement and the new right

It has been argued, particularly for the US, that the new right took advantage of the anti-abortion and pro-family counter-movements that emerged as a response to the successes of second wave feminism in the early 1970s (Luker, 1984; Petchesky, 1986; Chafetz and Dworkin, 1987; Buechler, 1990; Staggenborg, 1991). Petchesky argues that:

> The campaign against abortion was taken up as the battering ram in a much broader offensive against nontraditional families, feminism, teenage sexuality, the welfare state, socialism, and every other target of the right. (Petchesky, 1986: 242)

Thus feminism and homosexuality replaced communism as the embodiment of evil for the new right and they both represented 'movements for transcendence of a patriarchal form of family and for sexual liberation' (Petchesky, 1986: 244). These movements, together with socio-economic and demographic changes which have resulted in the male breadwinner family constituting only a minority of families at any one time in most advanced industrial societies, 'represent a genuine threat to the family system and sexual morality the new right is seeking to preserve' (Petchesky, 1986: 246). With the advent of the Thatcher administration in 1979, Reagan's election victory in the US in 1980 and the earlier election of the Fraser government in Australia in 1975, the ideas of the new right began to dominate the political agenda. This made it that much more difficult for the feminist movement to bring about changes in state policy and, arguably, the two contending movements demonstrated that issues surrounding the family and sexuality were controversial and therefore potential vote losers. This in itself was likely to make governments reluctant to move in either direction and, despite the strong right-wing rhetoric in favour of the male breadwinner family and in opposition to women's access to fertility control, radical policy change, even in the US where the countermovement appeared to be strongest, has not been forthcoming. Indeed, in both the US and Britain, it is the economic policies of the new right that have been more successfully implemented than their moral agenda.

The rhetoric of the pro-family counter-movement has it that state intervention in the family fatally weakens it by undermining the role of fathers as financial providers and undermining the role of mothers as full-time carers. The traditional family, therefore, can be strengthened by withdrawing state support. This has happened to a considerable extent in both Britain and the US with the retrenchment of welfare provision but has not resulted in a reinstatement of the male breadwinner family. Rather it has led to increased child and family poverty, women's wages have become even more essential to their families and the numbers of lone mothers have continued to rise thereby increasing welfare dependency. Thus the free market economic policies of the new right tend to undermine 'the social institutions favoured by cultural conservatives' (Garner, 1996: 126). Petchesky goes so far as to argue that the social conservatives have completely misread the situation and that their:

Rejection of the now dominant ideology of the 'working mother', their determination to bring women back into the home, represents a basic misunderstanding of current economic realities, including the long-range interests of the capitalist class as a whole, which continues to rely heavily on a (sex-segregated) female labour force. (Petchesky, 1986: 275)

This assessment may be correct, and it may also be the case that the new right has been much more successful in implementing its economic than its moral agenda. There have, nevertheless, been important policy developments which reflect the moral agenda of the new right and which are attempts to restrict women's sexual freedom and to scapegoat family forms which deviate from the male breadwinner/female dependant model. In Britain, although attempts to restrict access to abortion have been successfully resisted, there are three issues which graphically illustrate the continuing support of the state for the heterosexual family. They are Section 28 of the Local Government Act 1988, the Human Fertilisation and Embryology Act (1990) and the Child Support Act (1991) which created the controversial Child Support Agency.

In 1988 the Conservative Government passed a new local government bill, Section 28 of which prohibited 'the promotion of homosexuality and pretend family relationships' by local authorities (Reinhold, 1994: 62). It also banned 'the teaching of the acceptability of homosexuality in schools' (Carabine, 1996: 74, fn7). This was part of the Tory onslaught on 'loony left' local authorities which also included the abolition of the Greater London Council and other metropolitan authorities in 1986. This reaction had been precipitated by the adoption by the Labour Party in Haringey, London, of a call in its 1986 manifesto 'for the "promotion of positive images of homosexuality" in local schools' (Reinhold, 1994: 61). Labour won the local elections and was subsequently accused of 'corrupting children, destroying the family, spreading AIDS, and contributing to social revolution' (Reinhold, 1994: 62). Their commitment to 'positive images' was picked up by the Conservative Party. When the Tory MP David Wiltshire introduced the amendment (later to become Section 28) in Parliament he claimed that he was 'motivated wholly by the principle of supporting normality... Homosexuality is being promoted at the ratepayers' expense, and the traditional family as we know it is under attack' (*Guardian*, 12/12/87 cited in Richardson, 1996: 17).

What is interesting about the ensuing debate and the fact that the 'normality' and 'naturalness' of the heterosexual family were being publicly contested is that, although the government succeeded in legislating against the 'promotion' of homosexuality, the fact that homosexual partnerships were being debated as a form of family, albeit a 'pretend' form of family, suggests that the hegemony of the 'normal' family constituted by a heterosexual married couple was no longer undisputed (Reinhold, 1994: 66). Indeed what had previously been naturalised was now seen to be socially constructed and its naturalness was in question (Cooper, 1995: 131). The debate can be understood, therefore, as an attempt to reinstate the dominance of the heterosexual family and to define lesbian and gay partnerships as deviant and as not entitled to the same social rights as are heterosexual couples. What is significant about it is that it exists at all; the hegemony of the heterosexual family has been challenged, and this has been achieved by the women's and gay rights movements of the 1960s and 70s.

The second issue, which is linked to this, is the issue of reproduction and parenting, an issue which was also publicly aired during the debate on Section 28 (Reinhold, 1994: 73). This debate questioned the seemingly 'natural' link between heterosexuality and human reproduction and demonstrated that bearing and rearing children is not the preserve of heterosexuals. However, heterosexual parenthood remains the officially sanctioned form. This is clear in the availability of treatment for infertility which is regulated by the Human Fertilisation and Embryology Act (1990). The Warnock Report,[3] which paved the way for the passage of this act, assumes that couples being treated for infertility will be heterosexual and 'living together in a stable relationship' (Warnock, 1984: 10 cited in Feldman, 1987: 27) and recommends that the suitability for parenthood of 'couples' applying for fertility treatment should be assessed by the medical practitioners involved. During parliamentary debate on the bill, amendments restricting access to fertility treatment to women living with a male partner were discussed but were not incorporated into the legislation. However, women who are in heterosexual relationships are much more likely to be able to obtain fertility treatment than women who are not. Thus, section 13 of the Human Fertilisation and Embryology Act stipulates that a woman:

> Should not have access to certain treatments including donor insemination, 'unless account has been taken of the welfare of any child who may be born as a result of that treatment (including the need of that child for a father)'. (cited in Richardson, 1993: 78)

Subsequent to the passage of this legislation, there was considerable public debate over the access of lesbians to donor insemination in clinics regulated by the Human Fertilisation and Embryology Act (Cooper, 1995). According to Richardson, this resulted in one of the few agencies which had been prepared to provide donor insemination to lesbians discontinuing the practice although Cooper suggests that very few clinics changed their practice as a result of this legislation (Richardson, 1993: 79; Cooper, 1995: 88). The debate in the media, which became a debate over 'virgin births', focused on the child's need for a father, and the woman at the centre of the controversy was labelled 'neurotic' because she did not want to have heterosexual sex (*Guardian*, 12/3/91). Thus it was attempting to reunite heterosexual sex, child birth and fatherhood in the public consciousness.

It is not only the separation of reproduction from heterosexual sex which has entered public consciousness but also the de-naturalising of motherhood; an issue which has emerged from developments in reproductive technology. The most graphic example of this is provided by the issues surrounding surrogacy and the difficulties of establishing who is the biological and, by implication, social mother. Is it the woman whose egg has been fertilised or the woman whose body nourishes the embryo? In this scenario the disjuncture between heterosexual sex and biological reproduction could not be more extreme and the difficulty of reasserting their indivisibility more obvious. Such developments have also brought the distinction between biological and social parenting into regular parlance, thus demonstrating the fact that motherhood and fatherhood are social constructs (Strathern, 1992: 155). Thus the attempts of the new right to re-establish the hegemony of the heterosexual family are being undermined not only by the women's movement but also by developments in medical technology.

The third policy development I wish to explore is the establishment of the Child Support Agency in 1993. This was designed to ensure that absent fathers provided financial support for their children in an attempt to reduce state expenditure on benefits for single mothers. Similar measures were introduced in the US in 1984 when Congress passed a resolution requiring states to introduce measures which would force biological fathers to provide financial support for their children (Abbott and Wallace, 1992: 114). Jennifer Millar argues that the British legislation is an attempt to reconstitute the male breadwinner/female dependant family after couples have separated (Millar, 1994: 33). The assumption is that single mothers should try and find part-time employment and that their income will be made up by contributions from their absent ex-partner together with benefit payments. This ensures that single mothers are extremely unlikely to be able to climb out of poverty but that they will no longer be maintained by the state. Millar observes that it is the absence of child care which prevents most single mothers from working and that this is not tackled by the Child Support Agency; I return to this later.

As Jane Millar points out, this legislation is based on the assumption that all children have two biological parents (something that is increasingly put into question by assisted reproduction), and that parents' obligations to their biological offspring override obligations to other children, such as step-children (Millar, 1994: 34). Recently there has been controversy about lesbian mothers and the requirements of the CSA that they disclose the name of the biological father in order that he may support his child; this is only possible where women have arranged their own artificial insemination. If donor insemination is carried out in clinics the sperm donors cannot be pursued in this way (*Guardian*, 14/5/97). Thus one of the outcomes of the CSA is to make it even more difficult for women, whatever their sexuality, to rear children independently of men unless they have access to their own full-time wage.

There has been much opposition to this legislation from left and right. Thus feminists criticise the Child Support Agency for restoring women's financial dependency on individual men rather than on the state, that is, with reconstituting oppressive gender relations, while Families Need Fathers attacks it for making it impossible for men to fulfil their breadwinner role in their second or subsequent marriages. No wonder the state has been reluctant to intervene in such a hotly contested area. Passing such unpopular legislation satisfies neither the women's movement nor the new right and may partly explain the policy stalemate characterising this area.

These three areas of policy show that while hegemonic definitions of 'the family' and appropriate familial roles for women and men have been challenged by the women's movement, these challenges have not been reflected in changing policies. Indeed, during the 1980s and early 1990s, the existence of a strong counter-movement with allies in government has ensured the domination of pro-family ideas and the inability of the women's movement to gain acceptance for feminist ideas about families, sexuality and the organisation of child care. Instead the moral panic about masculinity has ensured that social policies continue to define single parents and gay couples as deviant and as a threat to the moral fabric of society, attempting to discourage them by denying them the rights enjoyed by so-called normal, heterosexual couples.

The evidence presented here seems to show that feminist social movements have had little impact on family policy. But why is this the case and what are the social forces which shape the policies of different welfare states? In order to explore this question, I compare child care policy in different societies and the ideologies underpinning it.

Child care and welfare state regimes

Child care policies differ markedly between different states. Thus far I have concentrated on developments in Britain and, to a lesser extent, the US where child care is defined as an individual rather than a collective issue and where pro-family counter-movements and new right governments have been in power. Here I wish to compare the development of child care policies in different types of welfare state in order to assess the impact of second wave feminism on this area of social policy.

In liberal welfare states such as Britain, the US and Australia, the decision to have children (or not) is defined as an individual, private matter and their care is the responsibility of parents. Historically, state-provided child care has been defined as a welfare issue, an intervention that is required when 'normal' families break down. A distinction can be made between states which leave child care provision to the market, those which see child care as an integral part of labour market policies, those which see child care as part of 'parenting or family policies' and those which define child care as something undertaken by women within the family (Fincher, 1996). These different orientations are apparent in the differences between British and US child care policies and those elsewhere.

The ideology which underpins state policy towards child care in Britain and the US defines the family as the private domain in which the state should not intervene except in emergency. The best form of child care for young children is provided by their mothers and, in Britain at least, there is considerable support for the view that mothers of children under 3 years old should be at home full time, financially supported by their child's father (Moss, 1991: 131). The assumption is, of course, that it is only heterosexual women with male partners who become mothers and that the family 'consists of a heterosexual, married couple and their own (genetic) children, conceived "naturally"' (Van Every, 1991/92: 63). Having and caring for children are regarded as private matters and state intervention is only warranted in the case of family breakdown. Consequently, state provision of day care is available only to children who are defined as being:

> In need because of some developmental problem or because of the social or economic circumstances of their families. Public day care therefore is only available where children or parents are deemed to be not coping or children are thought to be at risk: children will not be considered for a place in publicly-funded care because their parents are employed, unless the parent concerned is a lone mother or father. (Moss, 1991;125)

The dearth of day care provision, however, means that it is not available for most single parents either.

These same assumptions underpin provision of day care to welfare recipients in the US where federally funded day care is available to lone parents in order to get them into paid employment; maternal employment is encouraged and there is no state support for lone mothers to stay at home (Phillips, 1991: 167). However, there is consistent opposition to federal funding for day care for 'normal' (that is, non-welfare) families who are expected to make their own arrangements. Thus in 1971 there was an attempt to extend federal support for day care to all families. Those pressing for this legislation argued that day care should be available as a right to all sections of the population. This legislation was supported through Congress by 'a broad coalition of labour, church, social welfare and citizen's organisations' but was vetoed by Nixon (Phillips, 1991: 177). This was because it was seen as weakening the family and 'as advocating "communal approaches to childrearing over against the family-centred approach"' (Phillips, 1991: 177).

Similar problems were encountered in Australia in the early 1970s. State concern with the labour supply and the demand of the economy for women workers led to the Child Care Act of 1972 which permitted federal funding of child care (Franzway *et al.*, 1989: 71). In 1975, however, the election of the right-wing Fraser government marked opposition to state intervention which was seen as undermining rather than supporting the family. Child care was viewed as a 'residual welfare service rather than a universal right' and the resourcing of child care was reduced and responsibility shifted to state level (Franzway *et al.*, 1989: 75). In Australia, the incorporation of the labour movement into the state together with the pressure brought to bear by femocrats means that child care tends to be seen as an employment issue. This means that when the economic situation deteriorates, it is child care which is seen as expendable (Franzway *et al.*, 1989). In liberal welfare state regimes, therefore, there is reluctance to intervene in the private sphere of the family and government policy supports individual, market-based solutions favouring those which approximate most closely to mother care, such as child minding in Britain or family day care in Australia.

This contrasts with other European and Scandinavian countries where child care tends to be seen either as an employment issue or as a family issue, or both in combination. The definition of child care as an employment issue is particularly clear in countries where socialist or social democratic political parties have been in power and where there have been situations of labour shortage. Thus, in Sweden there is a longstanding commitment on the part of the state to provide child care in order that women can combine parenting with paid employment. In this way the state accepts a collective responsibility for child care in order to support family life and to facilitate women's participation in paid employment. Indeed, in Denmark and Sweden child care policies were developed in the 1930s as part of an attempt to 'increase the number of children by improving the health and living standards of families' (Borchorst, 1990: 168). There was thus a pro-natalist strand to this policy as well as one of facilitating women's employment. In France also child care policy in the 1970s and 80s developed in response to a perceived need to encourage child birth and, at the same time, to facilitate the combination of parenthood and paid employment (Hantrais, 1994). It therefore recognized women's increasing partic-ipation in the workforce and, at the same time, the undesirability of falling fertility levels. Similar concerns dictated policy in the former German Democratic Republic. Nowhere, however, has there been a significant move away from the view that child care is women's work. Women either take care of their own children in the privacy of their own home, or take care of other women's children in a variety of settings, both public and private, for very low rates of pay (Melhuish and Moss, 1991). And in countries such as Germany and the Republic of Ireland the state continues to encourage mothers to provide full-time child care for their own children at home (Lewis, 1993; Hantrais, 1994). It is probably Sweden that has moved furthest towards de-gendering care work by providing paid parental leave to fathers as well as mothers, but it is still overwhelmingly women who take this leave and therefore retain the major responsibility for care of very young children.

What these examples suggest is that child care has come to be seen as an employment issue where labour movements are strong and incorporated into processes of policy formation and where socialist or social democratic parties have achieved political power. In countries where labour movements are not fully incorporated into the state and where liberal ideologies of individualism and the privacy of the domestic sphere predominate, there is considerable reluctance on the part of the state to intervene in the family and solutions to the problem of combining paid employment and motherhood are left to individuals and the market. Thus the major differences between Sweden and Britain in relation to child care policy have been attributed to the hegemony of social democracy, the associated commitment to equality within the Swedish labour movement and its incorporation into the processes of policy making (Borchorst, 1990; Ruggie, 1984). In contrast, the British labour movement has been characterised by a familial ideology which leads to its supporting part-time working for mothers of young children rather than their incorporation into the workforce on the same basis as men; and it has remained marginal to the policy-making process (Ruggie, 1984).

These two contrasting approaches to child care policy can be linked to Esping-Anderson's social democratic and liberal welfare state regimes and the different ideologies underpinning state activity, particularly activity which crosses the public/private divide (Fincher, 1996; Randall, 1996: 492). As Esping-Anderson argues, these philosophies owe a considerable amount to the class alliances on which political parties are based and which thereby shape the form of the welfare state. Thus welfare state regimes which are dominated by the working class are more likely to provide child care as part of universal welfare provision than others. In contrast, conservative welfare state regimes appear actively to support 'the authority of the husband regarding decision-making in respect of children, divorce and whether the wife takes paid work' (Lewis, 1993: 15) but to vary in their child care policies. Thus France combines pro-natalist policies with policies which facilitate women's employment and Germany encourages mothers to stay at home. It appears, therefore, that the influence of the labour movement on the state has had considerable impact on child care policies.

The influence of the women's movement on child care policy is rather more difficult to discern. Franzway *et al.* argue that in Australia the pressure exerted by femocrats has been important in keeping the issue alive and in securing federal funding for public child care provision. Borchorst, however, in discussing developments in Britain and Scandinavia, comments that the feminist movement 'has not acted as a strong pressure group in relation to child care' (Borchorst, 1990: 174), a view with which Vicky Randall concurs (1996: 492). In Britain feminist campaigning on nursery provision moved onto the terrain of the local state and into economic organisations at the end of the 1970s. This was a result of the priority given to nursery provision by socialist feminists and their orientation towards the labour movement and employment. This means that much of their work during the 1980s is not visible in the form of autonomous organisation, although it is apparent in the commitment of employers and trade unions to child care. This fragmented and piecemeal approach is difficult to document and may contribute to the impression that the feminist movement has been conspicuously absent from the child care debate. However, the activities of feminists within organisations in pursuit of an equal opportunities agenda, together with Britain's membership of the EC and the election of a Labour government in 1997 in the context of skills shortages, have resulted in child care becoming a political issue in ways which it was not during the 1970s. Thus in 1989 the EC declared a policy interest in 'reconciling work and family life and sharing family responsibilities' (Hantrais, 1994: 137) and in 1990, the British government removed the tax on employers' subsidies for workplace nurseries (Moss, 1991: 122). Conservative governments have consistently resisted any extension of parental leave to fathers and have opposed EC directives on child care (Hantrais, 1994: 155). However, since 1997 the Labour Government (which includes an unprecedented number of feminists) has committed itself to extending parental leave and developing a national child care strategy in order to enable parents to 'achieve a good balance between working and family life' (DfEE, 1998: 10). They want to expand parental choice through facilitating the provision of a variety of forms of child care. Thus the commitment is to flexible patterns of employment and caring, for both women and men, rather than to state-funded provision of child care. Lone mothers are to be encouraged into paid employment through the provision of appropriate child care and training, thereby reducing dependence on the state. There is thus a move within Britain towards an acceptance of maternal employment as something that is here to stay, and a recognition that steps need to be taken to enable both women and men to combine paid employment with parenting. However, under the rhetoric of parental choice, a variety of individual solutions is likely to continue.

Child care, however, continues to be defined as an employment issue and is associated with the labour movement. This makes it difficult for it to be defined unequivocally as a feminist issue in the way that fertility control and violence against women can be. This may also explain its lack of centrality even within the women's movement and the development of policies with very little feminist input and which are frequently explicitly anti-feminist. Evidently feminism has not managed to shift the framework of understanding of child care in the way that it has with the issues of fertility control and violence against women.

This apparent lack of influence of feminist social movements on child care policies can be seen as relating to the fact that it addresses issues of redistribution. Child care is expensive and its provision by the state requires resources which would have to come from employers and men. It is also a role change issue because it raises questions about the gendering of care work and men's involvement in the domestic sphere, that is, it problematises the gender division of labour within the domestic sphere and demands its transformation. In addition there has been a strong anti-feminist counter-movement in support of the traditional family and full-time mothering. Where it has been influential, as in Britain and the US, its presence has ensured that a situation of stalemate is maintained as governments have been faced with two contending social movements embodying diametrically opposed prescriptions for family life in general and child care and sexuality in particular. Indeed, one of the outcomes of the women's movement in relation to family policy has been the emergence of a strong counter-movement which, during the 1980s, contributed to a lack of change in child care policies despite the continuing economic need for women's participation in the workforce.

Child care, however, now seems to be on the political agenda in a way in which it was not in the 1970s. This is to do both with the EC and changing socio-economic and demographic circumstances. This demonstrates that even if issues are defined as important by social movements, unless the political and socio-economic circumstances are propitious, they are unlikely to reach agenda status. Thus in considering the impact of social movements on social policy it is important to consider not only the political opportunity structure, which was unfavourable in Britain and the US throughout the 1980s, but also the material circumstances of changing patterns of marriage and family formation and economic structure. Child care is now on the political agenda and, in Britain there are signs of significant policy change. However, as we saw in Chapter 6, the direction of change may be influenced as much by right-wing definitions of parental responsibility and moral values as it is by feminist definitions of child care as a right. And even feminists have become more pragmatic in their approach, conceding that choice is important in child care and that market solutions are an acceptable way forward. This represents a considerable change from the early days of the movement and can be seen as part of the process of incorporation and issue perversion that occurs when social movements move onto the terrain of the state.

In this chapter we have seen that it is much more difficult for social movements to bring about policy change in areas which involve role change and resource redistribution and that such attempts are likely to provoke counter-movements. This leads to a policy stalemate. However, it is also the case that where the issue of child care is defined as a labour market issue and as necessary to support the family, state provision is more likely to be forthcoming. It is clear that the nature of the state and the class alliances on which it is based are crucial in determining policies in this area, together with the needs of the economy for female labour. In addition, the presence of a strong counter-movement militates against any change in policy, particularly in the area of the family and sexuality. Ironically the pro-family counter-movement was itself a product of second wave feminism.

In conclusion it can be said that the definitions of child care developed within other social movements have been more influential for policy in this area than the definitions emerging from the feminist movement. Thus child care is defined by the labour movement and within socialist ideology as an employment issue and, secondarily, as a gender issue. Child care is necessary in order to enable women to participate in employment on the same terms as men. The population movement defines child care in terms of fertility levels and sees its public provision as a means of halting the decline in fertility levels associated with women's increasing employment. Thus child care is a means of enabling women to combine bearing and rearing children with participation in paid employment, it is a way of supporting the family rather than undermining it. For the new right child care is seen as a moral issue revolving around definitions of motherhood and fatherhood and attempts to stop the 'decline' of the family. It is seen as further evidence of the state's disastrous interference in family life, removing responsibilities from families and enabling women to abandon full-time motherhood and men to abandon fatherhood in any social sense altogether. Feminism, on the other hand, defines child care as a social right and exposes the gendered nature of care work, arguing that the whole organisation of child care in advanced capitalist societies needs to be transformed in the direction of greater parity between women and men in both the private and public spheres. In different societies different definitions of child care have shaped the policy agenda, but it seems that the feminist definition has so far failed to influence significantly the development of child care or family policy despite the questions it has raised about hegemonic definitions of 'the family'.

Chapter 10

Conclusions

It is clear from the material presented in the previous pages that the way feminist social movements interact with the state to bring about social change is complicated and needs to be understood on many different levels. In this final chapter I focus on the theoretical issues which have emerged from my discussion of particular areas of policy change and explore their implications for understanding the relation between social movements and the state. I look first at the relationship between feminist social movements and their socio-economic and demographic context. I then discuss the involvement of feminist social movements in struggles over meanings and resources and the implications of this for their characterisation as cultural and/or political. Third, I discuss the organisational and political context of these struggles and the way this modifies and transforms feminist demands. Finally, I explore the relation between feminist social movements, social structures and the state and revisit the question of the constitution and representation of political interests which I raised at the beginning of the book.

Socio-economic change

The socio-economic context in which social movements are located provides the material basis for their emergence and sets limits on their effectivity at the level of policy change. Chapter 4 located the emergence of feminist social movements in the context of changes in capitalist economies which led to women's increasing participation in the workforce, increasing levels of education and decreasing fertility levels. These changes increased women's access to resources in the form of cultural capital, wages and time – cultural capital because of increased educational levels, wages because of increased participation in paid employment and time because of decreased involve-

ment in child bearing and rearing. In addition women were challenging state control of their fertility by resorting to illegal abortions
where other methods of fertility control failed. These changing material conditions and practices provide part of the context for the emergence of feminist social movements. Thus the expansion of the
service sector of the economy and the welfare state and the increasing need for women in the workforce provided a favourable environment for feminist social movements to press for gender equality
in employment. Likewise, fertility control was an issue on which
reform was lagging behind women's actual practice. In the context of
women's increasing participation in the workforce the legitimacy of
keeping women out of public places by means of violence or the
threat of violence is questionable. These can be seen as role-equity
issues and relate to gender inequality in the public sphere. On the
other hand, issues which are perceived as relating to the private
domain, such as child care, have proved more resistant to change,
particularly as they involve a struggle over the distribution of
resources between women and men and between classes. Questions
of role change are also raised by women's reproductive rights; the
ongoing debates around abortion illustrate this point graphically and
suggest that although socio-economic change has led to a reduction
in levels of fertility, the extent to which women should have
autonomous control over their fertility is a highly contested issue
which threatens 'traditional' gender arrangements and views of
the world.

Together with socio-economic and demographic change there
have also been cultural shifts which are manifest in value changes
and associated changes in identity. Thus, as we saw in Chapter 4,
prior to the emergence of second wave feminism a shift in values
was beginning to take place which reflected changing patterns of
family formation and employment, particularly decreasing fertility
levels and increasing female participation in the workforce.
Women's involvement in the public domain of paid employment
and their comparison with men on the basis of equality rather than
difference, enabled conceptions of gender equality to become
dominant and assume a legitimacy which they could not have had if
women were perceived primarily as domestic creatures occupying
the private realm. Value shifts, or cultural change, were therefore
occurring prior to the emergence of the women's movement.
Women's increasing participation in employment and decreasing
levels of fertility, as well as increasing women's independent access
to resources, made available to them other sources of identity

besides that of wife and mother. These changes therefore began to alter the balance of power between women and men at home and at work; a process which feminist social movements have taken further. This suggests that changing gender relations are both cause and consequence of feminist social movements.

Meanings and resources

Social movement theory argues that contemporary social movements are involved in the creation of new meanings and ways of understanding the world and that they do this by redefining or reframing issues in ways that expose previously invisible power relations. This analysis clearly applies to feminist social movements. Thus the definitions that emerged from the women's movement have created a completely new way of understanding the social world, as one that is structured by gendered power relations as well as by relations of class, ethnicity and sexuality. The different definitions put forward by the women's movement challenge dominant meanings and understandings of the world. Their very existence renders problematic and questionable issues which might previously have been thought to be unquestionable. Thus feminist social movements are about meaning and making visible previously invisible gendered power relations. In this way they challenge hegemonic definitions of social reality which render these relations invisible and therefore unchallengeable.

Feminist definitions are, however, in competition with others and it is only to the extent that they become hegemonic that they have a significant impact on social policy. Male violence towards women, for instance, has been successfully redefined in feminist terms as involving an abuse of power rather than as being due to men's uncontrollable sexual urges for which women are in some inexplicable way responsible. There is, however, an ongoing conflict over ways of defining male violence. Thus the criminal justice system defines the issue as one of dysfunctional families and individual pathology while the women's movement defines it as an issue of gendered power relations. Similarly, the definition of abortion as a woman's right is in competition with other definitions such as the religious definition of it as a moral issue and the medical definition of it as a health issue. The definition that is enshrined in legislation is the medical definition although the feminist definition has had a significant impact on the terms of the policy debate. Child care is also defined by the women's movement as a right but has been incorporated into policy as an employment issue. Defining it in this way has the effect of reproducing women's responsibility for child care and encouraging individual solutions which challenge neither gender divisions of labour nor familial ideology. And although feminist researchers have provided ample evidence of the way in which access to resources is gendered, these insights have not led to a redefinition of poverty. It continues to be defined in individual terms and policies are shaped by assumptions that men's access to full-time wages is more important to the well being of families than is women's. Where this is not the case, as in Sweden, this is due to the hegemony of social democracy and its commitment to equality, including gender equality. These conflicting definitions represent a struggle over meaning and have implications for policy change.

Whether feminist definitions become hegemonic is affected by the alliances which are formed in specific policy areas. This means that although feminist social movements are active in redefining issues and attempting to influence the policy agenda, they are not usually solely responsible for the issue attaining agenda status. This makes it unlikely that feminist definitions and policy prescriptions will prevail. Thus the women's movement has worked in alliance with the labour movement over issues such as gender equality and child care whereas in fighting for reproductive rights the medical profession and population movement are key players. Indeed, because the medical definition of abortion as a health issue is enshrined in legislation, the medical profession and, through it the state, regulates access to abortion despite its being defined as a woman's right by second wave feminism. The only area in which the women's movement has not been in alliance is the area of male violence. Although here its engagement with the state and its requirement for resources has led to conflict over ways of defining male violence against women. Feminist social movements are therefore engaged in struggles with other political actors and with the state over meaning and this affects the extent to which feminist definitions become hegemonic.

What is significant about many feminist definitions is that they question the public–private distinction which underpins the liberal state. It is those issues which can be accommodated within the discourse of liberalism, such as equality, which are more easily translatable into policy change than those which challenge its very foundation. This is evident in the way that equal opportunities policies have been implemented, limiting them to the short rather than the long agenda. As we saw in Chapter 5, implementing the short agenda enables women to participate in the public domain on men's terms and within existing power relations. The long agenda brings so-called 'private' issues into the public domain and, in the course of attempting to implement it, power relations and the distribution of resources on which they are based are challenged. Thus equal opportunities do not simply involve the removal of discrimination and disadvantages suffered by individual women in the sphere of paid employment but require a reordering of gender relations within the private, domestic sphere as well as in the public sphere of paid employment. Similarly domestic violence is defined as a public issue with which the state should be involved. These feminist definitions therefore illustrate the intimate connections between gendered divisions of labour within the home and within the workforce and feminist strategies for change involve changing men's behaviour as well as women's. Thus most of the issues which appear to be role equity issues which do not threaten existing distributions of resources, if taken to their logical conclusion, constitute a fundamental challenge to existing gender relations.

In the sphere of policy implementation it is clear that feminist activity is crucial. Without it rights remain on paper and have relatively little impact on women's daily lives or on gender relations. Thus feminists have been involved in the implementation of equal opportunities policies and the implementation of policies towards 'victims' of violence. In both cases they have challenged the distribution of resources which underpins inequitable gender relations and have had some success in bringing about redistribution. This, however, is difficult to achieve, not only because it requires a shifting of the prevailing hegemony but also because it gives rise to resistance. This was evident within organisations, where resistance from men was provoked by attempts to implement change, and is also evident at the societal level with the emergence of counter-movements.

Notwithstanding this resistance, feminist social movements have challenged women's access to resources both within organisations and on a societal level. Thus the refuge movement has successfully increased the independent access of mainly poor women to resources such as housing and welfare benefits (resources which are controlled by the state) while the equality legislation and the equal opportunities policies to which it gave rise have increased the access of women to resources in the form of wages. These changes threaten men's control over resources within households and their monopoly of highly paid jobs and provide some women with the wherewithal to escape from dependency on men. Through activities such as these which increase women's access to resources, feminist social movements are empowering women.

Feminist social movements are therefore involved in struggles on two levels: over meanings and over the distribution of resources within society. This implies that they are both cultural and political, something which existing social movement theory finds difficult to accommodate. Analyses which represent feminist social movements in purely cultural terms distort the women's movement and, in their extreme forms, do violence to it by removing feminists and feminism from it. It is hard to reconcile purely cultural analyses of social movements with the experience of the women's movement, just as it is to reconcile purely political interpretations. Both elements are intertwined in contemporary feminism and they have implications for each other, cultural change affects political practice and political and policy changes affect cultural practice. This is just as true of other social movements, including the labour movement, as it is of feminist social movements.

Identities

Social movement theory argues that the construction of collective identities is a crucial part of social movement formation and mobilisation. The process of identity construction has been linked to structural inequalities, thereby providing a means of theorising the connection between social structures and processes of mobilisation. As we have seen, the changes which preceded the emergence of second wave feminism made available to women identities other than that of wife and mother. This made it possible for women to compare themselves with men and to perceive their situation as unequal, thus leading to the formation of feminist collective identities which challenged existing gender relations and identities and the unequal distribution of resources on which they are based. It is also important to consider the relation of identities to structural inequalities when looking at resistance to feminist social movements, whether this be within organisations or in the form of counter-movements. Both can be seen as attempts to resist the redistribution of power and resources in women's favour and both take the form of defending identities perceived as under threat by such redistribution. The most obvious identity to be threatened is that of the male breadwinner. This demonstrates that challenging gender inequalities and the way resources are distributed between women and men has implications for the gender identities which are supported by existing arrangements. Thus in order to bring about changes in gender relations such that women are no longer subordinate to men, changes in gender identities are necessary; such change is painful and difficult. This is evident in the ongoing struggles within the armed forces, the most repressive part of the state, over sexual harassment and the challenge this poses to masculinist culture. The cultural organisation of the state is being challenged by women moving into these areas of employment and coming up against an extremely heterosexist culture which is very resistant to change and which mobilises a brutal armoury to keep women out. Male workers within organisations resist any diminution in their power and status precisely by resorting to sexual jokes and sexual harassment. As we have seen, it is not only men's identities which are under threat. Women, both within the workforce and within the home, may experience feminism as undermining their identity, particularly if they are full-time mothers dependent on a male breadwinner. Thus the pro-family counter-movement experiences feminist social movements as undermining the 'traditional' family and the identities of male breadwinner, female dependant and full-time mother which go with it. Authority and power are associated with masculinity and male identity within the home and within the workplace. Men therefore resist changes which threaten to undermine this, whether this be women assuming positions of power and authority at work or women taking fertility decisions into their own hands.

Feminist social movements, therefore, contribute to changes in behaviour and identity through their involvement in the implementation of policies and by increasing women's access to resources. It is unequal access to resources which provides the structural basis for so-called traditional gender identities. This means that any redistribution of resources is likely to be experienced as a threat to existing gender identities, a threat which engenders resistance.

Organisations

As we have seen the organisational forms adopted by second wave feminism are highly variable. They neither all conform to a rational-bureaucratic model nor are they devoid of organisational structure and in a continual state of flux. However, they are affected by the organisational context within which they operate and the necessity of engaging with the state. Feminist social movements operate a dual strategy of working within and outside existing organisations. Thus they have created autonomous, feminist organisations as well as moving into non-feminist organisations; the former tend to be associated with radical feminism and the latter with socialist and liberal feminism.

The existence of autonomous organisations, such as rape crisis centres or women's refuges, legitimates feminist political practice and feminist forms of service delivery in the eyes of the local and national state. However, some forms of feminist organising can be delegitimated if they are not prepared to submit to the authority of the state. In the US, for instance, some feminist rape crisis centres were unable to survive because they were not prepared to compromise their principles in order to receive state funding. Thus even within autonomous organisations compromise is often necessary to ensure survival.

A process of compromise is even more apparent within non-feminist organisations. As we have seen, feminist activists are present within organisations such as trade unions, political parties and pressure groups and have had an impact on the policy agenda and policy formation, but in the process feminist demands have been changed. This raises the issue of how feminist goals are transformed in the process of engagement with the state. There are several ways in which this can happen. Issues can be redefined such that feminist definitions are not the ones that become policy. This happened to a considerable extent in relation to the abortion issue where feminist demands were transformed or perverted in the course of being incorporated into legislation. Political parties, all with their own interests and constituencies, were in control of the legislative process and (as we saw in the case of Italy) ensured that the final legislation did not enshrine a woman's right to abortion and was therefore not feminist. As we have already seen alliances affect the way in which issues reach the political agenda and subsequent policy formation. Especially where feminist social movements are only one interest among many, feminist demands are not likely to emerge unscathed from the policy-making process. Feminists working within organisations are at the forefront of this process of compromise. Thus in order to make equal opportunities policies acceptable within capitalist organisations they are being redefined in terms of efficiency and cost-effectiveness. In other words the organisation's priorities and mode of functioning transforms feminist demands into something which is reconcilable with the requirements of capitalist production. On the other hand, the presence of feminists within organisations is important in translating issues into policy and in ensuring that policies are implemented, albeit in a transformed form. These compromises and transformations mean that although feminist social movements have clearly had a major impact on the formation and implementation of social policies, this impact has often been in ways which bear little resemblance to the original demands of second wave feminism.

The impact of feminist demands on policy is also affected by which part of the state feminist social movements are engaged with. Thus it appears to be easier for feminist organisations to maintain some control over the policy agenda and policy implementation if they are loosely tied to the voluntary or welfare sector of the state than if they engage with the more repressive arms of the state such as the criminal justice system. This became clear when comparing the refuge movements in Britain and the US. In Britain refuges receive funding from the welfare sector of the state which is less masculinised, less repressive and more peripheral than the criminal justice system which is where funding for US refuges is located. Similarly, the conflict over abortion rights takes place largely on the legal terrain, part of the masculinised, core, repressive state apparatus. These differences point to the contradictions within the state. Some parts of it are more enabling than others. Thus in Britain during the 1980s local government facilitated the development of social movement organisations while central government provided a hostile terrain for social movement activity. Likewise it appears to be easier to challenge the gender order and modify the distribution of resources in the peripheral areas of the state than the core areas where power is more jealously guarded and resistance to change is more entrenched. These differences mediate the impact of feminist social movements on policy change in different areas and also suggest that the state can be involved in facilitating and repressing social movement activity, often at the same time.

Engagement with the state is essential for feminist movements because the state regulates access to the resources that women need in order to be able to change gendered relations of power. But the nature of this engagement depends on the nature of the state and this affects both the tactics used by the women's movement and the forms of organisation adopted. Thus where the state is open, with a pluralist system and weak political parties, feminist interest groups and policy networks are likely to form, while in systems where political parties are strong and based on pre-existing social movements, feminist social movements are likely to attempt to influence political parties and the labour movement or to organise autonomously. Of course these forms of organising are not mutually exclusive. Thus, in the US and Australia, both of which have relatively open states, feminists have been incorporated into state bureaucracies and, in the US, feminist policy networks and bureaucratic, professional organisations are a feature of the women's movement. In Britain, in contrast, where direct access to the state is more difficult, large sections of the women's movement have moved into left-of-centre political parties and the labour movement. It is by influencing them that pressure can be brought to bear on the state. In Germany and Italy the women's movement has remained largely autonomous.

Although engaging with the state entails compromise, no engagement is likely to render the movement ineffective in improving women's access to resources. However, in engaging with the state feminist social movements are incorporated into the system. Thus refuges can be seen as part of the voluntary sector of the state while femocrats are part of the state bureaucracy. Such incorporation lends legitimacy to the state and reduces the ability of feminist social movements to maintain a critical stance towards it. Indeed, incorporation of feminist issues may ensure that feminist social movements do not emerge in the first place. It also ensures that feminist interests are represented within the state, albeit in transformed forms.

Structures

From our discussion thus far it is clear that feminist social movements raise fundamental questions about the way society is structured. Many of their demands and activities problematise the public–private divide and challenge the unequal distribution of resources between women and men. They have also had structural impacts on society in so far as they have challenged the gender ordering of social institutions. This has been seen in the implementation of equal opportunities policies and the associated cultural and organisational changes as well as in the increased representation of women within political parties and government. Thus feminist involvement in the British Labour Party resulted in the proportion of women MPs increasing from 9.2 per cent before the 1997 election to 18.4 per cent after it (Norris and Lovenduski, 1993: 46). This can be seen as a direct outcome of second wave feminism and its response to the election of the first Thatcher administration in 1979. The women's movement has therefore had a significant impact on forms of representation and resulted in the ongoing incorporation of feminist interests into left-of-centre political parties. Second wave feminism has also resulted in gender issues becoming an explicit dimension of the political process. Thus the support of the Republican party for the anti-abortion lobby has been identified as contributing to its defeat in the 1992 presidential election.

From this it is clear that second wave feminism has had an impact on the political opportunity structure, both by engaging with other social movements and political parties, thereby influencing their policies and forms of organisation, and by contributing to policy change. However, its relation to the way society is structured also needs to be considered, particularly as one of its aims was to end women's oppression.

Existing social movement theory relates the emergence of contemporary social movements to structural transformations in advanced capitalist society; these transformations are conceptualised in terms of class, though, which makes it rather difficult to incorporate feminist social movements into this framework. Even those who relate feminist social movements to patriarchal structures conceptualise their emergence as a result of changes in the demand for female labour brought about by changes in capitalism. As we have seen, the most fruitful attempts to explain the emergence of contemporary social movements and the representation of non-class-based interests within the state involve mobilising a concept of civil society. New social movements are seen as being located within civil society while the 'old' social movement (the labour movement) is located within the economy. The relations structuring these two spheres of society provide the material basis for the construction of interests and their representation within the state. This, however, maintains the public–private distinction which has been problematised by feminist social movements, allocating gender relations and the constitution of gender interests to the private sphere and class relations and interests to the public sphere. Thus the structure of the economy is seen as giving rise to class relations and political movements and parties while the structure of civil society, which includes the family, gives rise to gender relations and cultural or social movements. The former are said to be engaged in a struggle over the distribution of resources and inclusion in the polity while the latter are concerned with meaning and the defence of civil society from encroachment by the state. The maintenance of this distinction reveals the fact that the epistemological insights of feminist social movements have not yet been integrated into social movement or state theory. Thus feminists argue that the economy and class-based social movements are gendered, and that the public–private dichotomy has to be overcome in any explanation of the constitution and representation of interests. Indeed feminist social movements emerge from gender divisions which are structured by unequal access to resources in both the public and private domains and the construction of feminist collective identities takes place on the basis of these structural inequalities in both spheres. Thus gender interests emanate from the economy and from civil society, or – using other concepts – the spheres of production and reproduction, the market and the family.

Feminist social movements represent and constitute women's interests on the basis of changing gender relations at this level. These changes are based on 'new' ways of being and behaving and are associated with shifts in cultural values. The 'old' ways of being, however, continue to exist and are also associated with cultural values embedded in material practices. The emergence of counter-movements and the fierce ideological debates about changing social policies indicate that feminist social movements do not represent the interests of all women and that change is more difficult in some areas of policy than others. Indeed, women's participation in anti-feminist counter-movements suggests that interests are not simply constituted on the basis of gender, pitting women against men, but on the basis of individuals' differential positioning in the social relations of production and reproduction. Thus women who are full-time mothers dependent on a male wage might feel their identity and interests to be threatened by feminist social movements rather than represented by them. It may therefore be more accurate to say that feminist rather than women's interests are constituted and represented by feminist social movements. The basis for this is declining levels of fertility and the widening of opportunities in the workforce, both of which reduce the importance of a maternal identity to women. These changes provide the material basis for feminist social movements and give rise to struggles over the distribution of the tasks of social reproduction and over the control of reproduction (understood as biological reproduction). Such struggles involve the construction and representation of political interests, not only within feminist/anti-feminist social movements but also within other social movements, political parties and the state. Through this process of representation, political interests based on gender relations are transformed and re/constituted. It is, however, the material social relations of production and reproduction and the associated distribution of resources which provide the basis for the emergence of feminist social movements and for the constitution and representation of feminist political interests. But whether or not feminist social movements emerge at all depends fundamentally on the state's ability to respond to changing gender relations and to represent the new gender interests to which such changes give rise.

We can therefore provide some sort of an answer to the question raised in Chapter 3 as to whether policy change is caused by social movements or whether both it and social movements are a response to socio-economic and cultural change. Socio-economic and cultural change is associated with changes in patterns of behaviour. The state, particularly in its welfare form, regulates the behaviour of populations in the spheres of production and reproduction. It may respond to changes in behaviour in these spheres by implementing policy change, thus pre-empting the emergence of social movements. Or it may delay implementing policy change, thus creating a situation where behaviour and ideas are at odds with social policies which attempt to regulate behaviour; such policies thereby lose their legitimacy. These circumstances give rise to social movements. There cannot, therefore, be an abstract theoretical answer to the question as to whether policy change is brought about by social movements or by socio-economic and cultural change. What can be said is that socio-economic and cultural change brings about a response from the state that results in changes in social policy. But the extent to which these changes are mediated by social movements depends fundamentally on the nature of the state. Thus social movements emerge as a result of socio-economic and cultural change and also hasten that change, but whether they emerge at all is dependent on the state.

Notes

Chapter 1 Theorising the State

1. There is a lack of clarity in Walby's specification of the relation between the material basis of patriarchy and patriarchal political interests. She argues that patriarchy exists in structures and practices and therefore has a material basis, and that political struggles are relatively autonomous from this material base (Walby, 1990). She seems here to be working within a fairly straightforward representational framework. However, complications arise when she specifies the structures that constitute patriarchy, one of which is the state. Thus the state is part of the material basis of patriarchy but at the same time represents, or is biased towards, patriarchal political interests; this implies that in this capacity it is relatively autonomous from the material base of patriarchy. Walby does not clarify how the state can be part of the material basis of patriarchy as well as being relatively autonomous from it. It appears that her attempts to avoid charges of essentialism have resulted in a certain amount of conceptual confusion.

Chapter 2 Theorising Social Movements

1. Historicity is defined as the 'overall system of meaning which sets dominant rules in a given society' or 'the capacity to produce an historical experience through cultural patterns' (Touraine, 1985:778). Perhaps Touraine's historicity is analogous to Gramsci's hegemony, both being concerned with culture and definitions of social reality and the way that social conflict has the potential to transform dominant definitions of social reality which are reproduced through cultural forms.
2. Although Melucci discusses networks elsewhere, conceptualising social movements as consisting of networks of 'groups and individuals sharing a conflictual culture and a collective identity' (Melucci, 1985:799), he does not speak specifically of recruitment networks. Here he refers to recruitment networks as providing the mobilisation potential of a movement. This formulation, which recognizes that the situation of a particular section of the population makes it likely to support specific social movements, allows the consideration of a structural basis for the formation of collective identity. This consideration appears to have been introduced into Melucci's work under the influence of RMT, specifically the work of Klandermans and his development of the concept mobilisation potential (Klandermans and Tarrow, 1988). It may not be coincidental that this concept appears in Melucci's contribution to a

volume edited by Klandermans and Tarrow who share Melucci's concern to explain the way structural change is transformed into collective action (Klandermans and Tarrow 1988:10). Mobilisation is proposed as the concept that can link structural and individual levels. Melucci does not speak of recruitment networks in terms which are quite so close to those of Klandermans in any other of his works.

3. A frame is defined as an 'interpretive schemata that simplifies and condenses the "world out there" by selectively punctuating and encoding objects, situations, events, experiences, and sequences of actions within one's present or past environment' (Snow and Benford, 1992:137).

Chapter 4 The Emergence of Second Wave Feminism

1. Readers interested in a history of second wave feminism should consult Freeman (1975) for the US, Banks (1986) for the US and Britain, Lovenduski and Randall (1993) for Britain, Kaplan (1992) for Western Europe and Scandinavia and Charles (1993, Chapter 9) for a useful comparative summary.

2. Here again definitional problems are apparent. Mary Ruggie, in her study of Britain and Sweden differentiates between the two defining the former as a 'liberal welfare model' and only the latter as corporatist (Ruggie, 1984:13).

3. This analogy, however, also has the effect of making black women invisible and facilitating the assumption that all women share a common experience of oppression (Spelman, 1988).

4. Kaplan's characterisation of the Swiss and German states as conservative and resistant to egalitarian reforms conflicts with Kriesi's categorisation of them. He distinguishes between the German and Swiss states arguing that the latter is weak and inclusive. It therefore incorporates oppositional issues before they have time to gather momentum and is associated with moderate mobilisation of large numbers of people. In contrast Germany is characterised as weak and exclusive and therefore likely to encourage moderate mobilisations of large numbers of people. This clearly does not hold for feminist social movements. There are similar problems with his characterisation of the Netherlands (Kriesi, 1995).

Chapter 5 Equal Opportunities

1. EC member states had agreed in 1961 to implement equal pay for equal work and the Equal Pay Directive was issued in 1975 (Buckley and Anderson, 1988:7), ten months before the Equal Pay Act came into force (Gregory, 1992:47). This directive, however, specified that women be paid the same as men for work of equal value, a provision which is not enshrined in the 1975 Equal Pay Act which only legislates for equal pay for the same or similar work.

2. This had originally been introduced in order to ensure that returning veterans of the Second World War would be able to find employment in a situation of chronic labour shortage (Blakemore and Drake, 1996:16).

3. A similar movement of activists into mainstream politics occurred in Australia where there was also a concern with equal opportunities policies and where the phenomenon of the femocrat emerged (Burton, 1991).

Chapter 6 Poverty

1. Townsend found that, 'More than half the poor were women and girls, and nearly two thirds of the poor were under 15 or over 65. Women were at a disadvantage at most, but not all ages.' The only age they were not was under 15 years (Townsend, 1979: 285).
2. This conception of poverty is stronger in the European tradition than the Anglo-Saxon one which concentrates on defining and measuring poverty in terms of a poverty line (income) and on a group of people who are below that line and therefore need assistance (Jordan, 1996).
3. In 1994 the House of Lords ruled that 'the application of differing qualifying conditions for part-timers in employment legislation discriminated against women contrary to European equal pay and equal treatment law.' Before this those working 8–16 hours a week had to have 5 years continuous service to qualify for rights under the employment protection legislation and if they worked under 8 hours a week they could not qualify at all. In February 1995 all hours of work thresholds were removed from the employment protection legislation but length of service thresholds still apply.

Chapter 7 Violence

1. Refuges were established in 1973–4 in the US and Australia (Schechter, 1982; McGregor and Hopkins, 1991; Dobash and Dobash, 1992) and in other countries, such as Germany and Sweden, later in the decade – 1978 in Sweden (Gelb, 1989: 172) and 1979–80 in Germany (Ferree, 1991/2: 54). Indeed, in Germany the impetus came not directly from the women's movement but from the state.
2. Women are in priority need if they have dependent children living with them, if they are pregnant, if they are vulnerable due to age, ill health or disability, or if they have become homeless due to a natural disaster.
3. In 1985, Welsh Women's Aid's housing officer carried out a piece of research which explored the policies and practices of local housing authorities towards women who presented to them as homeless as a result of domestic violence (J. Taylor, 1989). In 1988 Welsh Women's Aid carried out a further study exploring the lack of suitable move-on accommodation for women and children leaving refuges. This was funded jointly by the Welsh Office and the Housing Corporation (as it then was).
4. The movements have also had an impact on policy implementation, affecting women's access to resources such as housing and the way they are treated within state agencies, particularly by the police and legal system. Indeed, changes in police practice have been pointed to as the 'chink... in the armour of the criminal justice system' which opens up possibilities for further change (Edwards, 1989; Lees with Gregory, 1997: 177). These movements can there-

fore be seen as challenging and transforming practices within the more masculinised parts of the state.

Chapter 8 Abortion

1. It is only in Scandinavia where abortion on request is legally granted to women, always within specific time limits, and where this right is backed up by adequate provision (Wiik, 1986; Kaplan, 1992). In other countries, such as the Netherlands, women have in effect been granted abortion on request although the legal position is slightly ambivalent.

Chapter 9 The Family

1. The Working Women's Charter was launched in 1974 and was aimed particularly at working within trade unions and trades councils, that is, the labour movement. The demand for free, 24-hour nurseries had been replaced by a demand for 'Improved provision of local authority day nurseries, free of charge, with extended hours to suit working mothers. Provision of nursery classes in day nurseries. More nursery schools' (Charles, 1979).
2. For a full account see Charles, 1979.
3. This report was produced by the Warnock Committee, set up in 1982 to explore the ethical and policy implications of advances in reproductive technology. The Report of the Committee of Enquiry into Human Fertilisation and Embryology was published in 1984 (Feldman, 1987: 26).

Bibliography

Abbott, P. and Wallace, C. (1992) *The Family and the New Right*, Pluto Perspectives: London/Boulder, Colorado.

Abrams, P. (1988) 'Notes on the difficulty of studying the state' in *Journal of Historical Sociology* **1**(1): 58–89.

Abrar, S. (1996) 'Feminist intervention and local domestic violence policy' in J. Lovenduski and P. Norris (eds) *Women in Politics*, Oxford University Press: Oxford, pp. 193–207.

Allen, J. (1990) 'Does feminism need a theory of the state?' in S. Watson (ed.) *Playing the State: Australian Feminist Interventions*, Verso: London, pp. 21–37.

Allen, S. (1997) 'Identity: feminist perspectives on 'race', ethnicity and nationality' in N. Charles and H. Hintjens (eds) *Gender, Ethnicity and Political Ideologies*, Routledge: London and New York, pp. 46–64.

Allen, T. (1996) 'The Nordic model of gender equality: the welfare state, patriarchy and unfinished emancipation' in V. Moghadam (ed.) *Patriarchy and Development*, Clarendon Press: Oxford, pp. 303–26.

Althusser, L. (1971) 'Ideology and ideological state apparatuses' in *Lenin and Philosophy*, New Left Books: London.

Arnold, G. (1995) 'Dilemmas of feminist coalitions: collective identity and strategic effectiveness in the battered women's movement' in M. M. Ferree and P. Y. Martin (eds) *Feminist Organizations: Harvest of the New Women's Movement*, Temple University Press: Philadelphia, pp. 276–90.

Bacchi, C. L. (1990) *Same Difference: Feminism and Sexual Difference*, Allen & Unwin: London.

Bagguley, P. (1992) 'Social change, the middle class and the emergence of "new social movements" ' in *Sociological Review* **40**(1): 26–48.

Banks, O. (1986) *Faces of Feminism: A Study of Feminism as a Social Movement*, Basil Blackwell: Oxford.

Barrett, M. (1980) *Women's Oppression Today*, Verso: London.

Barrett, M. and McIntosh, M. (1985) 'Ethnocentrism and socialist-feminist theory' in *Feminist Review* **20**: 23–47.

Barron, J. (1990) *Not Worth the Paper? The Effectiveness of Legal Protection for Women and Children experiencing Domestic Violence*, WAFE: Bristol.

Barry, U. (1988) 'Abortion in the Republic of Ireland' in *Feminist Review* **29**: 57–63.

Bassnett, S. (1986) *Feminist Experiences: The Women's Movement in Four Cultures*, Allen & Unwin: London.

Batiot, A. (1986) 'Radical democracy and feminist discourse' in D. Dahlerup (ed.) *The New Women's Movement: Feminism and Political Power in Europe and the USA*, Sage: London, pp. 85–102.

Beckwith, K. (1987) 'Response to feminism in the Italian parliament: divorce, abortion, and sexual violence legislation' in M. F. Katzenstein and C. M. Mueller (eds) *The Women's Movements of the United States and*

Western Europe: Consciousness, Political Opportunity, and Public Policy, Temple University Press: Philadelphia, pp. 153–71.

Beresford, P. and Green, D. (1996) 'Income and wealth: an opportunity to reassess the UK poverty debate' in *Critical Social Policy* **16**(1): 95–109.

Beynon, H. (1975) *Working for Ford*, E P Publishing: Wakefield.

Birnbaum, P. (1988) *States and Collective Action; The European Experience*, Cambridge University Press: Cambridge.

Blakemore, K. and Drake, R. (1996) *Understanding Equal Opportunities Policies*, Harvester Wheatsheaf: Hemel Hempstead.

Blum, L. M. (1992) 'Gender and class in comparable worth' in P. Kahn and E. Meehan (eds) *Equal Value/Comparable Worth in the UK and the USA*, Macmillan: Basingstoke, pp. 95–115.

Blumberg, R. L. (ed.) (1991) *Gender, Family and Economy: The Triple Overlap*, Sage: London.

Boggs, C. (1986) *Social Movements and Political Power: Emerging Forms of Radicalism in the West*, Temple University Press: Florida.

Boneparth, E. (1982) 'A framework for policy analysis' in E. Boneparth (ed.) *Women, Power and Policy*, Pergamon: Elmsford New York, pp. 1–14.

Borchorst, A. (1990) 'Political motherhood and child care policies: A comparative approach to Britain and Scandinavia' in C. Ungerson (ed.) *Gender and Caring: Work and Welfare in Britain and Scandinavia*, Harvester Wheatsheaf: Hemel Hempstead, pp. 160–78.

Borchorst, A. (1994) 'Welfare state regimes, women's interests and the EC' in D. Sainsbury (ed.) *Gendering Welfare States*, Sage: London, pp. 26–44.

Borchorst, A. and Siim, B. (1987) 'Women and the advanced welfare state – a new kind of patriarchal power?' in A. Showstack-Sassoon (ed.) *Women and the State*, Hutchinson: London, pp. 128–57.

Bott, E. ([1957] 1971) *Family and Social Network*, 2nd edn, Social Science paperbacks, Tavistock Publications: London.

Bouchier, D. (1983) *The Feminist Challenge: The Movement for Women's Liberation in Britain and the United States*, Macmillan: Basingstoke.

Brand, K.-W. (1990) 'Cyclical aspects of new social movements: waves of cultural criticism and mobilization cycles of new middle-class radicalism' in R. J. Dalton and M. Kuechler (eds) *Challenging the Political Order: New Social and Political Movements in Western Democracies*, Polity Press: Oxford, pp. 23–42.

Brannen, J. and Moss, P. (1987) 'Dual earner households: women's financial contributions after the birth of the first child' in J. Brannen and G. Wilson (eds) *Give and Take in Families: Studies in Resource Distribution*, Allen & Unwin: London, pp. 75–95.

Brannen, J. and Wilson, G. (eds) (1987) *Give and Take in Families: Studies in Resource Distribution*, Allen & Unwin: London, pp. 75–95.

Brenner, J. and Laslett, B. (1991) 'Gender, social reproduction, and women's self-organisation: considering the U.S. welfare state' in *Gender and Society*, **5**(3): 311–33.

Bright, C. and Harding, S. (1984) 'Processes of statemaking and popular protest: an introduction' in C. Bright and S. Harding (eds) *State-making and Social Movements: Essays in History and Theory*, University of Michigan Press: Ann Arbor, pp. 1–15.

Brownmiller, S. (1986) *Against our Will: Men, Women and Rape*, Penguin: Harmondsworth.

Bruegel, I. and Kean, H. (1995) 'The moment of municipal feminism: gender and class in 1980s local government' in *Critical Social Policy* 44/45, **15**(2/3): 147–69.

Bryan, B., Dadzie, S. and Scafe, S. (1985) *The Heart of the Race: Black Women's Lives in Britain*, Virago: London.

Bryson, V. and Lister, R. (1994) *Women, Citizenship and Social Policy*, University of Bradford Applied Social Studies/Joseph Rowntree Foundation.

Buckley, M. and Anderson, M. (1988) 'Introduction: problems, policies and politics' in M. Buckley and M. Anderson (eds) *Women, Equality and Europe*, Macmillan: Basingstoke, pp. 1–19.

Buechler, S. M. (1990) *Women's Movements in the United States: Woman Suffrage, Equal Rights, and Beyond*, Rutgers University Press: New Brunswick and London.

Buechler, S. M. (1993) 'Beyond resource mobilization? Emerging trends in social movement theory' in *The Sociological Quarterly* **34**(2): 217–35.

Buechler, S. M. (1995) 'New social movement theories' in *The Sociological Quarterly* **36**(3): 441–64.

Burton, C. (1985) *Subordination: Feminism and Social Theory*, Allen & Unwin: London.

Burton, C. (1991) *The Promise and the Price*, Allen & Unwin: London.

Bush, D. M. (1992) 'Women's movements and state policy reform aimed at domestic violence against women: a comparison of the consequences of movement mobilization in the U.S. and India' in *Gender and Society* **6**(4): 587–608.

Buswell, C. (1992) 'Training girls to be low-paid women' in C. Glendinning and J. Millar (eds) *Women and Poverty in Britain: the 1990s*, Harvester Wheatsheaf: Hemel Hempstead, pp. 79–94.

Canel, E. (1992) 'New social movement theory and resource mobilization: the need for integration' in W. K. Carroll (ed.) *Organizing Dissent: Contemporary Social Movements in Theory and Practice*, Garamond Press: Toronto, pp. 22–51.

Carabine, J. (1996) 'Heterosexuality and social policy' in D. Richardson (ed.) *Theorising Heterosexuality*, Open University Press: Buckingham, Philadelphia, pp. 55–74.

Carroll, W. K. (1992) 'Introduction: social movements and counter-hegemony in a Canadian context' in W. K. Carroll (ed.) *Organizing Dissent: Contemporary Social Movements in Theory and Practice*, Garamond Press: Toronto, pp. 1–19.

Carter, A. (1988) *The Politics of Women's Rights*, Longman: Harlow.

Castells, M. (1983) *The City and the Grassroots: A Cross-cultural Theory of Urban Social Movements*, Edward Arnold: London.

Chafetz, J. and Dworkin, G. (1987) 'In the face of threat: organized antifeminism in comparative perspective' in *Gender and Society* **1**(1): 33–60.

Chancer, L. S. (1987) 'New Bedford, Massachusetts, March 6, 1983–March 22, 1984: The "before and after" of a group rape' in *Gender and Society* **1**(3): 239–60.

Charles, N. (1979) An Analysis of the Ideology of Women's Domestic Role and its Social Effects in Modern Britain, unpublished PhD thesis, University of Keele.

Charles, N. (1990) 'Women – advancing or retreating?' in R. Jenkins and A. Edwards (eds) *One Step Forward? South and West Wales Towards the Year 2000*, Gomer Press: Llandysul, pp. 83–94.

Charles, N. (1991) *The Funding of Women's Aid Services to the Community: A Research Peport*, Welsh Women's Aid: Cardiff.

Charles, N. (1993) *Gender Divisions and Social Change*, Harvester Wheatsheaf: Hemel Hempstead.

Charles, N. (1994a) 'Domestic violence, homelessness and housing: the response of housing providers in Wales' in *Critical Social Policy* **14**(2): 36–52.

Charles, N. (1994b) 'The housing needs of women and children escaping domestic violence' in *Journal of Social Policy* **23**(4): 465–87.

Charles, N. (1995) 'Feminist politics, domestic violence and the state' in *Sociological Review* **43**(4): 617–40.

Charles, N. and Davies, C. (1997) 'Contested communities: the refuge movement and cultural identities in Wales' in *The Sociological Review* **45**(3): 416–36.

Charles, N. with Jones, A. (1993) *The Housing Needs of Women and Children Escaping Domestic Violence*, Tai Cymru/Housing for Wales: Cardiff.

Charles, N. and Kerr, M. (1988) *Women, Food and Families*, Manchester University Press: Manchester.

Cockburn, C. (1983) *Brothers: Male Domination and Technological Change*, Pluto Press: London.

Cockburn, C. (1991) *In the Way of Women*, Macmillan: Basingstoke.

Cohan, A. (1986) 'Abortion as a marginal issue: the use of peripheral mechanisms in Britain and the United States' in J. Lovenduski and J. Outshoorn (eds) *The New Politics of Abortion*, Sage: London, pp. 27–48.

Cohen, J. L. (1985) 'Strategy or identity: new theoretical paradigms and contemporary social movements' in *Social Research* **52–4**: 663–716.

Coleman, K. (1988) 'The politics of abortion in Australia: freedom, church and state' in *Feminist Review* **29**: 75–97.

Colgan, F. and Ledwith, S. (1996) 'Women as organisational change agents' in S. Ledwith and F. Colgan (eds) *Women in Organisations: Challenging Gender Politics*, Macmillan: Basingstoke.

Collins, P. H. (1990) *Black Feminist Thought*, Unwin Hyman: Boston, London.

Collinson, D. L., Knights, D. and Collinson, M. (1990) *Managing to Discriminate*, Routledge: London and New York.

Connell, R. W. (1990) 'The state, gender and sexual politics: theory and appraisal' in *Theory and Society* **19**: 507–44.

Cook, J. and Watt, S. (1992) 'Racism, women and poverty' in C. Glendinning and J. Millar (eds) *Women and Poverty in Britain: the 1990s*, Harvester Wheatsheaf: Hemel Hempstead, pp. 11–23.

Coontz, S. and Henderson, P. (eds) (1986) *Women's Work, Men's Property: The Origins of Gender and Class*, Verso: London.

Cooper, D. (1994) *Sexing the City: Lesbian and Gay Politics within the Activist State*, Rivers Oram Press: London.

Cooper, D. (1995) *Power in Struggle: Feminism, Sexuality and the State*, Open University Press: Milton Keynes.

Coote, A. and Campbell, B. (1982) *Sweet Freedom: The Struggle for Women's Liberation*, Picador: London.

Costain, A. (1981) 'Representing women: the transition from social movement to interest group' in *Western Political Quarterly* **34**: 100–13.

Costain, A. N. (1992) *Inviting Women's Rebellion: A Political Process Interpretation of the Women's Movement*, Johns Hopkins University Press: Baltimore.

Costain, A. N. and Costain, W. D. (1987) 'Strategy and tactics of the women's movement in the United States: the role of political parties' in M. F. Katzenstein and C. M. Mueller (eds) *The Women's Movement of the United States and Western Europe: Consciousness, Political Opportunity, and Public Policy*, Temple University Press: Philadelphia, pp. 196–214.

Coward, R. (1997) 'Sign of the crimes' in the *Guardian*, 24/7/97.

Crompton, R. and Harris, F. (1998) 'Explaining women's employment patterns: "orientations to work" revisited' in *The British Journal of Sociology* **49**(1): 118–36.

Crompton, R. and Le Feuvre, N. (1992) 'Gender and bureaucracy: women in finance in Britain and France' in M. Savage and A. Witz (eds) *Gender and Bureaucracy*, Blackwell/*The Sociological Review*: Oxford, pp. 94–123.

Dahlerup, D. (1986) 'Introduction' in D. Dahlerup (ed.) *The New Women's Movement: Feminism and Political Power in Europe and the USA*, Sage: London, pp. 1–25.

Dahlerup, D. (1987) 'Confusing concepts – confusing reality: a theoretical discussion of the patriarchal state' in A. Showstak-Sassoon (ed.) *Women and the State*, Hutchinson: London, pp. 93–127.

Dale, J. and Foster, P. (1986) *Feminists and State Welfare*, Routledge & Kegan Paul: London.

Daly, M. (1994) 'Comparing welfare states: towards a gender-friendly approach' in D. Sainsbury (ed.) *Gendering Welfare States*, Sage: London, pp. 101–17.

Dartmouth Park Hill, London (1982) 'Not so much a day nursery' in M. Rowe (ed.) *Spare Rib Reader*, Penguin Books: Harmondsworth, pp. 112–19.

Davies, H. and Joshi, H. (1994) 'Sex, sharing and the distribution of income' in *Journal of Social Policy* **23**(3): 301–40.

Davin, D. (1992) 'Population policy and reform: the Soviet Union, Eastern Europe and China' in S. Rai, H. Pilkington and A. Phizacklea (eds) *Women in the Face of Change*, Routledge: London and New York, pp. 79–104.

Davis, A. (1982) *Women, Race and Class*, The Women's Press: London.

de Leonardis, O. (1993) 'New patterns of collective action in a "post-welfare" society: the Italian case' in G. Drover and P. Kerans (eds) *New Approaches to Welfare Theory*, Edward Elgar: Aldershot, pp. 177–89.

della Porta, D. and Rucht, D. (1995) 'Left-libertarian movements in context: a comparison of Italy and West Germany' in J. C. Jenkins and B. Klandermans (eds) *The Politics of Social Protest: Comparative Perspectives on States and Social Movements*, UCL Press: London, pp. 229–72.

Dennis, N. and Erdos, G. (1993) *Families Without Fatherhood*, Choice in welfare series no. 12, IEA Health and Welfare Unit: London.

Department for Education and Employment, Social Security, Ministers for Women (1998) *Meeting the Childcare Challenge*, Cm 3959: London: HMSO.

Dex, S. (1988) *Women's Attitudes Towards Work*, Macmillan: Basingstoke.

Dobash, R. and Dobash, R. (1992) *Women, Violence and Social Change*, Routledge: London and New York.

Dominelli, L. (1991) *Women Across Cultures: Feminist Comparative Social Policy*, Harvester Wheatsheaf: Hemel Hempstead.

Donzelot, J. (1979) *The Policing of Families*, Hutchinson: London.

Doyal, L. (1981) *The Political Economy of Health*, Pluto Press: London.

Dunne, G. (1997) *Lesbian Lifestyles: Women's Work and the Politics of Sexuality*, Macmillan: Basingstoke.

The Economist, 22/2/92.

Eder, K. (1993) *The New Politics of Class: Social Movements and Cultural Dynamics in Advanced Societies*, Sage: London.

Edwards, J. and Mckie, L. (1993/4) 'The European Economic Community – a vehicle for promoting equal opportunities in Britain?' in *Critical Social Policy* **13**(3): 51–65.

Edwards, S. (1989) *Policing 'Domestic' Violence: Women, the Law and the State*, Sage: London.

Einhorn, B. (1993) *Cinderella Goes to Market: Citizenship, Gender and Women's Movements in East Central Europe*, Verso: London.

Eisenstein, H. (1991) *Gender Shock: Practising Feminism on Two Continents*, Allen & Unwin: Sydney.

Eisenstein, H. (1995) 'The Australian femocratic experiment: a feminist case for bureaucracy' in M. M. Ferree and P. Y. Martin (eds) *Feminist Organizations: Harvest of the New Women's Movement*, Philadelphia: Temple University Press, pp. 69–83.

Elliott, R. (1984) 'How far have we come? Women's organisation in the unions in the United Kingdom' in C. Cockburn (ed.) 'Trade unions and the radicalising of socialist feminism' in *Feminist Review* **16**: 64–73.

Epstein, B. (1990) 'Rethinking social movement theory' in *Socialist Review* **20**: 35–65.

Esping-Anderson, G. (1990) *The Three Worlds of Welfare Capitalism*, Polity Press: Oxford.

Eyerman, R. and Jamison, A. (1991) *Social Movements: A Cognitive Approach*, Polity Press: Oxford.

Faragher, T. (1985) 'The police response to violence against women in the home' in J. Pahl (ed.) *Private Violence and Public Policy*, Routledge & Kegan Paul: London, pp. 110–24.

Feldman, R. (1987) 'The politics of the new reproductive technologies' in *Critical Social Policy* **7**(1): 21–39.

Ferguson, K. E. (1984) *The Feminist Case Against Bureaucracy*, Temple University Press: Philadelphia.

Ferree, M. M. (1987) 'Equality and autonomy: feminist politics in the United States and West Germany' in M. F. Katzenstein and C. M. Mueller (eds) *The Women's Movements of the United States and Western Europe: Consciousness, Political Opportunity, and Public Policy*, Temple University Press: Philadelphia, pp. 172–95.

Ferree, M. M. (1991/2) 'Institutionalising gender inequality: feminist politics and equality offices' in *German Politics and Society* **24**(Winter): 53–67.

Ferree, M. M. (1992) 'The political context of rationality: rational choice theory and resource mobilization' in A. D. Morris and C. M. Mueller (eds) *Frontiers in Social Movement Theory*, Yale University Press: New Haven, CT, pp. 29–52.

Ferree, M. M. and Hess, B. B. (1985) *Controversy and Coalition: The New Feminist Movement*, G K Hall: Boston.

Ferree, M. M. and Martin, P. Y. (1995) *Feminist Organizations: Harvest of the New Women's Movement*, Philadelphia: Temple University Press.

Fincher, R. (1996) 'The state and child care: an international review from a geographical perspective' in K. England (ed.) *Who Will Mind the Baby:*

Geographies of Child Care and Working Mothers, Routledge: London, pp. 143–66.

Finegold, K. and Skocpol, T. (1984) 'State policy and industry: from business recovery to the Wagner Act in America's New Deal' in C. Bright and S. Harding (eds) *State-making and Social Movements: Essays in History and Theory*, University of Michigan Press: Ann Arbor, pp. 159–92.

Flammang, J. A. (1987) 'Women made a difference: comparable worth in San Jose' in M. F. Katzenstein and C. M. Mueller (eds) *The Women's Movements of the United States and Western Europe: Consciousness, Political Opportunity, and Public Policy*, Temple University Press: Philadelphia, pp. 290–309.

Fletcher, R. (1995) 'Silences: Irish women and abortion' in *Feminist Review* **50**: 44–66.

Flora, P. and Heidenheimer, A. J. (eds) (1987) *The Development of Welfare States in Europe and America*, Transaction: New Brunswick and London.

Foley, M. (1994) 'Professionalising the response to rape' in C. Lupton and T. Gillespie (eds) *Working with Violence*, Macmillan: Basingstoke, pp. 39–54.

Franzway, S., Court, D. and Connell, R. W. (1989) *Staking a Claim: Feminism, Bureaucracy and the State*, Polity Press: Oxford.

Freeman, J. (1975) *The Politics of Women's Liberation*, David McKay: New York.

Freeman, J. (1983) 'Introduction' in J. Freeman (ed.) *Social Movements of the 60s and 70s*, Longman: New York and London.

Freeman, J. (1987) 'Whom you know versus whom you represent: feminist influence in the Democratic and Republican parties' in M. Katzenstein and C. Mueller (eds) *The Women's Movements of the United States and Western Europe*, Temple University Press: Philadelphia, pp. 215–44.

French, K. (1995) 'Men and locations of power: why move over?' in C. Itzin and J. Newman (eds) *Gender, Culture and Organizational Change*, Routledge: London and New York, pp. 54–67.

Friedan, B. (1965) *The Feminine Mystique*, Penguin: Harmondsworth.

Fuszara, M. (1991) 'Will the abortion issue give birth to feminism in Poland?' in M. Maclean and D. Groves (eds) *Women's Issues in Social Policy*, Routledge: London and New York, pp. 205–28.

Gamson, W. A. (1992) 'The social psychology of collective action' in A. D. Morris and C. M. Mueller (eds) *Frontiers in Social Movement Theory*, Yale University Press: New Haven, CT, pp. 53–76.

Garner, R. (1996) *Contemporary Movements and Ideologies*, McGraw-Hill: New York.

Gelb, J. (1987) 'Social movement "success": A comparative analysis of feminism in the United States and the United Kingdom' in M. F. Katzenstein and C. M. Mueller (eds) *The Women's Movements of the United States and Western Europe: Consciousness, Political Opportunity, and Public Policy*, Temple University Press: Philadelphia, pp. 267–89.

Gelb, J. (1989) *Feminism and Politics: A Comparative Perspective*, University of California Press: Berkeley.

Gelb, J. and Palley, M. (1982) *Women and Public Policies*, Princeton: Princeton University Press.

Giddens, A. (1990) *The Consequences of Modernity*, Polity Press: Oxford.

Gillespie, T. (1994) 'Under pressure: rape crisis centres, multi-agency work and strategies for survival' in C. Lupton and T. Gillespie (eds) *Working with Violence*, Macmillan: Basingstoke, pp. 15–38.

Ginsburg, N. (1979) *Class, Capital and Social Policy*, Macmillan: Basingstoke.

Ginsburg, N. (1992) *Divisions of Welfare* Sage: London, Newbury Park, New Delhi.

Glendinning, C. and Millar, J. (1991) 'Poverty: the forgotten Englishwoman – reconstructing research and policy on poverty' in M. Maclean and D. Groves (eds) *Women's Issues in Social Policy*, Routledge: London and New York, pp. 20–37.

Goffman, E. (1974) *Frame Analysis: An Essay on the Organization of Experience*, New York: Harper.

Goggin, M. L. (ed.) (1993) *Understanding the New Politics of Abortion*, Sage: Newbury Park, London, New Delhi.

Goldberg, G. S. (1990) 'The United States: feminization of poverty amidst plenty' in G. S. Goldberg and E. Kremen (eds) *The Feminization of Poverty – Only in America*, Greenwood Press: New York, pp. 17–58.

Goldberg, G. S. and Kremen, E. (eds) (1990a) *The Feminization of Poverty – Only in America*, Greenwood Press: New York.

Goldberg, G. S. and Kremen, E. (1990b) 'The feminization of poverty: discovered in America' in G. S. Goldberg and E. Kremen (eds) *The Feminization of Poverty – Only in America*, Greenwood Press: New York, pp. 1–15.

Gordon, C. (ed.) (1980) *Power/Knowledge*, Pantheon Books: New York and Harvester Press: Brighton.

Gough, I. (1979) *The Political Economy of the Welfare State*, Macmillan: Basingstoke.

Graham, H. (1987) 'Women's poverty and caring' in C. Glendinning and J. Millar (eds) *Women and Poverty in Britain*, Harvester Wheatsheaf: Hemel Hempstead, pp. 221–40.

Gramsci, A. (1971) *The Prison Notebooks*, Lawrence & Wishart: London.

Green, E., Hebron, S. and Woodward, D. (1990) *Women's Leisure, What Leisure?*, Macmillan: Basingstoke.

Gregory, J. (1987) *Sex, Race and the Law*, Sage: London.

Gregory, J. (1992) 'Equal value/comparable worth: national statute and case law in Brtain and the U.S.A.' in P. Kahn and E. Meehan (eds) *Equal Value/Comparable Worth in the UK and the USA*, Macmillan: Basingstoke.

Guardian 12/3/91, 11/3/95, 3/4/95, 9/1/96, 24/2/96, 14/5/97, 24/10/97.

Habermas, J. (1981) 'New social movements' in *Telos* **49**: 33–7.

Hadley, J. (1994) 'God's bullies: attacks on abortion' in *Feminist Review* **48**: 94–113.

Hakim, C. (1995) 'Five feminist myths about women's employment' in *The British Journal of Sociology* **46**(3): 429–55.

Halford, S. (1992) 'Feminist change in a patriarchal organisation: the experience of women's initiatives in local government and implications for feminist perspectives on state institutions' in M. Savage and A. Witz (eds) *Gender and Bureaucracy*, Blackwell: Oxford/*The Sociological Review*, pp. 155–85.

Halva-Neubauer, G. A. (1993) 'The state after Roe: no "paper tigers"' in M. L. Goggin (ed.) *The New Politics of Abortion*, Sage: Newbury Park, London, New Delhi, pp. 167–89.

Hanmer, J. (1977) 'Community action, women's aid and the women's liberation movement' in M. Mayo (ed.) *Women in the Community*, Routledge & Kegan Paul: London, pp. 91–108.

Hanmer, J. (1978) 'Violence and the social control of women' in G. Littlejohn, B. Smart, J. Wakeford and N. Yuval-Davis (eds) *Power and the State*, Croom Helm: London, pp. 217–38.

Hantrais, L. (1994) 'Comparing family policy in Britain, France and Germany' in *Journal of Social Policy* **23**(2): 135–60.

Harkness, S., Machin, S. and Waldfogel, J. (1995) Evaluating the Pin Money Hypothesis: The Relationship Between Women's Labour Market Activity, Family Income and Poverty in Britain, LSE welfare state programme discussion paper 108.

Harriss, K. (1989) 'New alliances: Socialist-feminism in the eighties' in *Feminist Review* **31**: 34–54.

Hartmann, H. (1986) 'The unhappy marriage of Marxism and feminism' in L. Sargent (ed.) *The Unhappy Marriage of Marxism and Feminism*, Pluto: London.

Hastings, S. (1992) 'Equal value in the local authorities sector' in P. Kahn and E. Meehan (eds) *Equal Value/Comparable Worth in the UK and the USA*, Macmillan: Basingstoke, pp. 215–29.

Hekman, S. (1990) *Gender and Knowledge: Elements of a Post-modern Feminism*, Polity Press: Oxford.

Held, D. (1983) 'Introduction: Central perspectives on the modern state' in D. Held *et al.* (eds) *States and Societies*, Martin Robertson: Oxford, pp. 1–55.

Held, D. *et al.* (eds) (1983) *States and Societies*, Martin Robertson: Oxford.

Hellman, J. A. (1987) 'Women's struggle in a workers' city: feminist movements in Turin' in M. F. Katzenstein and C. M. Mueller (eds) *The Women's Movements of the United States and Western Europe: Consciousness, Political Opportunity, and Public Policy*, Temple University Press: Philadelphia, pp. 111–31.

Hellman, S. (1987) 'Feminism and the model of militancy in an Italian Communist Federation: challenges to the old style of politics' in M. F. Katzenstein and C. M. Mueller (eds) *The Women's Movements of the United States and Western Europe: Consciousness, Political Opportunity, and Public Policy*, Temple University Press: Philadelphia, pp. 132–52.

Hernes, H. (1987) 'Women and the welfare state: the transition from private to public dependence' in A. Showstack-Sassoon (ed.) *Women and the State*, Hutchinson: London, pp. 72–92.

Himmelweit, S. (1988) 'More than a woman's right to choose?' in *Feminist Review* **29**: 38–56.

HMSO (1979) *Britain 1979: An Official Handbook*, HMSO: London.

Hobson, B. (1994) 'Solo mothers, social policy regimes, and the logics of gender' in D. Sainsbury (ed.) *Gendering Welfare States*, Sage: London, pp. 170–87.

Hubback, J. (1957) *Wives who Went to College*, Heinemann: London.

Huberts, L. W. (1989) 'The influence of social movements on government policy' in B. Klandermans (ed.) *Organizing for Change: Social Movement Organizations in Europe and the U.S.*, International Social Movement Research, vol. 2, JAI Press Inc: Greenwich, CT, London, Oxford, pp. 395–426.

Hughes, M., Mayall, B., Moss, P., Perry, J., Petrie, P. and Pinkerton, G. (1980) *Nurseries Now: A Fair Deal for Parents and Children*, Penguin Books: Harmondsworth.

Hunt, S. A., Benford, R. D., Snow, D. A. (1994) 'Identity fields: framing processes and the social construction of movement identities' in E. Laraña, H. Johnston and J. R. Gusfield (eds) *New Social Movements: From Ideology to Identity*, Temple University Press: Philadelphia, pp. 185–208.

Hyde, C. (1995) 'Feminist social movement organizations survive the New Right' in M. M. Ferree and P. Y. Martin (eds) *Feminist Organizations: Harvest of the New Women's Movement*, Temple University Press: Philadelphia, pp. 306–22.

Inglehart, R. (1990) *Culture Shift in Advanced Society*, Princeton University Press: Princeton, NJ.

Itzin, C. (1995) 'The gender culture in organizations' in C. Itzin and J. Newman (eds) *Gender, Culture and Organizational Change*, Routledge: London and New York, pp. 30–53.

Jarman, J. (1991) 'Equality or marginalisation: the repeal of protective legislation' in E. Meehan and S. Sevenhuijsen (eds) *Equality Politics and Gender*, Sage: London, pp. 142–53.

Jenkins, J. C. (1995) 'Social movements, political representation, and the state: an agenda and comparative framework' in J. C. Jenkins and B. Klandermans (eds) *The Politics of Social Protest: Comparative Perspectives on States and Social Movements*, UCL Press: London, pp. 14–35.

Jenkins, J. C. and Klandermans, B. (eds) (1995) *The Politics of Social Protest: Comparative Perspectives on States and Social Movements*, UCL Press: London.

Jenkins, S. (1991) 'Poverty measurement and the within-household distribution: agenda for action' in *Journal of Social Policy* **20**(4): 457–83.

Jenson, J. (1987) 'Changing discourse, changing agendas: political rights and reproductive policies in France' in M. F. Katzenstein and C. M. Mueller (eds) *The Women's Movements of the United States and Western Europe: Consciousness, Political Opportunity, and Public Policy*, Temple University Press: Philadelphia, pp. 64–88.

Jessop, B. (1982) *The Capitalist State*, Martin Robertson: Oxford.

Jewson, N. and Mason, D. (1986) 'The theory and practice of equal opportunity policies: liberal and radical approaches' in *The Sociological Review* **34**(2): 307–29.

Johnston, H. and Klandermans, B. (eds) (1995) *Social Movements and Culture*, UCL Press: London.

Johnston, H., Laraña, E. and Gusfield, J. R. (1994) 'Identities, grievances and new social movements' in E. Laraña, H. Johnston and J. R. Gusfield (eds) *New Social Movements: From Ideology to Identity*, Temple University Press: Philadelphia, pp. 3–35.

Jones, S. (1997) Still a Mining Community: Gender and Change in the Upper Dulais Valley, unpublished PhD thesis, University of Wales Swansea.

Jordan, B. (1996) *A Theory of Poverty and Social Exclusion*, Polity Press: Oxford.

Kaplan, G. (1992) *Contemporary Western European Feminism*, UCL Press: London.

Katzenstein, M. F. and Mueller, C. M. (eds) (1987) *The Women's Movements of the United States and Western Europe: Consciousness, Political Opportunity, and Public Policy*, Temple University Press: Philadelphia.

Keane, J. (1993) Introduction in J. Keane (ed.) *Civil Society and the State: New European Perspectives*, Verso: London.

Kelly, L. (1995–6) 'Zero Commitment' in *Trouble and Strife* **32**: 9–16.

Ketting, E. and Van Praag, P. (1986) 'The marginal relevance of legislation relating to induced abortion' in J. Lovenduski and J. Outshoorn (eds) *The New Politics of Abortion*, Sage: London, pp. 154–69.

Klandermans, B. (1986) 'New social movements and resource mobilisation: the European and the American approach' in *Journal of Mass Emergencies and International Disasters*, special issue, *Comparative Perspectives and Research on Collective Behaviour and Social Movements* **4**: 13–37.

Klandermans, B. (1988) 'The formation and mobilization of consensus' in B. Klandermans, H. Kriesi and S. Tarrow (eds) *From Structure to Action: Comparing Social Movement Research Across Cultures*, International Social Movement Research, vol. 1, JAI Press: Greenwich, CT, pp. 173–97.

Klandermans, B. and Tarrow, S. (1988) 'Mobilising into social movements: synthesising European and American approaches' in B. Klandermans, H. Kriesi and S. Tarrow (eds) *From Structure to Action: Comparing Social Movement Research Across Cultures*, International Social Movement Research, vol. 1, JAI Press: Greenwich, CT, pp. 1–38.

Klatch, R. (1988) 'Coalition and conflict among women of the New Right' in *Signs* **13**: 671–94.

Klein, E. (1984) *Gender Politics*, Harvard University Press: Cambridge, MA.

Klein, E. (1987) 'Diffusing of consciousness in the United States and Western Europe' in M. F. Katzenstein and C. M. Mueller (eds) *The Women's Movements of the United States and Western Europe: Consciousness, Political Opportunity and Public Policy*, Temple University Press: Philadelphia, pp. 23–43.

Koven, S. and Michel, S. (1990) 'Womanly desires: maternalist politics and the origins of welfare states in France, Germany, Great Britain and the United States, 1880–1920' in *American Historical Review* **95**(4): 1076–108.

Kriesi, H. (1989) 'New social movements and the new class in the Netherlands' in *American Journal of Sociology* **94**(5): 1078–116.

Kriesi, H. (1995) 'The political opportunity structure of new social movements: its impact on their mobilization' in J. C. Jenkins and B. Klandermans (eds) *The Politics of Social Protest: Comparative Perspectives on States and Social Movements*, UCL Press: London, pp. 167–98.

Kriesi, H., Koopmans, R., Dyvendak, J. W. and Giugni, M. G. (1995) *New Social Movements in Western Europe: A Comparative Analysis*, UCL Press: London.

LA/2665a, *Sexual Harassment: A Code of Practice*, Association of University Teachers, May 1985.

Labour Party (1995) *Peace at Home*, a Labour Party consulation on the elimination of domestic and sexual violence against women, the Labour Party: London.

Labour Party Feminists (1984) 'The women's movement and the Labour Party: an interview with Labour Party feminists' in *Feminist Review* **16**: 75–87.

Land, H. (1983) 'Poverty and gender: the distribution of resources within the family' in M. Brown (ed.) *The Structure of Disadvantage*, SSRC/DHSS Studies in deprivation and disadvantage 12, Heinemann Educational: London, pp. 49–71.

Laraña, E., Johnston, H. and Gusfield, J. R. (eds) (1994) *New Social Movements: From Ideology to Identity*, Temple University Press: Philadelphia.

Lash, S. and Urry, J. (1987) *The End of Organised Capitalism*, Polity Press: Oxford.

Lawrence, E. and Turner, N. (1997) New Social Movements and Equal Opportunities Work, paper presented to the BSA conference, York, April.

Lees, S. (1997) *Ruling Passions: Sexual Violence, Reputation and the Law*, Open University Press: Milton Keynes.

Lees, S. with Gregory, J. (1997) 'In search of gender justice: sexual assault and the criminal justice system', Chapter 9, in S. Lees *Ruling Passions: Sexual Violence, Reputation and the Law*, Open University Press: Milton Keynes.

Leidner, R. (1991) 'Stretching the boundaries of liberalism' in *Signs* **16**(2): 263–89.

Leira, A. (1993) 'Mothers, markets and the state: a Scandinavian "model"?' in *Journal of Social Policy* **22**(3): 329–47.

Levine, P. (1987) *Victorian Feminism, 1850–1900*, Hutchinson Education: London.

Levitas, R. (1996) 'The concept of social exclusion and the new Durkheimian hegemony' in *Critical Social Policy* **16**(1): 5–20.

Lewis, J. (1992) *Women in Britain Since 1945*, Blackwell: Oxford.

Lewis, J. (1993) 'Introduction: Women, work, family and social policies in Europe' in J. Lewis (ed.) *Women and Social Policies in Europe: Work, Family and the State*, Edward Elgar: Aldershot, pp. 1–24.

Lewis, J. and Piachaud, D. (1987) 'Women and poverty in the 20th century' in C. Glendinning and J. Millar (eds) *Women and Poverty in Britain*, Harvester Wheatsheaf: Hemel Hempstead, pp. 28–52.

Lister, R. (1990) 'Women, economic dependancy and citizenship' in *Journal of Social Policy* **19**(4): 445–67.

Lister, R. (1997) *Citizenship: Feminist Perspectives*, Macmillan: Basingstoke.

Llewelyn Davis, M. ([1915] 1978) *Maternity: Letters from Working Women*, Virago: London.

London Edinburgh Weekend Return Group (1980) *Up Against the State*, Pluto Press: London.

Lovenduski, J. (1986a) *Women and European Politics: Contemporary Feminism and Public Policy*, Wheatsheaf Books: Brighton.

Lovenduski, J. (1986b) 'Parliament, pressure groups, networks and the women's movement: the politics of abortion law reform in Britain (1967–83)' in J. Lovenduski and J. Outshoorn (eds) *The New Politics of Abortion*, Sage: London, pp. 49–66.

Lovenduski, J. and Norris, P. (1993) *Gender and Party Politics*, Sage: London, Thousand Oaks, New Delhi.

Lovenduski, J. and Randall, V. (1993) *Contemporary Feminist Politics: Women and Power in Britain*, Oxford University Press: Oxford.

Luker, K. (1984) *Abortion and the Politics of Motherhood*, University of California Press: Berkeley.

Lupton, C. (1994) 'The British refuge movement: the survival of an ideal?' in C. Lupton and T. Gillespie (eds) *Working with Violence*, Macmillan: Basingstoke, pp. 55–74.

Lustiger-Thaler, H. and Shragge, E. (1993) Social movements and social welfare: the political problem of needs' in G. Drover and P. Kerans (eds) *New Approaches to Welfare Theory*, Edward Elgar: Aldershot, pp. 161–76.

McCarthy, J. D. and Zald, M. N. (1987) 'Resource mobilization and social movements: a partial theory' in M. N. Zald and J. D. McCarthy (eds) *Social Movements in an Organizational Society*, Transaction Books: New Brunswick (US) and Oxford (UK).

McGregor, H. and Hopkins, A. (1991) *Working for Change: the Movement Against Domestic Violence*, Allen & Unwin: Sydney, Australia.

Machin, S. and Waldfogel, J. (1994) The Decline of the Male Breadwinner: Changing Shares of Husbands' and Wives' Earnings in Family Income, LSE Welfare State Programme Discussion Paper 103.

McIntosh, M. (1978) 'The state and the oppression of women' in A. Kuhn and A. Wolpe (eds) *Feminism and Materialism*, Routledge & Kegan Paul: London.

McIntosh, M. (1981) 'Feminism and social policy' in *Critical Social Policy* **1**(1): 32–42.

Mackay, F. (1996) 'The zero tolerance campaign: setting the agenda' in J. Lovenduski and P. Norris (eds) *Women in Politics*, Oxford University Press: Oxford, pp. 208–22.

MacKinnon, C. (1989) *Towards a Feminist Theory of the State*, Harvard University Press: London.

Maguire, D. (1995) 'Opposition movements and opposition parties: equal partners or dependent relations in the struggle for power and reform?' in J. C. Jenkins and B. Klandermans (eds) *The Politics of Social Protest: Comparative Perspectives on States and Social Movements*, UCL Press: London, pp. 199–228.

Maguire, S. (1988) '"Sorry love" – violence against women in the home and the state response' in *Critical Social Policy* **8**(2): 34–45.

Malos, E. and Hague, J. (1993) *Domestic Violence and Housing: Local Authority Responses to Women and Children Escaping Violence in the Home*, WARE and School of Applied Social Studies, University of Bristol.

Mama, A. (1989) *The Hidden Struggle: State and Voluntary Sector Responses to Violence Against Black Women in the Home*, London Race and Housing Research Unit.

Mansbridge, J. (1986) *Why We Lost the ERA*, University of Chicago Press: Chicago.

Marshall, T. H. (1950) *Citizenship and Social Class and Other Essays*, Cambridge University Press: Cambridge.

Martin, P. Y. (1990) 'Rethinking feminist organizations' in *Gender and Society* **4**: 182–206.

Marx, K. (1970) *Capital*, vol. 1, Lawrence & Wishart.

Marx, K. and Engels, F. (1973) 'Manifesto of the Communist Party' in *Selected Works*, vol. 1, Lawrence & Wishart.

Matthews, N. (1994) *Confronting Rape: the Feminist Anti-rape Movement and the State*, Routledge: London and New York.

Matthews, N. (1995) 'Feminist clashes with the state: tactical choices by state-funded rape crisis centers' in M. M. Ferree and P. Y. Martin (eds) *Feminist Organizations: Harvest of the New Women's Movement*, Temple University Press: Philadelphia, pp. 291–305.

Mayo, M. and Weir, A. (1993) 'The future for feminist social policy?' in R. Page and J. Baldock (eds) *Social Policy Review 5*, Social Policy Association, pp. 35–57.

Meehan, E .M. (1985) *Women's Rights at Work: Campaigns and Policy in Britain and the United States*, Macmillan: Basingstoke.

Melhuish, E. C. and Moss, P. (eds) (1991) *Day Care for Young Children*, Routledge: London.

Melucci, A. (1980) 'The new social movements: a theoretical approach' in *Social Science Information* **19**: 199–226.

Melucci, A. (1984) 'An end to social movements? introductory paper to the sessions on 'New movements and change in organizational forms' in *Social Science Information* **23**: 819–35.

Melucci, A. (1985) 'The symbolic challenge of contemporary movements' in *Social Research* **52**: 789–816.

Melucci, A. (1988) 'Getting involved: identity and mobilization in social movements' in B. Klandermans, H. Kriesi and S. Tarrow (eds) *From Structure to Action*, pp. 329–48.

Melucci, A. (1989) *Nomads of the Present: Social Movements and Individual Needs in Contemporary Society*, Hutchinson Radius: London.

Melucci, A. (1995) 'The process of collective identity' in H. Johnston and B. Klandermans (eds) *Social Movements and Culture*, UCL Press: London, pp. 41–63.

Meyer, D. S. and Whittier, N. (1994) 'Social movement spillover' in *Social Problems* **41**(2): 277–98.

Meyer, M. (1995) 'Social-movement research in the United States: a European perspective' in S. M. Lyman (ed.) *Social Movements: Critiques, Concepts, Case-Studies*, Macmillan: Basingstoke, pp. 168–95.

Meyer, T. (1994) 'The German and British welfare states as employers: patriarchal or emancipatory?' in D. Sainsbury (ed.) *Gendering Welfare States*, Sage: London, pp. 62–81.

Middleton, S. Ashworth, K. and Braithwaite, I. (nd) *Small Fortunes: Spending on Children, Childhood Poverty and Parental Sacrifice*, Joseph Rowntree Foundation: York.

Miliband, R. (1973) *The State in Capitalist Society*, Quartet Books: London.

Millar, J. (1994) 'State, family and personal responsibility: the changing balance for lone mothers in the United Kingdom' in *Feminist Review* **48**: 24–39.

Millar, J. (1996) 'Women, poverty and social security' in C. Hallett (ed.) *Women and Social Policy: An Introduction*, Harvester Wheatsheaf: Bath, pp. 52–64.

Millar, J. and Bradshaw, J. (eds) (1996) *Social Welfare Systems: Towards a Research Agenda*, Bath Social Policy Papers no. 24/ESRC.

Millar, J. and Glendinning, C. (1987) 'Invisible women, invisible poverty' in C. Glendinning and J. Millar (eds) *Women and Poverty in Britain*, Harvester Wheatsheaf: Hemel Hempstead, pp. 3–27.

Millar, J. and Glendinning, C. (1992) '"It all really starts in the family": gender divisions and poverty' in C. Glendinning and J. Millar (eds) *Women and Poverty in Britain: the 1990s*, Harvester Wheatsheaf: Hemel Hempstead, pp. 3–10.

Mishra, R. (1981) *Society and Social Policy: Theories and Practice of Welfare*, 2nd edn, Macmillan: Basingstoke.

Mitchell, J. (1986) 'Reflections on twenty years of feminism' in J. Mitchell and A. Oakley (eds) *What is Feminism?*, Blackwell: Oxford, pp. 34–48.

Mooers, C. and Sears, A. (1992) 'The "new social movements" and the withering away of state theory' in W. K. Carroll (ed.) *Organizing Dissent: Contemporary Social Movements in Theory and Practice*, Garamond Press: Toronto, pp. 52–68.

Moore, B. (1967) *Social Origins of Dictatorship and Democracy*, Allen Lane, Penguin Press: Harmondsworth.

Morgan, P. (1995) *Farewell to the Family? Public Policy and Family Breakdown in Britain and the USA*, Choice in Welfare Series no. 21, IEA Health and Welfare Unit: London.

Morgen, S. (1995) '"It was the best of times, It was the worst of times": emotional discourse in the work cultures of feminist health clinics' in M. M. Ferree and P. Y. Martin (eds) *Feminist Organizations: Harvest of the New Women's Movement*, Temple University Press: Philadelphia, pp. 234–47.

Morris, A. D. and Mueller, C. M. (eds) (1992) *Frontiers in Social Movement Theory*, Yale University Press: New Haven, CT.

Morris, J. (1991) *Pride Against Prejudice: A Personal Politics of Disability*, The Women's Press: London.

Morris, L. (1990) *The Workings of the Household*, Polity Press: Oxford.

Mosesdottir, L. (1995) 'The state and the egalitarian, ecclesiastical and liberal regimes of gender relations' in *The British Journal of Sociology* **46**(4): 623–42.

Moss, P. (1991) 'Day care for young children in the United Kingdom' in Melhuish E. C. and Moss P. (1991) *Day Care for Young Children*, Routledge: London, pp. 121–41.

Mosse, G. (1985) *Nationalism and Sexuality: Middle-Class Morality and Sexual Norms in Modern Europe*, University of Wisconsin Press: Madison, WI.

Mossuz-Lavau, J. (1986) 'Abortion policy in France under governments of the Right and Left (1973–84)' in J. Lovenduski and J. Outshoorn (eds) *The New Politics of Abortion*, Sage: London, pp. 86–104.

Mueller, C. M. (1987) 'Collective consciousness, identity transformation, and the rise of women in public office in the United States' in M. F. Katzenstein and C. M. Mueller (eds) *The Women's Movements of the United States and Western Europe: Consciousness, Political Opportunity, and Public Policy*, Temple University Press: Philadelphia, pp. 89–108.

Myrdal, A. and Klein, V. (1968) *Women's Two Roles: Home and Work*, Routledge: London.

New Earnings Survey (1997) Office for National Statistics, HMSO: London.

Nollert, M. (1995) 'Neocorporatism and political protest in the Western democracies: a cross-national analysis' in J. C. Jenkins and B. Klandermans (eds) *The Politics of Social Protest: Comparative Perspectives on States and Social Movements*, UCL Press: London, pp. 138–64.

Norris, P. (1987) *Politics and Sexual Equality: The Comparative Position of Women in Western Democracies*, Wheatsheaf: Brighton.

Norris, P. and Lovenduski, J. (1993) 'Gender and party politics' in J. Lovenduski and P. Norris (eds) *Gender and Party Politics*, Sage: London.

Novak, T. (1995) 'Rethinking poverty' in *Critical Social Policy* 44/45, **15**(2/3): 58–74.

O'Connell, J. (1993) 'Gender, class and citizenship in the comparative analysis of welfare states: theoretical and methodological issues' in *The British Journal of Sociology* **44**(3): 501–18.

Offe, C. (1984) *Contradictions of the Welfare State*, Hutchinson: London.

Offe, C. (1985) 'New social movements: challenging the boundaries of institutional politics' in *Social Research* **52**(4): 817–68.

Offe, C. (1990) 'Reflections on the institutional self-transformation of movement politics: a tentative stage model' in R. J. Dalton and M. Kuechler (eds) *Challenging the Political Order*, Polity Press: Oxford, pp. 232–50.

Olofsson, G. (1988) 'After the working class movement? An essay on what's "new" and what's "social" in the new social movements' in *Acta Sociologica* **31**: 15–34.

Outshoorn, J. (1986a) 'The rules of the game: abortion politics in the Netherlands' in J. Lovenduski and J. Outshoorn (eds) *The New Politics of Abortion*, Sage: London, pp. 5–26.

Outshoorn, J. (1986b) 'The feminist movement and abortion policy in the Netherlands' in D. Dahlerup (ed.) *The New Women's Movement: Feminism and Political Power in Europe and the USA*, Sage: London, pp. 64–84.

Outshoorn, J. (1991) 'Is this what we wanted? Positive action as issue perversion' in E. Meehan and S. Sevenhuijsen (eds) *Equality Politics and Gender*, Sage: London, pp. 104–21.

Pahl, J. (1985) *Private Violence and Public Policy: The Needs of Battered Women and the Response of the Public Services*, Routledge & Kegan Paul: London.

Pahl, J. (1989) *Money and Marriage*, Macmillan: Basingstoke.

Patel, P. (1997) 'Third wave feminism and black women's activism' in H. S. Mirza (ed.) *Black British Feminism: A Reader*, Routledge: London and New York.

Pateman, C. (1988) *The Sexual Contract*, Polity Press: Oxford.

Pateman, C. (1989) *The Disorder of Women*, Polity Press: Oxford.

Pateman, C. (1992) 'Equality, difference, subordination: the politics of motherhood and women's citizenship' in G. Bock and S. James (eds) *Beyond Equality and Difference: Citizenship, Feminist Politics, Female Subjectivity*, Routledge: London and New York.

Pember Reeves, M. ([1913] 1984) *Round About a Pound a Week*, Virago: London.

Perrigo, S. (1986) 'Socialist-feminism and the Labour Party: some experiences from Leeds' in *Feminist Review* **23**: 101–8.

Petchesky, R. (1986) *Abortion and Woman's Choice*, Verso: London.

Phillips, D. (1991) 'Day care for young children in the United States' in E. C. Melhuish and P. Moss (1991) *Day Care for Young Children*, Routledge: London, pp. 161–184.

Pierson, C. (1991) *Beyond the Welfare State? The New Political Economy of Welfare*, Polity Press: Oxford.

Pierson, C. (1996) *The Modern State*, Routledge: London and New York.

Pisciotta, E. E. (1986) 'The strength and powerlessness of the new Italian women's movement: the case of abortion' in D. Dahlerup (ed.) *The New Women's Movement: Feminism and Political Power in Europe and the USA*, Sage: London, pp. 26–47.

Piven, F. F. and Cloward, R. A. (1992) 'Normalizing collective protest' in A. D. Morris and C. M. Mueller (eds) *Frontiers in Social Movement Theory*, Yale University Press: New Haven, CT, pp. 301–25.

Pizzey, E. (1974) *Scream Quietly or the Neighbours Will Hear*, Penguin: Harmondsworth.

Plotke, D. (1990) 'What's so new about new social movements?' in *Socialist Review* **20**: 35–65.

Pringle, R. and Watson, S. (1992) 'Fathers, brothers, mates: the fraternal state in Australia' in S. Watson (ed.) *Playing the State: Australian Feminist Inverventions*, Verso: London, pp. 229–43.

Quest, C. (ed.) (1992) *Equal Opportunities: A Feminist Fallacy*, Choice in Welfare no. 11, IEA Health and Welfare Unit: London.

Quest, C. (ed.) (1994) *Liberating Women... From Modern Feminism*, Choice in Welfare no. 19, IEA Health and Welfare Unit: London.

Rai, S., Pilkington, H. and Phizacklea, A. (eds) (1992) *Women in the Face of Change: the Soviet Union, Eastern Europe and China*, Routledge: London and New York.

Ramsay, K. and Parker, M. (1992) 'Gender, bureaucracy and organizational culture' in M. Savage and A. Witz (eds) *Gender and Bureaucracy*, Blackwell/*The Sociological Review*: Oxford, pp. 253–76.

Randall, V. (1986) 'The politics of abortion in Ireland' in J. Lovenduski and J. Outshoorn (eds) *The New Politics of Abortion*, Sage: London, pp. 67–85.

Randall, V. (1996) 'Feminism and child daycare' in *Journal of Social Policy* **25**(4): 485–505.

Ransome, P. (1992) *Antonio Gramsci: A New Introduction*, Harvester Wheatsheaf: Hemel Hempstead.

Rees, T. (in press) *Women and Work: 25 Years of Equality Legislation in Wales*, University of Wales Press: Cardiff.

Rees, T. (1992) *Women and the Labour Market*, Routledge: London and New York.

Reinelt, C. (1995) 'Moving onto the terrain of the state: the battered women's movement and the politics of engagement' in M. M. Ferree and P. Y. Martin (eds) *Feminist Organizations: Harvest of the New Women's Movement*, Temple University Press: Philadelphia, pp. 84–104.

Reinhold, S. (1994) 'Through the parliamentary looking glass: 'real' and 'pretend' families in contemporary British politics' in *Feminist Review* **48**: 61–79.

Richardson, D. (1993) *Women, Motherhood and Childrearing*, Macmillan: Basingstoke.

Richardson, D. (1996) 'Heterosexuality and social theory' in D. Richardson (ed.) *Theorising Heterosexuality*, Open University Press: Buckingham, Philadelphia, pp. 1–20.

Ristock, J. (1990) 'Canadian feminist social service collectives: caring and contradictions' in L. Albrecht and R. Brewer (eds) *Bridges of Power*, New Society: Philadelphia, pp. 172–81.

Rodriguez, N. M. (1988) 'Transcending bureaucracy: feminist politics at a shelter for battered women' in *Gender and Society* **2**(2): 214–27.

Roseneil, S. (1995) *Disarming Patriarchy: Feminism and Political Action at Greenham*, Open University Press: Milton Keynes.

Rosenthal, M. G. (1990) 'Sweden: promise and paradox' in G. S. Goldberg and E. Kremen (eds) *The Feminization of Poverty – Only in America*, Greenwood Press: New York, pp. 129–55.

Rosenthal, N. and Schwarz, M. (1989) 'Spontaneity and democracy in social movements' in B. Klandermans (ed.) *Organizing for Change: Social Movement Organizations in Europe and the United States*, International Social Movement Research, A research annual, vol. 2, JAI Press Inc: Greenwich, CT, London.

Rothschild-Whitt, J. (1979) 'The collectivist organization: an alternative to rational-bureaucratic models' in *American Sociological Review* **44**: 509–27.

Rowbotham, S. (1973) *Woman's Consciousness, Man's World*, Penguin Books: Harmondsworth.

Rowbotham, S. (1989) *The Past Is Before Us*, Pandora: London.

Rowbotham, S., Segal, L. and Wainwright, H. (1980) *Beyond the Fragments: Feminism and the Making of Socialism*, Merlin: London.

Rucht, D. (1988) 'Themes, logics and arenas of social movements: a structural approach' in B. Klandermans, H. Kriesi and S. Tarrow (eds) *From Structure to*

Action: Comparing Social Movement Research Across Cultures, International Social Movement Research, vol. 1, JAI Press: Greenwich, CT, pp. 305–28.

Ruggie, M. (1984) *The State and Working Women,* Princeton University Press: Princeton, New Jersey.

Ruggie, M. (1987) 'Workers' movements and women's interests: the impact of labor-state relations in Britain and Sweden' in M. F. Katzenstein and C. M. Mueller (eds) *The Women's Movements of the United States and Western Europe: Consciousness, Political Opportunity, and Public Policy*, Temple University Press: Philadelphia, pp. 247–266.

Safa, H. (1996) 'Gender inequality and women's wage labour: a theoretical and empirical analysis' in V. M. Moghadam (ed.) *Patriarchy and Development*, Clarendon Press: Oxford, pp. 184–219.

Sainsbury, D. (1994) 'Women's and men's social rights: gendering dimensions of welfare states' in D. Sainsbury (ed.) *Gendering Welfare States*, Sage: London, pp. 150–69.

Savage, M. (1992) 'Women's expertise, men's authority: gendered organizations and the contemporary middle class' in M. Savage and A. Witz (eds) *Gender and Bureaucracy*, Blackwell/*The Sociological Review*: Oxford, pp. 124–51.

Schechter, S. (1982) *Women and Male Violence: The Visions and Struggles of the Battered Women's Movement*, South End Press: Boston.

Schnell, F. (1993) 'The foundations of abortion attitudes: the role of values and value conflict' in M. L. Goggin (ed.) *Understanding the New Politics of Abortion*, Sage: Newbury Park, pp. 23–43.

Scott, A. (1990) *Ideology and the New Social Movements*, Unwin Hyman: London.

Scott, H. (1984) *Working Your Way to the Bottom: The Feminization of Poverty*, Pandora: London.

Scott, J. (1994) *Poverty and Wealth: Citizenship, Deprivation and Privilege*, Longman: London.

Seccombe, W. (1993) *Weathering the Storm: Working-class Families from the Industrial Revolution to the Fertility Decline*, Verso: London.

Segal, L. (1987) *Is the Future Female? Troubled Thoughts on Contemporary Feminism*, Virago: London.

Siim, B. (1987) 'The Scandinavian welfare states – towards sexual equality or a new kind of male domination?' in *Acta Sociologica* **30**(3/4): 255–70.

Siim, B. (1988) 'Towards a feminist rethinking of the welfare state' in K. Jones and A. Jonasdottir (eds) *The Political Interests of Gender: Developing Theory and Research with a Feminist Face*, Sage: London, 160–86.

Sly, F., Price, A. and Risdon, A. (1997) 'Trends in labour market participation of ethnic groups: 1984–1996' in *Labour Market Trends*, Office for National Statistics, August: 295–303.

Smart, C. (1989) *Feminism and the Power of Law*, Routledge: London.

Smith, D. (1988) *The Everyday World as Problematic: A Feminist Sociology*, Open University Press: Milton Keynes.

Snell, M. (1986) 'Equal pay and sex discrimination' in *Feminist Review* (ed.) *Waged Work: A Reader*, Virago: London, pp. 12–39.

Snow, D. A. and Benford, R. D. (1992) 'Master frames and cycles of protest' in A. D. Morris and C. M. Mueller (eds) *Frontiers in Social Movement Theory*, Yale University Press: New Haven, CT, pp. 133–55.

Snow, D. A., Burke Rochford Jr, E., Warden, S. K. and Benford, R. D. (1986) 'Frame alignment process, micromobilization and movement participation' in *American Sociological Review* **51**: 464–81.

Social Justice (Commission on Social Justice) (1994) *Social Justice: Strategies for National Renewal*, Report of the Commission on Social Justice, Vintage: London.

Spalter-Roth, R. and Schreiber, R. (1995) 'Outsider issues and insider tactics: strategic tensions in the women's policy network during the 1980s' in M. M. Ferree and P. Y. Martin (eds) *Feminist Organizations: Harvest of the New Women's Movement*, Temple University Press: Philadelphia, pp. 105–27.

Spelman, E. V. (1988) *Inessential Woman: Problems of Exclusion in Feminist Thought*, Women's Press: London.

Spring Rice, M. ([1939] 1981) *Working-class Wives*, Virago: London.

Staggenborg, S. (1991) *The Pro-choice Movement: Organization and Activism in the Abortion Conflict*, Oxford University Press: New York, Oxford.

Staggenborg, S. (1995) 'Can feminist organizations be effective?' in M. M. Ferree and P. Y. Martin (eds) *Feminist Organizations: Harvest of the New Women's Movement*, Temple University Press: Philadelphia, pp. 339–55.

Stephens, E. (1982) 'Out of the closet into the courts' in M. Rowe (ed.) *Spare Rib Reader*, Penguin Books: Harmondsworth, pp. 91–8.

Strathern, M. (1992) 'The meaning of assisted kinship' in M. Stacey (ed.) *Changing Human Reproduction*, Sage: London, pp. 148–69.

Tarrow, S. (1983) *Struggling to Reform: Social Movements and Policy Change During Cycles of Protest*, Western Societies Paper no. 15, Cornell University: Ithaca, NY.

Tarrow, S. (1994) *Power in Movement: Social Movements, Collective Action, and Politics*, Cambridge University Press: Cambridge.

Taylor, J. (1989) *The Answer is Maybe and That's Final*, Welsh Women's Aid.

Taylor, V. (1989) 'Social movement continuity: the women's movement in abeyance' in *American Sociological Review* **54**: 761–75.

Taylor, V. and Whittier, N. (1992) 'Collective identity in social movement communities: lesbian feminist organization' in A. D. Morris and C. M. Mueller (eds) *Frontiers in Social Movement Theory*, New Haven, CT: Yale University Press, pp. 104–29.

Therborn, G. (1977) 'The rule of capital and the rise of democracy' in *New Left Review* **103**: 3–41.

Therborn, G. (1989) 'States, population and productivity' in P. Lassman (ed.) *Politics and Social Theory*, Routledge: London and New York, pp. 62–84.

Tilly, C. (1984) 'Social movements and national politics' in C. Bright and S. Harding (eds) *State-making and Social Movements: Essays in History and Theory*, University of Michigan Press: Ann Arbor, pp. 297–317.

Tilly, C. (1988) 'Social movements old and new' in L. Kriesberg and B. Misztal (eds) *Social Movements as a Factor of Change in the Contemporary World, Research in Social Movements, Conflict and Change*, vol. 10, JAI Press: Greenwich, CT, pp. 1–18.

Tilly, L. A. and Gurin, P. (eds) (1990) *Women, Politics and Change*, Russell Sage: New York.

Titmuss, R. (1974) *Social Policy: An Introduction*, Allen & Unwin: London.

Touraine, A. (1977) *The Self-production of Society*, University of Chicago Press: Chicago.

Touraine, A. (1981) *The Voice and the Eye: An Analysis of Social Movements*, Cambridge University Press: Cambridge.

Touraine, A. (1985) 'An introduction to the study of social movements' in *Social Research* **52**(4): 749–87.

Touraine, A. (1992) 'Beyond social movements?' in *Theory, Culture and Society* **9**(1): 125–45.

Townsend, P. (1979) *Poverty in the United Kingdom*, Penguin: Harmondsworth.

Townsend, P. (1993) *The International Analysis of Poverty*, Harvester Wheatsheaf: Hemel Hempstead.

Tribe, L. H. (1990) *Abortion: The Clash of Absolutes*, Norton: New York.

Tucker, K. H. (1991) 'How new are new social movements?' in *Theory, Culture and Society* **8**: 75–98.

Van Every, J. (1991/2) 'Who is "the family"? The assumptions of British social policy' in *Critical Social Policy* **11**(3): 62–75.

Vaughan, P. (1970) *The Pill on Trial*, Penguin: Harmondsworth.

Vogler, C. (1994) 'Money in the household' in M. Anderson, F. Bechhofer and J. Gershuny (eds) *The Social and Political Economy of the Household*, SCELI, Oxford University Press: Oxford, pp. 225–66.

Wajcman, J. (1996) 'Women and men managers' in R. Crompton, D. Gallie and K. Purcell (eds) *Changing Forms of Employment: Organisations, Skills and Gender*, Routledge: London and New York, pp. 259–77.

Walby, S. (1986) *Patriarchy at Work*, Polity: Oxford.

Walby, S. (1990) *Theorising Patriarchy*, Basil Blackwell: Oxford.

Walby, S. (1994) 'Is citizenship gendered?' in *Sociology* **28**(2): 379–95.

Walby, S. (1996) 'The "declining significance" or the "changing forms" of patriarchy?' in V. Moghadam (ed.) *Patriarchy and Development*, Clarendon Press: Oxford, pp. 19–33.

Walby, S. (1997) *Gender Transformations*, Routledge: London and New York.

Walker, A. (1983) 'Care for elderly people: a conflict between women and the state' in J. Finch and D. Groves (eds) *A Labour of Love: Women, Work and Caring*, Routledge & Kegan Paul: London, pp. 106–28.

Warnock, M. (1984) *Report of the Committee of Enquiry into Human Fertilisation and Embryology*, DHSS, Cmnd 9314, HMSO: London.

Watson, S. (1992) 'Femocratic feminisms' in M. Savage and A. Witz (eds) *Gender and Bureaucracy*, Blackwell/*The Sociological Review*: Oxford, pp. 186–204.

Webb, J. and Liff, S. (1988) 'Play the white man: the social construction of fairness and competition in equal oppportunity policies' in *The Sociological Review* **36**(3): 532–51.

Weber, M. (1970) 'Politics as a vocation' in H. H. Gerth and C. Wright Mills (eds) *From Max Weber: Essays in Sociology*, Routledge & Kegan Paul: London.

Weir, A. (1977) 'Battered women: some perspectives and problems' in M. Mayo (ed.) *Women in the Community*, Routledge & Kegan Paul: London, pp. 109–20.

Welsh Women's Aid (1990) *Annual Report 1989–1990*, Welsh Women's Aid.

Welsh Women's Aid (1992) *Annual Report 1991–1992*, Welsh Women's Aid.

Welsh Women's Aid (nd) *Homes Fit for Heroines*, Welsh Women's Aid.

Westergaard, J. and Resler, H. (1976) *Class in a Capitalist Society: A Study of Contemporary Britain*, Penguin: Harmondsworth.

Whitting, G. (1992) 'Women and poverty: the European context' in C. Glendinning and J. Millar (eds) *Women and Poverty in Britain: The 1990s*, Harvester Wheatsheaf: Hemel Hempstead.

Wiik, J. (1986) 'The abortion issue, political cleavage and the political agenda in Norway' in J. Lovenduski and J. Outshoorn (eds) *The New Politics of Abortion*, Sage: London, pp. 139–53.

Williams, F. (1990) *Social Policy: A Critical Introduction*, Polity Press: Oxford.

Williams, F. (1994) 'Social relations, welfare and the post-Fordism debate' in R. Burrows and B. Loader (eds) *Towards a Post-Fordist Welfare State?*, Routledge: London and New York.

Wilson, E. (1977) *Women and the Welfare State*, Tavistock: London.

Wilson, E. (1980) *Only Halfway to Paradise: Women in Post-war Britain 1945–1968*, Tavistock: London.

Wilson, F. L. (1990) 'Neo-corporatism and the rise of new social movements' in R. J. Dalton and M. Kuechler (eds) *Challenging the Political Order: New Social and Political Movements in Western Democracies*, Polity Press: Oxford.

Wishand, B. (1981) *Swedish Women on the Move*, ed. and trans. by J. Rosen, Stockholm: The Swedish Institute.

Witz, A. and Savage, M. (1992) 'The gender of organizations' in M. Savage and A. Witz (eds) *Gender and Bureaucracy*, Blackwell/*The Sociological Review*: Oxford, pp. 3–62.

Yeatman, A. (1990) *Bureaucrats, Technocrats, Femocrats: Essays on the Contemporary Australian State*, Allen & Unwin: Sydney.

Zald, M. N. (1992) 'Looking backward to look forward: reflections on the past a future of the resource mobilization research program' in A. D. Morris and C. M. Mueller (eds) *Frontiers in Social Movement Theory*, Yale University Press: New Haven, CT, pp. 326–48.

Zopf, P. E. (1989) *American Women in Poverty*, Greenwood Press: New York.

Index